HARVARD HISTORICAL STUDIES

Published under the direction
of the Department of History
at the charge of the Henry
Warren Torrey Fund and of
the Charles Warren Center for
Studies in American History

Volume XC

Hon. Josiah Quincy, by Gilbert Stuart. 1826.

Josiah Quincy

1772 - 1864

The Last Federalist

ROBERT A. McCAUGHEY

Harvard University Press   Cambridge, Massachusetts   1974

In Memory of My Father

The work was well considered and diligently labored. The hopeless design, or the vain desire, of pleasing everybody was not mine. Those, who think history and eulogy are terms identical, and those whose maxim is 'de mortues nil nise bonum' will be dissatisfied in advance.

—Josiah Quincy, commenting on his
History of Harvard University

Preface

"It is the misfortune of American biography," James Russell Lowell wrote in 1867, "that it must needs be more or less provincial." The remark was intended less as literary criticism than historical commentary.

Wanting any great and acknowledged centre of national life and thought, our expansion has hitherto been rather aggregation than growth; reputations must be hammered out thin to cover so wide a surface, and the substance of most hardly holds out to the boundaries of a single State. Our very history wants unity, . . . A sense of remoteness and seclusion comes over us as we read, and we cannot help asking ourselves, 'Were *not* these things done in a corner?'

Josiah Quincy spent his life doing things in a corner of Massachusetts. His eight years in Washington as a Federalist congressman confirmed rather than qualified his essential provincialism. Boston, which he served as mayor, and Harvard College, over which he presided — these, not the nation, were the beneficiaries of his most important public labors. Nor can his stubborn espousal of Federalist sentiments long after the party's demise, involvement with the problems of urban life when most Americans were transfixed by the opportunities of the frontier, and commitment to collegiate order and scholarship during an era suspicious of one and scornful of the other, permit any claims to be made on his behalf as a "representative" of his age.

Yet one can discern from his life as from the lives of such equally provincial contemporaries as DeWitt Clinton of New York, John C. Calhoun of South Carolina, Thomas Hart Benton of Missouri, or even that "archetypal" American, Andrew Jackson of Tennessee, clues to a more comprehensive understanding of the many-threaded history of antebellum America. Born into the colonial aristocracy and schooled in its elitist ethic of public service, Quincy lived to see that aristocracy displaced and its ethic repudiated. That Boston, supposedly protected from the winds of democratic change which swept across the frontier and whistled through the streets of newer

American cities, provides the principal setting for his life, enhances the diagnostic value of his biography. Where better to observe the clash of deferential forms of eighteenth-century public life and Jacksonian egalitarianism than in what Alexander Hamilton called "the citadel of sound principles"?

This is the second full-scale biographical study of Josiah Quincy. The first, Edmund Quincy's *Life of Josiah Quincy,* differs from the standard nineteenth-century filial biography in one important respect: it is the work of an accomplished writer. Moreover, because Edmund had access to materials, no longer extant, relating to his father's congressional career, his book continues to serve as a valuable primary source for the Jeffersonian era. My indebtedness is evidenced in my notes.

In its interpretation, however, Edmund's *Life of Josiah Quincy* conforms to a recognizable genre of nineteenth-century biography. Resistance to change and an uncompromising refusal to countenance new notions are depicted as Quincy's signal virtues. Political defeats are cherished more than victories, proof that he never succumbed to the crowd. Over half the book is given to his father's eight years in Congress with the result that it slights his subsequent municipal and academic careers. Edmund later made explicit a conviction that is implicit in the biography: that his father's place in American history would rest not upon his successes as mayor of Boston, president of Harvard, or even as an anti-slavery agitator in the 1850's, but upon his actions in Congress. It was consistent with the author's interpretation that these actions met with almost universal popular disapproval and overwhelming political opposition.

"How like a rock from the Quincy quarries your father stood among those stormy waves," Oliver Wendell Holmes wrote to Edmund after reading his *Life of Josiah Quincy.* A later and more critical perusal prompted Vernon L. Parrington, in his categorizing way, to dismiss the subject as "an example of stalwart and antiquated Federalism." Still later, and more appreciatively, Samuel Eliot Morison called him "a colonial whig, born too late."

But he was more than that. Intransigence was neither Quincy's most characteristic trait nor the one that merits further consideration. While he lacked sympathy with and often understanding of developments taking place during his long lifetime, he never turned away from them in disgust. At times he could sound like the most hidebound of reactionaries but seldom the "opted-out" dissident. In order to satisfy an inherited sense of public responsibility to his fellow citizens, he had, in some measure, to accommodate his beliefs to theirs, to adapt his commitment to continuity to their passion for change. He made no more accommodations than required and sometimes made too few; that he made any illustrates the conflicting imperatives that gave his life its dynamic tension and retrospective significance. Though Josiah Quincy never fully resolved the question of how to remain true to his elitist beliefs and yet retain a functional role in a society that rejected them, he did keep working at it.

Acknowledgments

Among the many debts incurred along the way, I owe a special one to Professor Donald Fleming. His kindly counsel and not-so-kindly critical skills have been made available to me at every point in this project, as has his scholarly example. I should also like to acknowledge the help of four other members of the Harvard History Department: Bernard Bailyn, Frank Freidel, Oscar Handlin, and Robert Lee Wolff.

Draft chapters have received detailed criticism from the following individuals: Bernard Barber, Stephen E. Koss, Chilton Williamson, all of Barnard College; Eric L. McKitrick, Columbia University; Richard C. Wade, City University of New York; Walter Muir Whitehill, Boston Athenæum. Editorial assistance was provided by Ann Louise McLaughlin, Madeleine Gleason, and Shana R. Conron. To all these people I wish to express my thanks — and apologies for not always following their sound advice.

Among the several librarians and archivists who proved helpful beyond the call of their official responsibilities. I should like to mention Miss Carolyn Jakeman, Houghton Library, Harvard University; Stephen T. Riley, Director, and Miss Winifred Collins, Massachusetts Historical Society; Lyman H. Butterfield and Marc Friedlaender, The Adams Papers; John Alden, Rare Book Room, Boston Public Library; Kimball C. Elkins and Harley P. Holden, Harvard University Archives; the staff and trustees of the Redwood Library, Newport, who allowed me to take up undisturbed residence all one summer.

Research costs for the project were defrayed by the United States Government through the National Defense Education Act, by the American Philosophical Society, the Barnard College Faculty Research Fund, and the Charles Warren Center for Studies in American History. To all these organizations I am grateful, both for their largesse and for their patience.

Parts of Chapters 6 and 7 have appeared in the *Political Science Quarterly,* and Chapter 8, in somewhat altered form, in the *William and Mary Law Review.* My thanks to the editors of both journals for permission to reproduce this material. Reproduction of the Gilbert Stuart portrait of Josiah Quincy is with the permission of the Museum of Fine Arts, Boston.

Finally, I wish to acknowledge the contributions of my wife, Ann, who took time from her own work to aid me in mine, first as critic and editor, last as typist and indexer, always as my spur and my happiness.

Robert A. McCaughey

Charles Warren Center
Harvard University
Cambridge, Massachusetts

Contents

Josiah Quincy, 1772 - 1864

1 / A Dubious Legacy

...besides diligence and application when young, it is indispensably necessary to the forming of *a distinguished career in public*, that truth should be the invariable object of your pursuit, and *your end*, the public good. These are maxims of wisdom, which I have every reason to think your Great Grandfather, as well as your dear deceased Father strictly adher'd to. . . .

–Josiah Quincy I, to his grandson
Josiah, on his eighth birthday

"From a Massachusetts point of view," Henry Adams once corrected an English journalist, "the Adamses are hardly a family at all; they are a creation of yesterday, barely a century old." The same he could not say, however, of his great-great-grandmother's family. "The Quincys are, strictly speaking, an old family. They belonged to the colonial aristocracy."[1]

Of Good Estate

No less a descendant than Abigail Adams served as the Quincy's first genealogist. Her principal feat in this capacity was to connect the family of her maternal grandfather, John Quincy, of Braintree, Massachusetts, to Robert de Quincey, Earl of Winchester, a signatory of the Magna Carta and a casualty of the Crusades. Her evidence, which consisted of little more than similar coats-of-arms, came to light during her researches in the 1780's while her husband served as American envoy to the Court of St. James's. "These matters have hitherto been of so little consideration in America," she noted in her journal; "scarcely any person traces their descent beyond the third generation by which means the Britains sometimes twit us for being descended from the refuse of their gaols and from transported convicts. . . . Can it be wondered at," she concluded, "that I should wish to trace an ancestor amongst the Signers of the Magna Carta?"[2]

Although English heralds insisted that the Earl of Winchester's lineage expired in 1321, nineteenth-century Bostonians generously conceded the Quincys their Norman ancestors. They proved stickier, however, when claims were put forth by the family's second

1

genealogist. Eliza Susan Quincy, Josiah's eldest daughter and his amanuensis, devoted the years after his death to establishing the Quincys' precedence in America. It had earlier been assumed that the Quincy name, in the person of Edmund Quincy, first came to Massachusetts in 1633, but Eliza insisted that Edmund had landed five years earlier on a reconnoitering trip. He then went back to Achurch, in Northamptonshire, sold his farm and dissolved his English connections, gathered up his family and *returned* to Massachusetts in 1633. Despite all her researches, Boston remained, and remains, unpersuaded.[3]

Still, 1633 was not a bad year. Governor Winthrop had welcomed Edmund and the other men "of good estate," including the Reverends John Cotton and Thomas Hooker, when the *Griffin* docked in Boston in early September. Made a freeman upon arrival and enrolled in the First Church by November, Edmund was elected the following spring to represent Boston at the first meeting of the General Court. Later the same year he helped secure for the Puritan community the legal title to the Shawmut peninsula upon which it was rearing itself.[4]

In 1635 he received a grant from the town to several thousand acres of land situated six miles to the south and already famous as the site of Thomas Morton's bacchanalian festivities. By the time Edmund moved his family out to Mount Wollaston (later Braintree, still later Quincy), Miles Standish had evicted Morton, pulled up his maypole, and chased off those "frolicking lasses in beaver coats." What remained were a few Moswetuset Indians and some of the best farmland in New England. By befriending the one, he secured title to most of the other, thereby establishing the landed base for the subsequent Quincy fortunes.[5]

Edmund "the Settler" died in 1635, leaving a wife and two children behind in the wilderness. All managed nicely. His wife Judith remarried and before her death in 1654 saw her daughter Judith married to John Hull, the Bay Colony's mintmaster and its richest citizen. An issue of this marriage, Hannah, was subsequently snapped up, along with a dowry of gold reportedly equal to her weight, by the diarist and later Chief Justice, Samuel Sewall. The second Edmund devoted most of his energies to the family estate in Braintree where he was accorded those offices reserved for men of standing in seventeenth-century Massachusetts. A colonel in the

Suffolk militia, representative to the General Court, and perennial moderator of the town meeting, it was Edmund his neighbors called upon, whether to warn children against cutting down trees in the Common, or, after the cashiering of Governor Edmund Andros in 1688, to serve on the Council of Safety.[6]

The last of Edmund II's nine children, yet another Edmund, carried the main family line into the eighteenth century and initiated two practices that were to be followed by six successive generations of Quincys: attending Harvard College and naming a son Josiah. Alternating between Braintree, where he served as justice of the peace, and Boston, the provincial capital, Edmund III quickly acquired other badges of colonial prominence. Governor Dudley commissioned him a colonel in the Suffolk militia in 1713; five years later Governor Shute appointed him a judge of the Superior Court, a post he held for twenty years. In 1738, while representing Massachusetts in a boundary dispute with New Hampshire, he died. The General Court gave his heirs a thousand acres of land in Lenox and had a monument erected over his English grave in recognition of his services. In addition to an estate of over £14,000, Edmund III left behind "an unblemished Reputation for *Wisdom, Justice*, and *Probity*."[7]

For more than a century the Quincys had experienced a steady accumulation of wealth and influence. A good start, the absence of profligate sons, and a knack for marrying well all helped. So had a willingness to serve in public office, the ability to do so effectively, at the same time capitalizing on the economic benefits that often went with such positions. Religious moderates and monetary conservatives, they were equally welcome at the Province House and among the other members of the gentry. Even in the highly unstable society of colonial Massachusetts, where fortunes and reputations could be lost on the turning of the evening tide, by the 1740's the Quincys had achieved the appearance of permanence.[8]

After graduating from Harvard in the 1720's, Edmund III's two sons, Edmund and Josiah, joined with their brother-in-law, Edward Jackson, to form the Boston mercantile firm of Quincy, Quincy, and Jackson. The partners prospered, in part because of such contacts as Governor William Shirley and in part because of the general wartime prosperity of the 1740's. Then, in the summer of 1748, they got lucky. The *Bethell*, a small privateer owned by the firm and sailing off Gibraltar, came upon the *Jesus Maria Joseph*, a Spanish treasure ship. The *Bethell*'s Captain Isaac Freeman gave chase to the larger but leaky *Jesus*, and under cover of night bluffed the Spanish captain into striking his colors without a shot being exchanged. "By daylight we had the last of the prisoners secured," Freeman wrote his employers; they "were ready to hang themselves on sight of our six wooden guns, and scarce enough men to hoist the topsails." Before cutting the *Jesus* loose, the *Bethell* crew relieved it of 161 chests of gold and silver. Each partner's share amounted to more than $100,000, making them among the richest men in the colonies.[9]

Losing interest in the business soon thereafter, Josiah Quincy dissolved his connections with the firm, sold his Boston house, and returned with his wife and four children to Braintree. There he intended to dabble in glass manufacturing, while satisfying "his passion for field sports" and his responsibilities as the presiding squire. Braintree received "the Colonel," as he wished to be called after being so commissioned in the Suffolk militia, with mixed feelings; many of his neighbors could not help but begrudge his windfall. Nonetheless, the town meeting acknowledged his rights to the office of moderator, held previously by his father, uncle, and grandfather. Beginning in 1754 he regularly represented the town in the General Court and served, along with two other Quincys, as one of its four justices of the peace.[10]

Nowhere is the Quincys' dominance of the Braintree scene more colorfully recorded than in John Adams' early diaries. "Most secretly despise him, hate him," he wrote of the Colonel in 1760, "but they fear him too." Adams, a struggling young lawyer, knew better than to run afoul of the town's leading citizen, pompous ass or no. Often he tried convincing himself that the Colonel's "friendship is not worth a wise man's seeking, nor his enmity worth fearing," but when an invitation came from the Colonel to go on "a fishing frolick," though he knew from past experience that it would be Quincy who fished while Adams rowed, he went.[11]

The Colonel's four children elicited the same scrutiny. Edmund, following graduation from Harvard in 1752, became a merchant of sorts in Boston. He much preferred the role of litterateur to that of businessman, which along with his liberal religious views did not escape critical notice in Braintree. Adams thought Ned enjoyed playing the heretic and had nothing good to say about him except that "he tells a story reasonably well."[12]

Samuel Quincy was a sophomore when Adams enrolled at Harvard in 1751. Although Sam's class rank (third of twenty) identified him as the son of an important personage and John's (fourteenth of twenty-four) did not, they became reasonably good friends. Both were admitted to the Boston bar in 1758, but whereas John took his legal career very seriously, Sam preferred "Cards, Fiddles, and Girls." While acknowledging Sam's "easy, social, and benevolent ways," Adams begrudged him the unearned edge his family name gave him over a nonentity like himself. "When I was young," he later reminisced with Thomas Jefferson, "the *Summum Bonum* in Massachusetts was to be worth ten thousand pounds Sterling, ride in a chariot, be colonel of a Regiment of Militia and hold a seat in his Majesty's Council." In the early 1760's it appeared doubtful that hard work alone would bring all those emblems of status to the son of a Braintree yeoman; Sam Quincy could expect them as a simple matter of inheritance.[13]

If the Colonel's two older sons convinced Adams that the Quincys lacked perseverance, his daughter demonstrated their lack of taste. Despite a concerted effort on John's part, complete with moonlight walks and solemn discussions about marital life, Miss Hannah Quincy made permanent bestowal of her affections elsewhere. Throughout the spring of 1759 the "tender and indulgent" Hannah welcomed his romantic advances only to become engaged the following year to Dr. Bela Lincoln, whom the rejected suitor described, not without feeling, as "boorish, ungentlemanly, impolite, ridiculous . . . hoggish, illbred, uncivil, haughty, coxcomb." Abigail Smith soon filled the void but Hannah's perfidy had hurt. It was another instance of the Quincy hauteur. Adams needed only the exposure provided in pre-Revolutionary Braintree to justify his lifelong suspicion of the high-born. As a somewhat mellowed old man he could write of the Quincys as only one of a dozen "Aristocratical Families" of colonial Massachusetts, but in his young manhood aristocrat and Quincy were synonymous.[14]

The Patriot

Ned Quincy died of a pulmonary condition in 1768, thirty-five and unmarried. In contrast, Hannah outlived two husbands to the age of ninety. After Dr. Lincoln's unmourned death in 1774, she married Ebenezer Storer, a man with an affinity for noble, nonremunerative activities. Only the intervention of President John Adams in 1797, providing Storer with a federal office, rescued his family from debt. Hannah's old suitor could not have failed to derive a certain satisfaction from this turn of events.[15]

Sam's end was still sadder. During the late 1760's he had drifted into the political orbit of Lieutenant Governor Thomas Hutchinson, the office of Solicitor General and the promise of a secret retainer to be derived from the Tea Tax sealing his allegiance to the Administration camp and earning him the enmity of the Patriots. When fighting broke out in 1775, he boarded the Dover-bound *Minerva* with dozens of other Boston Loyalists. "I am but a passenger," he wrote to his family, "and must follow the fortunes of the day." He never returned to Boston; his Hanover Street house was successively occupied, plundered, confiscated as Loyalist property and sold at public auction. In 1780 he took up residence in the West Indies where he had purchased a royal office. There he died in 1789.[16]

Sam provided the Quincys with their Loyalist; no Massachusetts family could later claim pre-Revolutionary eminence without at least one. Nonetheless, he had acted without his family's approval. The Colonel, whose support of the Patriots was unequivocal, had been less shocked by his son's decision to "enlist as a sycophant under the obnoxious Hutchinson" than sadly confirmed in his estimate of Sam's worth. There was no reason, however, for the Quincys to feel incriminated by the defection of a single member; by the time Sam sidled up the ladder of the *Minerva*, the family had already contributed a martyr to the Revolutionary cause.[17]

So different in personality was Josiah Quincy Jr. from the rest of the Colonel's children, one is tempted to query consanguinity. While Sam acknowledged his own "permanent passion" to be "a love of Ease and Retirement," he prophesied that his younger brother, "carried out by the zeal and fervor of imagination, strength of Genius, and love of Glory, shall snatch at the wreaths of fame through the turmoils of *public action*." The brilliant and fragile child of his parents' middle years, Josiah never experienced an extended period of good health. The "delicacy of his constitution" represented a standing concern of his family and friends, and may have accounted for the absolute seriousness with which he approached all he did during his short life.[18]

Following a brilliant four years at Harvard, capped by his 1763

Commencement English Oration on "Patriotism," Josiah took up the study of law with enthusiasm and industry. He read in the Boston office of Oxenbridge Thatcher and so impressed this leader of the Massachusetts bar that the bulk of the office's business was soon in his hands. By 1767, only a year after being admitted to practice before the Inferior Court, he had one of the biggest practices in Boston.[19]

As early as 1768 Josiah Jr. could report to his father that "I am out of a temptation to the meaner vices, and in that state, which to one of my temper, is the happiest human nature can boast, an independency, save on God and myself, for a decent support through life." Nor did his engagement to Abigail Phillips, the eldest daughter of one of Boston's leading merchants, cloud his material prospects. Yet even at this point, only twenty-four and on the threshold of a promising legal career, he had premonitions of early death. He insisted that his life, if short, be guided by "the hope of quitting the stage with that best human standard of true worth, the general approbation of my countrymen."[20]

Such hopes had already drawn him into the political tumult. Under the pen-name "Hyperion," the first of many he used during his polemical career, Quincy entered the lists in the fall of 1767 with a series of letters to the *Boston Gazette*. Blasting Parliament for the revenue and judicial legislation it was about to impose following the repeal of the Stamp Act, he identified the colonists' cause with that of the English revolutionaries of the seventeenth century and dismissed the present English government as their "degenerate progeny." He then warned his fellow Bostonians against "these venal hirelings" who represented the crown locally. "When they endeavour to make us 'perceive our inability to oppose our mother country,' " Quincy concluded, "let us boldly answer: In defence of our civil and religious rights, we dare oppose the world." All this in 1767.[21]

Historians of the American Revolution have generally acknowledged Quincy's contributions in bringing the colonial pot to a boil, though some have doubted his sincerity in doing so. This was Thomas Hutchinson's view as well; rather than take seriously the excitable young man's charges, he dismissed Quincy as a "Wilkes manqué." Certainly no one can deny the violence of his rhetoric. A passage from his *Observations on . . . the Boston Port Bill* (1774) will serve as an illustration:

Hath not Britain (fallen from her pristine freedom and glory) treated America, as Castile did Arragon? Have not Britons imposed on our necks the same yoke which the Castilians imposed on the happy Arragonese? Yes! I speak it with grief,—I speak it with anguish,—Britons are our oppressors: I speak it with shame,—I speak it with indignation,—*we are slaves.*

Yet, as John Adams said, Quincy was "always impetuous and vehement." No less than his public statements, his letters to his father resound with charges against "the obnoxious tools of the British ministry," while his travel journals attest to his almost paranoid fears of corruption in America and unchecked luxury in England. With his physical condition in precipitous decline after the fall of 1772, he repudiated the politics of accommodation as personally unacceptable.[22]

However much an emotional revolutionary, Quincy remained an ideological conservative. The urgency that informed his politics emanated less from what he believed could be gained by vigorous action than from what he feared would be lost without it. He read John Locke and Algernon Sidney, John Trenchard and Thomas Gordon, Mrs. Macaulay and other English radical theorists, not to devise a program but to muster a defense for prevailing practices. The political liberties for which they argued—extended suffrage, frequent elections, actual representation, checks on the executive—he already enjoyed, as had four generations of Massachusetts Quincys. Only after 1763, when fiscal considerations and imperial pretensions in England seemed to threaten these liberties, did Quincy and his fellow colonists move to articulate an ideology.[23]

What made revolutionaries out of both Josiah Quincys was British meddling with the colonial *status quo.* Any alteration in long-standing arrangements, not only commercial but religious, military, legislative, and legal, was viewed as a challenge to their favored place in the community. From their perspective, British imperial policy could easily be interpreted as a conspiracy designed to displace those families who had secured themselves a measure of permanence atop the shaky social pyramid that was colonial Massachusetts. In this context Josiah Quincy Jr.'s otherwise curious definition of the goal of "independence" takes on meaning: "to restrain, to a certain degree, the instability of fortune."[24]

Quincy's revolutionary fervor never became confused with egalitarianism. Like most eighteenth-century "radicals," he did not question the basic economic and social ordering of England and the colonies. While in London in 1774, he made plans, "if the affairs of America should terminate speedily in the freedom and peace of the country," to bring back with him indentured servants to develop the family holdings out in Lenox. Even his well-known antipathy to slavery, as revealed in his "Southern Journal," was based not on any belief in the right of blacks to political freedom but on his fear that the institution rendered Southern whites unfit to govern themselves. Josiah Quincy I owned slaves in Braintree, a fact that seems to have caused Josiah Jr. little discomfort.[25]

Nor does he qualify as a democrat. The ideal polity of his admired English theorists—"a broad, propertied, oligarchy, in which the lower orders should clearly know and accept their places"—was his as well. Like his father, he felt a paternalistic affection for the yeomen of New England, but farmers elsewhere, he discovered during his travels in 1773, "cut a very different figure," while most of "the middling order" were "odious characters."[26]

Quincy feared the colonial mob as much as English meddling; both he believed capable of bringing on disorder. He came away from the Stamp Act riots in 1765 convinced that in all of history there had never been "a more flagrant instance to what a pitch of infatuation an incensed populace can arise." Later, when Sam Adams urged that mobs be encouraged to intimidate merchants who reneged on the nonimportation pledges, Quincy warned him against "groundlessly enflaming the minds of the People." Twice in 1770, in *Rex v. Richardson* and in the Boston Massacre Trial, he defended Englishmen who stood up to "the rabble." Indeed, at times Quincy seemed to be arguing that only a break with England would avert mob rule. The most serious charge made against Parliament in his *Observations on the Boston Port Bill* was its persistence in policies that had earlier provoked mob violence. Bostonians were not "a tumultuous, disorderly people," but how much longer would they remain so? One might reverse Carl Becker's familiar apothegm and argue that Quincy insisted on home rule in order to assure the continuation of those who ruled at home.[27]

In the fall of 1774 Quincy went to England to confer with friends of the American cause and to make a final determination for the Continental Congress of Parliament's intentions. After several months there, he sailed back across the Atlantic, already "far gone with a consumption," only to die on April 26, 1775, a few hours after the *Boston Packet* tied up at Gloucester. No one ever found out what he learned, but by then it did not matter. A week earlier Minutemen and British troops had clashed on the road between Lexington and Concord.[28]

Although he died before American independence had been achieved, Josiah Quincy Jr. has received his due share of the credit for bringing it about. He was, according to John Lowell, "assuredly the most extraordinary man whom our Revolution brought to notice." His wish to die with "the general approbation of my countrymen" had been granted. Like A. E. Housman's young athlete, the thirty-one-year-old Patriot might have been "a smart lad, to slip betimes away," leaving behind still another Josiah Quincy to cope with a nation that his generation's political audacity had made possible—perhaps inevitable.[29]

Preparations in the Traditional Mode

"Though some of them were remarkably distinguished," the Colonel informed his eight-year-old grandson, "I indulge the pleasing hope, that by your assiduity and perseverance . . . you will one day equal at least, if not surpass your predecessors in every respect." Born on February 4, 1772, in the upstairs bedroom of his father's house on Marlborough Street in Boston's then fashionable North End, this sixth generation Quincy first opened his eyes on the final days of the colonial era. The recent repeal of the Townshend Acts had for the moment quieted things down in Boston, but the storm brewing since the early 1760's continued to gather force. When it broke in 1775 Josiah Quincy was three years old and fatherless.[30]

Despite his early death, Josiah Quincy Jr. had left behind for his son a considerable legacy. There was the Quincy name, long respected in Massachusetts and now honored throughout America because of his efforts on behalf of the Revolutionary cause. And, of course, there were his books. "To my son Josiah when he shall reach the age of fifteen years," his will directed,

Algernon Sidney's Works in a large quarto, John Locke's Works in 3 Vols. in Folio, Lord Bacon's Works in 4 Vol. in Folio, Gordon's Tacitus in 4 Vol., Gordon's Sallust, Cato's Letters by Gordon and Trenchard and Mrs. Macaulay's History of England. May the Spirit of Liberty rest upon him.

These well-thumbed volumes and the English radical political thought they contained had served the father well; when he composed his will in 1774 he knew no reason why they should not likewise serve his son. Had the Revolution he helped set in motion gone only as far as he envisioned, perhaps they would have.[31]

The most striking aspect of Josiah's early training is the assumption on the part of those responsible for it that the Revolution changed nothing. Loyalist pamphleteers had prophesied that anarchy would follow hard on a break with England, but the Colonel never took them seriously. The war was making the reputations of a few heretofore marginal Massachusetts families, like the Adamses and the Cabots, while in the upper ranks of the old colonial order a number of openings had been created by Tory emigrations, yet neither phenomenon need affect the basic hierarchical structure of the society. Having supported the Patriots in 1775 "to combat the enemies of the British Constitution in its Purity," the Colonel believed their success only confirmed his family's ascendancy. He had good reason to believe so. His commission as justice of the peace, granted in 1757 and then voided in 1775 with the closing of the colonial courts, had been promptly reissued by the new state government in 1777. Similarly, his views continued to be deferred to at the Braintree town meeting; in 1781 he was chosen to draw up the town's instructions on revising the new state constitution. Presumably the other emblems of the family's status were equally secure.[32]

Grandfather Quincy offered much advice on the boy's education, insisting that it be "in the traditional mode," but Grandfather Phillips paid the bills. Following her husband's death, Abigail fell back on the resources of her father, William Phillips, described by a Boston Tory in 1775 as "a deacon of the Old South Meeting . . . an occasional moderator of Town Meetings. . . . Formality and a Presbyterian Face are his ornaments." His branch of the Phillipses came from Andover, twenty miles north of Boston, where his father, the Reverend Samuel Phillips, dominated the religious and political scene for much of the eighteenth century. William, like his father, subscribed to a harshly Calvinistic version of Christianity, which did not prevent his becoming one of New England's most successful merchants and one of its most vigorous supporters of the Revolution.[33]

It did make him, however, something less than an indulgent

grandfather. Abigail's objections notwithstanding, he decided to send his six-year old grandson away to boarding school. A nephew, Samuel Jr., had been trying since graduating from Harvard in 1771 to set up a boarding school in Andover. Other members of the family had supported the project from the beginning, whereas Uncle William's interest coincided with the arrival of his rambunctious grandson into his household. In 1777 he joined his two brothers and provided sufficient backing for Samuel's venture. The following spring Phillips Academy opened with Josiah Quincy its youngest student.[34]

Except for an anti-classical bias, Samuel's academic views were thoroughly conservative. He wanted only the sons of the wealthy at Andover. "The happiness of such a child [a rich one] is as great consequence as that of a poor child," he reasoned, "his opportunity for doing good greater." When a few charity students were eventually admitted, Samuel made it clear that the motive had been Christian kindness, not incipient egalitarianism.[35]

A principal reason for establishing the school out in Andover was the belief that a proper Calvinist atmosphere might be better maintained there than in Boston. All the Phillipses viewed with horror the advances made by Arminianism in the capital. Even the Quincys were infected; Ned had joined Jonathan Mayhew's very liberal West Church while Josiah Jr. had regarded Charles Chauncy, a somewhat more secretive anti-Trinitarian, as both his religious and his political advisor. By packing Josiah off to Andover, Grandfather Phillips hoped, in addition to getting him out of his hair, to rescue the boy's soul.[36]

Josiah spent eight long years at Andover. Eliphalet Pearson, the school's first headmaster and a thoroughgoing Calvinist, with Ezekiel Cheever's *Accidence* in one hand and a switch in the other, did what he could to "promote True Piety and Virtue" in the heart of his terrified charge. More than seventy years later Quincy looked back on his Andover days without a trace of nostalgia, remembering most clearly "the severe discipline to which I was subjected" and the unending drudgery of the schoolwork. In 1785 Pearson advised Mrs. Quincy against sending her son on to Harvard, certifying him as incapable of sustained study. The student's evaluation of the headmaster was equally severe: "distant and haughty in his manners, fear was the only impression I received from his treatment of myself and others."[37]

William Phillips' hopes that Andover would make a good Calvinist out of his grandson went unrealized. On the contrary, the boy reacted negatively to the school's religious orthodoxy and rejected the harsh God Pearson kept before his eyes. In later life, without ever describing himself as such, Quincy became a Unitarian, finding the rational theology of William Ellery Channing far more appealing than the fire and brimstone favored by his Phillips relatives. He summarized his religious creed in 1854:

From the doctrines with which metaphysical divines have chosen to obscure the word of God,—such as predestination, election, reprobation, &c.,—I turn with loathing to the refreshing assurance which, to my mind, contains the substance of revealed religion,—'In every nation, he who feareth God, and worketh righteousness, is accepted of Him.'

Comforting as such an irenic view of Christianity was in Quincy's old age, the Phillipses would have thought it blasphemy.[38]

The Andover years were not an unmitigated disaster. Josiah managed to memorize enough Greek and Latin from Pearson, an accomplished classicist, to provide the basis for a life-long interest in both languages. James Walker, a classics professor at Harvard before becoming its president in 1853, thought Quincy a better Latin scholar than any of his predecessors in the Harvard presidency, an opinion that must have caused a stir beneath Increase Mather's gravestone. Moreover, the close discipline under which he toiled yielded dividends later. Like his father, he was a high-strung and excitable human being, temperamentally prone to rash actions. He managed to offset this trait in some degree by a huge capacity for work. A man of great energy, his many accomplishments owed less to any intellectual brilliance than to a capacity to drive himself to the point where the dullest and most intractable materials became vitally interesting. "I am not apt to be startled at labor," he wrote in 1804, "nature having been plain in her intimations that she intended me for *the dray*." First intimations came at Andover.[39]

A final benefit derived from Phillips Academy was the friends he made there. As intended by its founders, the school immediately became the preferred repository for the sons of Massachusetts' first families. His cousin and life-long friend, John Phillips, later a prominent state legislator, first mayor of Boston, and father of Wendell Phillips, was a fellow student. Quincy also shared his schoolboy rigors with John Lowell, subsequently a lawyer, philan-

thropist, and dyspeptic Federalist pamphleteer, and with John
Thornton Kirkland, afterwards Quincy's minister and his predecessor
in the Harvard presidency. Like them he survived Andover and, in
the summer of 1786, effected his escape to the welcome freedom of
Cambridge.[40]

For most Bostonians in the last quarter of the eighteenth century,
college meant Harvard. Dartmouth and Brown were still too new to
attract students outside their immediate environs while Yale and
Princeton, despite their specifically Calvinist orientations, had yet to
develop an eastern Massachusetts clientele. Moreover, Harvard was
one matter upon which the Phillipses and the Quincys were in
agreement; eleven of the former and ten of the latter had already
preceded Josiah to Cambridge.[41]

The college had passed unscathed through the Revolution—and
unreformed. In size and function it differed remarkably little from
the Harvard of the 1760's when Josiah Jr. attended, or, for that
matter, from the Harvard of the Colonel's undergraduate days in the
1720's. Its patrons remained those few, principally Boston families
desirous of exposing their sons to a measure of learning before
starting them into professional life. The college's governance continued to be, as it had been since 1650, in the hands of a
self-perpetuating Corporation (President, Treasurer, and five
Fellows), with a Board of Overseers, comprised of state officials and
Congregationalist ministers, which possessed a seldom-used veto.
Rather than being altered by the break with England, this arrangement had been affirmed by the 1780 Massachusetts Convention.[42]

Academically, any changes since the Revolution had undoubtedly
been for the worse. The "humorless, cold" President Joseph Willard
was far less effective in the classroom, and less often found in one,
than Edward Holyoke. With the retirement in 1779 of John Winthrop, Hollis Professor of Mathematics and Natural Philosophy,
Harvard lost its only internationally recognized scholar; it would not
have another until Benjamin Peirce in the 1840's. Teaching responsibilities fell principally on a half-dozen tutors, whose knowledge of
the prescribed subjects was scarcely greater than the students'. John
Quincy Adams, who entered Harvard in 1786 as a sophomore, after
having studied at two European universities, judged it "fit only for
idle fellows."[43]

Whatever its shortcomings, the Freshman Quincy found much to like about Harvard. After Andover, he appreciated its lack of close supervision and its religious latitudinarism—not that he took advantage of either. Compared with most of his classmates, he was a model of circumspection and propriety. Except for being docked occasionally for missing morning chapel, his behavior was exemplary. Years later he would speak of Joseph Dennie, an incorrigible disturber-of-the-peace and later publisher of the *Port Folio*, as a college pal, but Dennie never regarded Quincy as among "the *good* lads of the class." Presumably his failure to congregate regularly with "the *good* lads" at the Blue Anchor Inn rendered him suspect. No matter, he had other friends and his own standards. "Through my youth and early manhood the main stay and stimulus to virtue," he recalled sixty years after graduation, "were my affection for my mother, and my respect and interest in the memory of my father, which she never ceased to impress on my heart, and to make a motive for my life."[44]

Just as he approved of Harvard's liberalism, he had no complaints about its academic fare. The college made little of competition; regular grades and written examinations were unheard of, and the infrequent public exercises conducted by alumni were *pro forma* affairs. While John Quincy Adams might rail at it, Quincy worked steadily through the curriculum, learning what he could and without taxing the limited resources of his tutors. In Greek he read Xenophon and a few books of the *Iliad*; in Latin some Sallust and Livy; Mathematics consisted of algebra and some arithmetic; Locke's *Essay concerning Human Understanding* was assigned in Metaphysics, and a treatise on astronomy in Natural Philosophy; a handful of other books and that was that. He did not break under the strain, but then neither did he later presume that college was the terminal point in the eduational process.[45]

The prevailing pedagogical system stressed oral recitations; frequent college-wide conferences encouraged students to develop their skills in public speaking. Quincy worked hard at this, and his efforts were rewarded when he was chosen English Orator for his 1790 Commencement. In later years he would be generally acknowledged as one of Boston's great orators, a description Daniel Webster confirmed by calling a speech Quincy made on the occasion of Boston's Bicentennial celebration the best he had ever heard. In this regard, at least, his four years at Harvard served him well.[46]

Preparations for public life did not end with graduation. It would be necessary, for example, to get a job. "In New England," a Bostonian later put it, "there is no consideration unless there is specific employment." Given Quincy's limited options and family tradition, that meant the law. Although Theophilus Parsons' Newburyport office was acknowledged as the best place to acquire legal training, he decided to do his apprenticeship closer to home. It was in William Tudor's Boston office, within hailing distance of his mother's house on Court Street, that Quincy spent three years casually perusing Coke and Blackstone.[47]

Quincy later faulted the apprenticeship system for failing to inspire in him "a love for his profession" and for quenching whatever "juvenile ardor" he brought to it. But this was hardly fair either to the system or to William Tudor; ardor, however juvenile, must exist before it can be quenched. For Quincy the study and practice of law represented a socially acceptable way of biding time while awaiting the opportunity for public responsibilities. He was admitted to the Suffolk bar in 1793 and handled a few cases each year before the Court of Common Pleas, until 1804 when he quietly closed his office permanently. He seems not to have bothered following the circuit courts about the state as did his more ambitious, more financially pressed colleagues. His name appeared on an 1802 list of Boston's "most prominent lawyers," but that was because of his "classical knowledge," "wit," and "integrity," and despite "size of practice." Seldom given to understatement, Quincy admitted later in life that he had "hung rather loosely on the profession."[48]

Other activities kept him from the office. The Wednesday Evening Club, founded in 1777 and easily the most select in Boston, welcomed Quincy to its table in 1797. A year later, at twenty-six, he became the youngest member of the Massachusetts Historical Society; a year after that, he was elected to the American Academy of Arts and Sciences. In 1801 he and several other Boston professionals founded the Society for the Study of Natural Philosophy. Discussions which he led at the Society's meetings on the air pump and the electrical spark, as well as on one occasion "a pleasing experiment" on the chemical affinities, understandably put a crimp in his law practice.[49]

Yet Quincy's financial situation was never so secure that it could be left unattended. He had no intention of devoting himself to money-getting, but realized that going broke would never do. Upon the Colonel's death in 1784, the Braintree farm became his; the bulk of the estate, however, went elsewhere. Because of a falling-out between his mother and her father, little would be forthcoming from the Phillips side. Fortunately for Quincy, the 1790's were boom years in Boston. Thanks to a thriving international trade, the town experienced an unprecedented influx of wealth that put Charles Bulfinch's architectural talents much in demand. By investing in Boston and South Shore real estate, as well as in such transportation ventures as the Neponset Turnpike and the Middlesex Canal, Quincy partook of the general prosperity. Though never a speculator on the scale of Harrison Gray Otis, he enjoyed considerable success as an investor in real estate. In view of the fact that realty values in Boston tripled every twenty years between 1800 and 1860, it required little more than longevity for him to become at his death one of the city's principal landholders. The other virtue of holdings in real estate was that it required little of his time, time he had earmarked for public affairs.[50]

"This young man," declared President John Adams following Quincy's visit with him in Philadelphia in January 1796, "is a rare instance of hereditary eloquence and ingenuity in the fourth generation. . . . He comes into life with every advantage of family, fortune and education." Accordingly, the President judged him "the first match in the United States" and commended him to his daughter Abby, though he conceded the possibility that "he may have left his heart in Boston." And so he had: with Miss Eliza Susan Morton who had visited there the summer before. The eldest daughter of John Morton, a leading New York merchant and financial backer of the Revolutionary cause, the twenty-two-year-old Eliza was introduced to all of Boston's eligible bachelors, Quincy prominently among them. A week after their meeting they became secretly engaged, and they were married on June 6, 1797, in New York City. The precipitate nature of their courtship notwithstanding, the marriage proved to be for both an unqualified success. During their fifty-three years together, Quincy remained devoted to her, while Eliza, in addition to bearing seven children and his idiosyncrasies, provided her often rash and emotionally unbending husband with sound counsel and unfailing support. He never discounted the importance of either.[51]

Preparations were now complete. Schooled in the approved eighteenth-century manner, instilled with a sense of public obligation, possessed of a measure of financial independence, professional credentials, and an eminently suitable wife, he was ready to take his place in the world. Because little in his life to this point had obliged him to question whether all these preparations had been made for a world different from the one that awaited him, and in which he would have to live, he stepped forward confidently.

2 / A Federalist from Principle

I am a Federalist because the men thus called, have been, under God, the means of great blessings to this country.

—Josiah Quincy, 1805

There was little of trauma attending Josiah Quincy's selection of a career. Family tradition and the fact of his father's political ambitions having been frustrated by early death pointed him toward public life, as did his own inclinations. "He is the only man among us," Harrison Gray Otis said of Quincy, "who had intended *ab initio* to pursue politics as a profession and who has qualified himself for that department." Assured of his calling, he began very early to think himself destined to become "a public man on a large and national scale." And with some reason. The year he entered politics, 1796, John Adams was elected President of the United States. If an Adams, why not a Quincy?[1]

Forced into the Lists

Quincy made his political debut in the prescribed Boston manner, by involving himself in the affairs of the Town Meeting. After two years on various *ad hoc* committees, he received his reward in 1798 when the Board of Selectmen appointed him Town Orator. A position held previously by Harrison Gray Otis and John Quincy Adams, it was a traditional springboard to elective office. The "powerful eloquence" of his Fourth of July Oration, a ringing defense of President Adams' policies and of his refusal to submit to French extortion, won for Quincy national as well as local notice. In the spring of 1800 he was elected to the School Committee, the most prestigious of the five semi-autonomous boards directing Boston's civic affairs. Later that spring he addressed the Charitable Fire Society, another sign of his rising political stock. At twenty-eight he seemed on his way.[2]

His political aspirations had much to commend them to Boston's Federalist leaders. A member of the socially prestigious and doctrinally moderate New South Church, Quincy was known as an enthusiastic churchman at a time when Federalists were coming to regard themselves as bulwarks of Christianity against the Jacobian deists and infidels who voted as Democratic-Republicans. His honorary degrees from Yale (1792) and Princeton (1796) served as religious no less than intellectual endorsement. Moreover, he looked the part of the Federalist candidate. An 1803 Gilbert Stuart portrait reveals him to have been strikingly handsome, with a full head of dark, curly hair, an aquiline nose, and a firm, graceful chin. Over six feet tall, with broad, sloping shoulders and an impressive physique which he would retain well into his eighties, Quincy merited the *New England Palladium*'s compliment: "Apollo views with honest pride / fav'rites all on Fed'ral side." As late as 1812 a British observer could describe Federalist officeholders, in contrast with the Republicans,* as "gentlemen of fortune, talents and education." In Josiah Quincy the Federalists had an ideal candidate.[3]

Personal qualifications aside, Quincy won his first nomination to Congress by default. Following Fisher Ames's retirement from the House in 1797 after four terms, the First Middle District had been represented in the Fifth Congress by the dashing realtor of Beacon Hill, Harrison Gray Otis. Only a month before the 1800 congressional elections, however, Otis announced that he would not stand for reelection; he had earlier promised his wife to drop out of politics "until I have made some addition to my fortune." Party leaders then turned to Thomas Handasyd Perkins, a prominent China merchant and active Federalist, but he declined because of "private concerns." Other names were brought forward, but the response was the same. Only then, with the election less than two weeks away, did they get around to inquiring whether Quincy might be available.[4]

This dearth of volunteers for Congress was symptomatic of the Massachusetts Federalist party. Even its most prominent leaders were disinclined to exchange the comforts and profits of Boston for the rigors and responsibilities of the nation's capital. Cosmopolitan Philadelphia under Federalist administrations had been one thing; "wilderness Washington," under the Republicans, promised to be quite another. However politically inclined, Boston Federalists like

---

*Although Quincy and his Federalist colleagues pejoratively referred to the Jeffersonians as "Democrats," they will be identified herein as Republicans to conform with historical usage.

Otis, Perkins, Timothy Bigelow and Christopher Gore owed their principal allegiance to their commercial activities. Accordingly, they preferred a seat in the General Court which carried the same prestige as a national office, if not more, without involving a comparable sacrifice in time and fortune. It was not coincidental that most early national officeholders from eastern Massachusetts came from outlying towns; Timothy Pickering of Newburyport, Fisher Ames of Dedham, and the Adamses were cases in point. Nor was it coincidental that both Ames and Pickering died penniless, while John Quincy Adams during his last years became financially dependent upon his son Charles Francis.[5]

Perhaps more than any other factor, young Quincy's willingness, indeed his eagerness, to serve in Congress distinguished him from what Richard Hildreth called "the merely mercantile Federalists of Boston." Unlike them, he viewed officeholding as a full-time job and had so arranged his life as to be dependent upon public responsibilities to give it meaning and substance. Throughout his public career he never hesitated to make the required financial sacrifices.[6]

On October 29, 1800, three days before the election, Federalists caucusing at the Boston Concert Hall "unanimously" endorsed Josiah Quincy, "a worthy descendant of Patriotic Leaders," for Congress. Although the *Independent Chronicle* tried to dismiss him as "too young and inexperienced," it hastened to assure its Republican readers that their candidate, Dr. William Eustis, a Revolutionary War veteran and twice Quincy's age, ran on his own, not "on the virtues of his father." "What the late Josiah Quincy *was*," the *Chronicle* said of Eustis in an imaginative bit of posthumous coat-tailing, "*He* is at the moment."[7]

Despite the short notice, Quincy ran well in his first bid for Congress, rolling up a larger majority in Boston than Caleb Strong, the Federalist gubernatorial candidate, only to lose East Sudbury and Hopkinton, Holliston and Medway, and thereby the election (2790 to 2468). Charges from both sides of balloting irregularities attested to the spiritedness of the canvass. In a year when Federalists were divided over the renomination of Adams for President and "the poison of disaffection" had thinned party ranks, Quincy's showing was recognized as impressive. Taking his defeat philosophically, he assumed he would be given another chance at Eustis.[8]

Now immersed in politics, Quincy gradually abandoned what

remained of his law practice, referring to it in 1802 as "my other vocation." He had in fact to wait four years before having a second try at Congress. The 1802 Federalist nomination went not to him but to John Quincy Adams, who, after returning from Prussia in 1801, won election to the Massachusetts Senate. Party leaders there soon found him unmanageable and, anxious to get rid of him, offered him the congressional nomination. Quincy, whose availability had been certified and who was already being taken for granted, was asked to step aside. He had no choice but to comply.[9]

Despite redistricting designed to favor the Federalists, Adams failed to unseat Eustis. "A rainy day lost me the election by forty or fifty votes," he complained in his diary. Four months later he was chosen by the General Court to fill the vacant seat in the United States Senate, and Quincy's claims on the congressional nomination were again acknowledged. But not until the spring of 1804 did party leaders see fit to provide him a place in the state senate where he might more respectably cool his heels.[10]

On November 2, 1804, he again found himself challenging Eustis, now a two-term incumbent. This time, however, though Jefferson carried the state and both the Middlesex and Norfolk congressional districts elected Republicans, Quincy increased his earlier Boston majority, carried normally Republican Charlestown, and cut into Eustis' rural support enough to win by ninety-five votes. He then promptly disavowed any personal interest in the position he had sought so diligently for four years. "I was, in a manner forced into the lists from a sense of duty," he wrote in acknowledgment of congratulations from a Connecticut friend, Oliver Wolcott Jr., "rather than from inclination, from a conviction, that if my friends and party could agree upon no other, who would be willing to go, that my situation was such, that I had no just reason to decline."[11]

In January 1805, as if still trying to persuade himself of his disinterestedness, he confided to his diary: "Sensible as I am of many deficiencies it would, perhaps, have been becoming in me to have declined the honour when proffered rather than have undertaken a life to which I may, upon trial, find myself inadequate." But then, casting aside such momentary misgivings, he concluded that his acceptance was less a matter of choice than a responsibility incumbent upon him as a Quincy.

I have been educated in a high sense of the duty I owe my country and the times
are such that as on the one hand they make political life, little desirable to one
of my sentiments, in politics, so on the other, they seem to lay peculiar
obligations upon one, who was conscious of no motives of unworthy ambition,
not to shrink from defending what ramparts yet remained about our liberties
and laws.[1 2]

These are more than the typical politician's disclaimers, even a
Federalist's. During the forty-five consecutive years that Quincy held
public or semi-public office, he sincerely believed that he did so out
of a compelling sense of duty and not from "any miserable ambition
for a feather." "As I enter on this trust without any lively
expectation," he told Wolcott following his election to Congress, "I
hope I shall be able to lay it down when my time comes, as soon it
will, without regret." He stood for elective office twenty-seven times,
and served in an appointive capacity for seventeen years, yet never
hesitated to attack the "wickedly aspiring" who swarmed about the
public trough. The fact that he reveled in the pomp and regalia of
office, was never happier than when using his talents and energies in
the public domain, and had neither an occupational alternative to
nor a psychological substitute for officeholding, seems never to have
given him pause. Unquestionably, an excess of righteousness, with its
corresponding tendency to judge others too harshly, constituted a
personal failing and would later prove a distinct political liability; at
the same time, his immunity from the self-doubts that plague less
secure men was his greatest virtue and ultimately enabled him to
become what James Russell Lowell called him: "A Great Public
Character."[1 3]

The Federalist Persuasion

By virtually all the standard determinants of party affiliation—
geography, economic circumstances, profession, social status, education—Quincy was a Federalist. Moreover, he claimed to be so by
inheritance, including his grandfather and father among "those who
gave us the Federal Constitution" and brought "great blessings to
this country." As a Harvard freshman he watched with approval as
Governor Bowdoin routed Captain Shays and his rural malcontents;
two years later he sat in the South Church balcony to witness the

debates over ratification of the Constitution, never forgiving Elbridge
Gerry for his opposition or John Hancock his waffling. As the
numbers of *The Federalist* appeared, he read them, or so he recalled
seventy-five years later, "with the enthusiasm of youth and . . . full
of joy and approbation, at its power and success in demolishing those
anti-Federal doctrines."[14]

The organizing impulse in the Massachusetts Republican party in
the 1790's has been attributed to a sense of alienation from "the
established authority," compounded by the belief that in the
Commonwealth that authority was intentionally thwarting the political and social aspirations of "ambitious though less favored citizens."
Clearly, Quincy identified with no such animus; his loyalties were
with the established authority and his politics committed to its
preservation. Boston had its Republicans, as the election returns
attested, but few could be found among the families, societies,
churches, and corporate directorships that constituted Quincy's
Boston. Like his father, he defined his political antagonists as those
who sought to disrupt the *status quo.* Thus, in his Fourth of July
Oration, which began with a quotation from *Observations on the
Boston Port Bill*, he identified the "Jacobins and Exclusive Patriots
of Ninety Eight" (i.e., the Jeffersonians) not with the Patriots of
1775 but with Governors Bernard and Hutchinson.[15]

Historians since Richard Hildreth have generally dealt harshly with
the Federalists. Following the lead of Charles A. Beard, most
twentieth-century students of early national politics have stressed the
size of their investment portfolios while ignoring their rhetoric.
Another historiographical tendency, equally dismissive, has been to
consider Federalism in exclusively political terms and thereby to
declare it extinct after 1800 outside of New England, where it
lingered on a bit longer reflecting only that musty corner of the
country's characteristic atavism. Both views, the materialistic and the
sectional, pass over the question of the ideological content of
Federalism.[16]

This charge does not apply to Louis Hartz, who, in *The Liberal
Tradition in America*, confronts the question of Federalist ideology
directly by insisting that there was no such thing. Finding no Filmer,
not even a Burke among them, Hartz concluded the Federalists were,
like their archetype John Dickinson, little more than "frustrated
liberals who wanted to lean on a bit of aristocracy." "Burke assailed

the revolutionary 'shopkeepers' of Paris," he noted, "and the continental reactionaries defined the commercial way of life as a satanic plot against God. Is this the mood of Alexander Hamilton? Of the Hartford Convention?" Persuaded that Hamilton lacked an anti-commercial bias, Hartz inducted him and his fellow Federalists into "the wealthy middle class." Similarly, with the Hartford Convention, by stressing its economic motives he could refer to its members as "Federalists" and "Whigs" interchangeably, both being variants of the genus "American liberal capitalist."[17]

Yet Hartz made his case too tidy by selecting as representative Federalists Hamilton, a most controversial figure even within his own party, and those exceedingly cautious politicians who trekked to Hartford in 1814. What of those Federalists who objected to Hamilton's schemes for encouraging domestic manufacturing? And what of those whose "fiery earnestness" eliminated them from consideration as delegates to Hartford and who prophesied that nothing would come out of the convention but "A GREAT PAMPHLET"? Some Federalists later became Whigs, but others abandoned national politics rather than abandon what they conceived to be Federalism's distinctive ideological persuasion. Josiah Quincy for one, who watched the Whigs from their emergence in the 1830's to their demise in the 1850's, never mistook them for the legatees of Federalism.[18]

Hartz's comparison of the American and European Right fails to recognize the native sources of a conservative persuasion. America had no medieval tradition but it did have a colonial experience which fostered the introduction of distinctive political arrangements. Moreover, at the time of the Revolution these arrangements acquired an ideological rationale different not only from those prevailing in Europe but from that later espoused by the Jeffersonians. Admittedly, the American ideological spectrum was much narrower than that of Napoleonic Europe, though wide enough so that one need not dismiss any discussion of these differences within the American context as hairsplitting. Nor is it necessary to deny the economically and socially self-serving aspects of the Federalist persuasion to suggest that it was more than a smoke screen to cover the machinations of tightfisted capitalists. "We are all Republicans, we are all Federalists," Thomas Jefferson proclaimed in 1801, but some of his contemporaries, including Quincy, remained unconvinced. And for those, the distinctiveness of the Federalist persuasion remained real and operative long after the party itself had disappeared.[19]

Whatever they may have lacked, Federalists had a very definite conception of what constituted a proper society: hierarchically ordered, positively governed, economically stable, institutionally rooted, geographically delimited, ethnically and religiously homogeneous. Conceived in a pre-industrial world, the Federalist persuasion presumed widespread suffrage as it presumed widespread ownership of property. Political leaders, however, were not to be drawn indiscriminately from all levels, but only from the uppermost tier, those whom Quincy called in 1798 "the best and most virtuous citizens." "I write to those only who are contented with being *well governed*," the Federalist John Lowell cautioned in 1812, "and who do not wish to be governors themselves." Federalism as a politically viable force survived only as long as that distinction retained popular meaning; as an ideology it survived as long as there were those who thought the distinction should have meaning.[20]

If this sounds like the ideal polity that revolutionaries like Josiah Quincy Jr. had defended against British meddling a generation earlier, the resonance is not coincidental. Although Federalists who came on the political scene after 1800 were reduced to performing an ideological rear-guard action, they tried to retain what they could of an essentially eighteenth-century conception of a properly ordered society in the burgeoning nineteenth. That they largely failed does not make them any less sincere or more self-serving than those who championed, or at least were more readily reconciled to, the egalitarian, individualistic, laissez-faire, expansive, ethnically and religiously heterogeneous society that America became instead.[21]

It is noteworthy that Quincy, throughout his public years and in his retirement, frequently cast himself in the role of the historian. Retrospection was for him as for most Federalists, indeed most conservatives, an essential intellectual activity. This has usually been attributed to filiopietism, but much more is involved. Quincy's inclination to render homage to the American past reflected his rejection of the radical's belief in the ultimate perfectibility of man and his misgivings about the liberal's faith in change. American history was not for him, as it was for Bancroft, the successive revelation of a divinely ordained plan that would culminate in universal salvation but a series of timely warnings against precisely such muddleheaded meliorism.[22]

As historian of the Quincy family, of Boston and several of its institutions, and of Harvard University, he was continually attracted to the Great Migration and the Revolution. They were in his mind the two truly heroic moments in American history and he never failed to depict them in terms of complete moral approbation. His defense of the Puritans is virtually absolute, from their conception of government and their views on religious toleration to their hostile attitude toward "strangers." And so laudatory could he become in discussing the Revolutionary era that John Adams once felt obliged to inform him that "it had as many poor creatures and selfish beings . . . in proportion, as you have among you." Sitting in a Republican Congress at the time, Quincy found this hard to believe.[2 3]

Aside from the prominence of Quincys in both, the major attraction of the Great Migration and the Revolution was that the participants displayed an abiding faith in what Edmund Morgan has recently delineated as "the Puritan Ethic." "Luxury, sensuality and spiritual pride" in Stuart England, according to Quincy, had obliged the Puritans to give up their homes and "dare the dangers of tempestuous and unexplored seas, the rigors of untried climates, the inhuman warfare of savage foes." Nearly one hundred and fifty years later the same "luxury, avarice, and lust of domination," this time emanating from the England of George III, prompted the Americans to declare their independence and risk the consequences of such an unprecedented act.[2 4]

Both ventures succeeded, Quincy believed, because the participants were able to turn their backs on corrupting material influences. They did so by a communal act of self-denial: in the first instance, by exchanging the comforts of their native England for wilderness America; in the second, by rejecting the commercial advantages and military security that went with colonial status. Each experiment, then, was accomplished by a frugal, liberty-loving people covenanting together and, guided by selfless leaders "called" to their places of authority, delivering themselves from the encroaching corruption.[2 5]

Unfortunately the virtues displayed in these struggles—self-denial, communal solidarity, loyalty to responsible leaders—were not readily transmissible. Just as the Puritans, having broken with England, saw many of their children succumb to indigenous forms of material corruption, Quincy believed his own generation to be in the throes of a post-Revolutionary slump. "Merciful and righteous have been the ways of Providence to our nation," he proclaimed in 1798. "It had crowned our cup high with bounties. The United States walked forth among the people of the earth, in the bloom and majesty of youth and freedom." But as before, "prosperity began to obliterate the principles of our forefathers, to corrupt their simple and pure manners, and to weaken their attachment to country, which was their distinguishing attribute." William Bradford's serpent yet lurked in the New England underbrush.[26]

Such rhetoric had been standard pulpit fare in Massachusetts since the jeremiads of the 1660's and permeated the pamphlets of the Revolutionary period, conspicuously those of Josiah Quincy Jr. That it persisted in the writings of Josiah Quincy underlines the ideological continuity between father and son, and between them and their Puritan ancestors. Five generations of prosperous Quincys had not erased the suspicion by a sixth that prosperity could be a source of personal corruption and the means by which a community or nation is destroyed. Throughout his life he remained sceptical of those who pointed to America's material abundance as evidence of wisdom and proof of durability. This scepticism, very much a part of what Quincy took to be the Federalist persuasion, revealed itself not only in his historical writing but in personal doubts about the ideological constancy of some of his fellow Federalists.[27]

Thick-Skinned Beasts Will Crowd Congress Hall

It is one of the ironies of Quincy's career as a Federalist politician that it began precisely at the moment party fortunes crested. President Adams' indignant response to the XYZ Affair in the spring of 1798 had momentarily transformed him from a colorless chief executive into a popular hero. Federalist majorities in New England legislatures were all increased by the April elections and even Thomas Jefferson acknowledged that the growth of "the popular movement" had been checked. "Americans have returned to their government," Quincy announced at the close of his Fourth of July Oration, "they have returned to the principles of their revolution." Unfortunately for him, they did not stay long.[28]

Republican successes in 1800 were not, Quincy thought at the time, cause for political despair. Jefferson's narrow victory and the election of a Republican Congress could both be explained by divisions within Federalist ranks. Like most Federalists, he assumed the Republicans incapable of directing the government. Once they revealed their ineptitude they would be removed from power, the Federalists permanently restored, and the 1800 elections dismissed as an aberration. But by the fall of 1801, with Jefferson safely through his first six months as President, Quincy began having second thoughts.[29]

"It is a curious fact," he conceded in September, "that the funds of the United States continue rising. . . . The confidence of monied men seems to increase exactly in proportion as the evidences of want of stamina in government multiply." The continued prosperity of businessmen who had previously thought the party of Hamilton held an exclusive patent on it, and the resultant growing popularity of Jefferson among them, indicated that the Republicans would not be as easily dislodged as he had earlier imagined. "I have been, I confess, more at a loss to account for this than for any other late occurrences, as it happened directly contrary to my expectations."[30]

By spring things were worse. "I will say nothing concerning the aspect of our political affairs," Quincy told Wolcott, "it is so gloomy that to say little would not do justice to my own feelings." What most perplexed him was that the Federalists, rather than contesting the Republicans' tightening grip on national affairs, seemed on the verge of collapse. Many New York and Boston merchants, the mainstay of the party in the 1790's, appeared ready to accommodate themselves to continued Republican rule. Even his friend Wolcott, Adams' Secretary of the Treasury and earlier an outspoken Federalist, Quincy noted only half-jokingly, "is sunk in the commission merchant . . . our political Mars has melted down his armour and put the metal out at interest and cares nothing about the din of this great world, except what is made by telling out nine per cent at his bank and five per cent at his counting house."[31]

Nowhere did Quincy find the indifference of Federalists more portentous than in the equanimity with which they received the news from France in July 1803 that the United States had bought Louisiana. While the Republican press trumpeted it as a Jeffersonian coup and urged quick approval by the Senate of the enabling bill, Federalist newspapers scarcely noted the transaction. Information reached Quincy in early September that New York's two leading Federalists, Alexander Hamilton and Rufus King, were "satisfied with the bargain" and would not speak against it. Even a number of Boston Federalists, he discovered, had "half a mind to support this treaty," a fact which only confirmed his fears that "the spirit of speculation, which is the evil genius of Americans," had invaded the two urban bulwarks of Federalism. By making Louisiana appear "a new bubble for the land office," Jefferson had successfully undercut partisan opposition to its acquisition. "This string," Quincy noted bitterly, "the friends of the administration continue to touch—not without effect."[32]

Historians have generally commended those Federalists who supported the Louisiana Purchase, if not for their patriotism, then for their eye for a bargain. Except for Henry Adams' sympathetic rendering of his grandfather's constitutional scruples over the way in which statehood was stipulated in the cession treaty (he applauded the Purchase), most commentators have dismissed Federalist objections as partisan and hypocritical. John Bach McMaster neatly summarized the consensual view: "they ought to have been ashamed." Admittedly, objections raised by some Federalists that Jefferson had been overcharged and that Louisiana's cost would bankrupt the country were absurd, while those of New England Federalists like Harrison Gray Otis who were anxious to protect investments in wilderness tracts in Maine and Vermont were disingenuous. Other objections, however, should not be so summarily dismissed because they reflect another of the distinctive ideological strains in the Federalist persuasion—anti-expansionism.[33]

"Admit this world into the Union," Senator William Plumer warned in October 1803, "and you destroy at once the whole weight and importance of the Eastern states." Quincy, too, feared the political implications of the Louisiana Purchase, interpreting the promise of statehood to those in the territory "as soon as possible" to mean that the older states would soon be overwhelmed by new ones in the South and West. But his fears ran deeper. A firm adherent to "the myth of New England exclusiveness," that its citizenry was uniquely qualified to sustain a republican government by virtue of its political experience and social homogeneity, Quincy believed the country could not possibly assimilate what Fisher Ames disdainfully called "this Gallo-Hispano-Indian-*omnium gatherum* of savages and adventurers" residing in Louisiana. "Should this precious treaty go into operation," he predicted six weeks before the Senate overwhelmingly ratified it, "I doubt not thick-skinned beasts will crowd Congress Hall, Buffaloes from the head of the Missouri and Alligators from the Red River. . . ."[34]

Beneath the sarcasm and barbaric imagery, Federalists like Ames and Quincy were raising serious questions, not only about the wisdom of doubling the size of the national domain but about the country's capacity to do so. Could any government ever hope to regulate such an expanse of territory? "By adding an unmeasured world beyond that river," Ames wrote, "we rush like a comet into infinite space. In our wild career, we may jostle some other world out of orbit, but we shall, in every event, quench the light of our own." Quincy put it more prosaically: by ignoring "the principle of compression," we abandon all hope of "consolidating and cementing our political building, so as to be safe without and comfortable within."[35]

Quincy had read *The Federalist* as an undergraduate, but failed to be persuaded by Madison's argument in "Number Ten" that size was a virtue in a republic. "The expanse of the country is, in a national point of view," he insisted as the United States prepared to add 828,000 square miles of territory, "already one of our great misfortunes." Rather than rendering factions ineffective as Madison had predicted, "the diversity of interests and intelligence, at present existing at the extremes and centre of our empire," Quincy argued, had "rendered government incapable of all regular and dignified involvement."[36]

The heart of Quincy's case against the expansionist ethic was that it denied an already distended nation the time to acquire an organic unity.

Even now our motion is not that of a man—that of a rational being, who has comprehensive views and master motives to give harmony and character to his actions; but it is like the motion of that toy which children call Jack-O-Malingo, whose head neither moves with his body, nor his limbs with either, nor with each other, but each flounders about as the trifling local ties happen to twitch it. . . . Can it then be wise to extend our surface;—to multiply the chances for local projects and interests?[37]

Federalists like Quincy are distinguishable from other nineteenth-century Americans not by the nostalgic element in their ideologies, equally discernible among Jeffersonians, Jacksonians, and Whigs, but by the fact that their remembered past was communal rather than individualistic. They longed for a return to community with its attendant obligations, and to positive, purposeful government, not atomistic independence and anarchic freedom. When Quincy complained that "our population is already spilt upon the face of the continent and can not be gathered up for any politial emergency," the tight New England community, with its town meeting, volunteer fire company, and militia ready to muster on the Common at a moment's notice served as his idealized model.[38]

Though certainly not all Federalists were as urbanized in their life styles as Quincy, they were generally more cosmopolitan than their relatively rustic Republican counterparts. In Boston, New York, Philadelphia, Baltimore, and even Charleston, Federalists continued to sponsor most of the culturally oriented activities long after they ceased controlling local politics. Furthermore, it was their patronage which sustained Harvard, Yale, Columbia, and Princeton well into the nineteenth century. Accordingly, their relatively more civilized and educated sensibilities found distinctly unappealing the primitive and isolated conditions that prevailed on the frontier. Yet Quincy feared those sensibilities were being ignored by Republicans all too willing to give the nation over to interminable frontier-breaking. "Are the spirit and strength of our people forever to be exhausted in the chase of savages until they reach the South Sea?" he lamented. "Shall they never have leisure to attain the wisdom and habits of regular life; or cease to confine all social activity to the cutting down of pines and the extirpation of wolves and woodchucks?"[39]

As Quincy feared, Jefferson's acquisition of Louisiana was a transforming event in the history of the United States. By committing the government to its settlement, development, and incorporation into the Union, he dramatically turned the country's attention inward, away from Europe but also away from the settled Atlantic seaboard. For the next fifty years a premium was placed on the "thick-skinned" American who went westward into the wilderness, carrying his history in his rucksack, his family in his wagon; a man who made do without institutions that made life more than the sum total of its material requirements, who lived without laws and demanded of his government only that he be left alone. These were at least the ascribed values of the American pioneer, perhaps those of a majority of nineteenth-century Americans, if the way in which both political parties by 1840 sought to identify with them is any indication. The ascendancy of these values following the Louisiana Purchase marks the point, even more definitively than the Revolution, where the eighteenth-century values of Federalists like Quincy became obsolete. But this is not to say that he abandoned them.[40]

Our Opponents Are Better Politicians

"Louisiana excites less interest than our Thanksgiving," Fisher Ames mordantly noted, a month after the Senate approved the cession treaty. "It is an old story." A few Federalists, however, thought it the last straw. At the instigation of Timothy Pickering, United States Senator from Massachusetts, several national legislators staying at Coyle's boardinghouse during the first session of the Eighth Congress decided the time had come for a separation of New England and New York from the Union. Throughout the winter of 1803-1804, Pickering, Senators James Hillhouse and Uriah Tracy of Connecticut, as well as Congressman Roger Griswold from the same state, and William Plumer of New Hampshire secretly tried to enlist others in their scheme for a "Northern confederacy."[41]

Some verbal sympathy but little tangible support was forthcoming and by the summer of 1804 the separatist conspiracy had collapsed. Pickering failed to interest the very Federalists he had most counted on, New Yorkers like Alexander Hamilton and Rufus King, George Cabot and Stephen Higginson from Massachusetts. Even Fisher Ames put off the secessionists with a wisecrack. "If Jacobinism makes haste," he told Pickering, "I may yet live to be hanged." Pickering would try again later, only to meet with the same patriotic opposition to his notions from some Federalists, and unalloyed indifference from others.[42]

Whereas Pickering's exasperation over the state of national affairs moved him to conspiracy, other Federalists simply dropped out. This second response, personified by Cabot and Higginson, and by John Jay in New York, was no less despairing than the secessionists', simply more fatalistic—thereby conceding Federalism's inability to contest Republicanism by the political rules of the Revolutionary era. Men of their generation proved too old and too inflexible to adjust to the new political order emerging in the late 1790's with the development of the popularly based, election-oriented Republican party. When Pickering conspired to destroy the Union and Cabot tossed up his hands and announced, "let the world ruin itself in its own way," they merely demonstrated their unwillingness to play politics according to the revised rules.[43]

Quincy knew nothing of the Northern Confederacy scheme and undoubtedly would have opposed it.* This is not to suggest that he viewed the course of political events since 1800 any less darkly than did the Timothy Pickerings, rather that their response reflected a desperation he did not fully share. Disengagement, as commended by Cabot's example, he thought no less extreme and, at his age, premature. Moreover, it was ill-suited to his temperament. "An individual who should retire from conversation with the world for the purpose of taking vengeance on it for some real or imaginary wrong," he once wrote, "would soon find himself grievously mistaken; notwithstanding the delusions of self-flattery, he would certainly be taught that the world was moving along just as well, after his dignified retirement, as it did while he intermeddled with its concerns."[44]

Republican successes at the polls had, however, obliged him to rethink some of his earlier political views. Like all Federalists in the 1790's he opposed a direct appeal to the voters, viewing it as destructive of the deferential society the party was committed to preserving. Federalists agreed "to stand" for office; they did not "run," and they condemned the elaborate organizations and aggressive electioneering tactics the Republicans had begun to introduce. In 1798, with the Federalists riding high, he solemnly warned his Fourth of July audience against the machinations of "an internal, depraved, ambitious, disappointed faction." In defending the Alien and Sedition Acts just passed, he conceded no middle ground where reasoned dissent or orderly opposition might exist: one supported the government or one was a traitor. By 1804, with the Federalists long out of national power and threatened with displacement even in Massachusetts, he had changed his mind.[45]

Quincy aligned himself with the younger Massachusetts Federalists who were determined to give their party a more popular veneer by copying Republican organizational and electioneering techniques. Accordingly, he criticized the "cautious politicians" of the older

*Although John Quincy Adams implicated virtually all his Federalist contemporaries in one secession scheme or another, he admitted to Quincy in 1829 that his doubts about him had no basis in fact.

generation and denounced their stated misgivings about electioneering as "merely an apology of inactivity." Like Harrison Gray Otis, Timothy Bigelow, and Thomas Handasyd Perkins, he and John Quincy Adams, though the latter with less certainty, thought that party fortunes could be recouped only if its leadership acknowledged the need to appeal to the voters for support. "A degree of organization has been effected in the opposite party," he complained to Adams, "unexampled, in this country, since the revolutionary committees of 1775." To Oliver Wolcott he put the situation in even bolder relief: "Our opponents are better politicians. . . . And until we can learn to contend like them, more upon party principles than many of us seem willing to do, we must be content to be governed by as arrant a set of villains as ever were the curse of a country."[4 6]

Adams, of course, soon passed beyond mere copying of forms and adopted the Democratic-Republican name and program. The local distress at his "apostasy" in 1807 was the price he willingly paid for the possibility of a national political career which, he had begun to recognize as early as 1802, did not exist for a Federalist. "Whatever the merits or demerits of the former [Federalist] administrations may have been," he told Rufus King, "there never was a system of measures more completely and irrevocably abandoned and rejected by the popular voice. . . . to attempt its restoration would be as absurd as to undertake the resurrection of a carcase seven years in its grave."[4 7]

Quincy's family had been too long and too intimately a part of Boston's elite for him to share John Quincy Adams' congenital suspicion of its leaders. Their shabby treatment of his father as President was something Adams never forgot nor forgave, and he felt not the least compunction in deserting their party when the opportunity presented itself. At the same time his many years in Europe had made him "an implacable American." They had also made him an insistent expansionist. Quincy lacked that wider perspective, that willingness to identify with all Americans rather than with just those of his section and class, which he might have acquired had he traveled abroad. More ambitious, more politically flexible, less circumscribed by his heritage and locale, Adams went on to become, as he predicted in 1803, " the man of my whole country," and President of the United States, whereas Quincy remained a Federalist and settled for being President of Harvard College. Though they remained friends, even during the period of Adams' ostracism from Boston society in 1808, Quincy took to his grave the belief that Adams had been wrong in siding with the Republicans, however politically rewarding it proved to be.[48]

His own approach to the problem was more modest. By convincing himself that Federalist setbacks were attributable to the "indifference or inactivity of our party," and by insisting that copying Republican forms could set matters right, he remained both politically engaged and locally respectable. "Although we have failed," he wrote following Jefferson's triumph in Massachusetts in 1804, "our labour is not lost." Indeed, once settled on this policy, he informed it with his own special fervor. "I find it impossible to conceive that anyone believes in his own politics or thinks them of any weight," Burke had intoned in *Thoughts on the Cause of the Present Discontents*, and Quincy faithfully copied into his journal, "who refuses to adopt the means of having them rendered into practice." Persuaded, Quincy went even further. "Nothing it seems to me can be politically good whose root springs from the other side of the political equator," he told Wolcott. "It will always be a root of bitterness. High authority tells us that a pure stream cannot issue from a corrupt fountain. Is it not as truly moral as political to choke up every course it takes?"[49]

One can easily exaggerate both the depth and the longevity of Quincy's commitment to the popular strategy advanced by Otis and the younger members of the Massachusetts Federalist party who soon came to dominate its Central Committee, but it is clear that he identified with their belief in legislative aggressiveness. "Men who hesitate at everything," he announced as he readied himself to beard the Republican lion in his own den, "contend at unequal odds with men who stick at nothing." Washington would find in him, for a time at least, one Federalist determined to even the odds.[50]

3 / The Politics of Exasperation

The present session of Congress is highly important and very interesting. But I think many of the friends of our Country will be much disappointed in the result. They have, in the impressive language of Scripture, *looked for much, but it came to little,* and in that perhaps their disappointment will be injurious.

—Senator William Plumer, January 22, 1806

It began auspiciously enough. A leisurely trip from Boston brought the new congressman, his wife, and their six-year-old daughter Eliza Susan to Washington in the early autumn of 1805. Finding lodgings proved surprisingly easy. An old Braintree neighbor, Judge William Cranch of the federal district court, invited the Quincys to share his home for the session, an invitation they promptly accepted. "I am delighted, as is Mrs. Q., with our situation," the thirty-three-year-old Federalist announced during his first month in the capital, "it is precisely what we both wish, in every respect."[1]

Whistling in the Dark

Family needs provided for, Quincy turned to those of his party. The essential problem facing the Federalists in 1805 was merely an aggravated version of that facing them since 1800: too many Republicans. Only in the federal judiciary did the party retain a substantial, though declining, presence. With Jefferson ensconced in the White House, the recipient of an overwhelming mandate for a second term, the Republicans monopolized the executive branch of the government. In addition, a sophisticated national party organization had transformed the President's personal popularity into ever-increasing Republican majorities in Congress. For every Federalist elected to the House of Representatives in 1804 there were four Republicans; over in the Senate the ratio was one to three. Only one Federalist in Congress represented a district south of the Potomac River or west of the Allegheny Mountains. As a Republican summed up the situation: "We are strong enough and have nothing to fear except from divisions among ourselves."[2]

In such divisions lay the Federalists' only hope. And as the Ninth Congress prepared to convene, there were reasons to believe it might not be an entirely futile hope. Having announced his intention not to stand for a third term, Jefferson opened the possibility of a scramble among various members of his Cabinet which could split the party into warring factions. With the bulk of his patronage dispensed, the President's capacity to contain such a scramble was problematical. Moreover, the very lopsidedness of his party's majority in Congress rendered it fractious, while the virtual disappearance of the Federalists as a creditable opposition removed what had earlier been a principal stimulus to party unity.[3]

Rumblings within Republican ranks had been heard during the previous Congress. Debates in the House during the spring of 1804 revealed the existence of a number of Southern Republicans grown restive after three years of close executive direction. Disturbed by the centralizing proclivities of Jefferson-in-power and angered by his growing reliance upon Northern Republican advice, some of the most disaffected Southerners ("Quids") threatened to resurrect the same states' rights issue the out-of-power Jefferson had used so successfully against the Federalists in the 1790's. To some observers at least, an ideological split along sectional lines seemed a distinct possibility. "One thing is certain," Samuel Taggart, a Federalist congressman from Massachusetts, concluded midway through the second session of the Eighth Congress; the Republicans "at present seem broken and divided, and do not act with their usual concert."[4]

The Ninth Congress opened as the Eighth had closed: with Republicans squabbling among themselves. Despite their overwhelming majority in the House they could not agree on a Speaker. Northern Republicans, hoping to unseat Nathaniel Macon of North Carolina, brought forward a candidate of their own, Joseph B. Varnum of Massachusetts. It took three ballots and some help from the Federalists before Macon won reelection. The closeness of the final vote, 58 to 50, lent plausibility to the optimistic view held by the new Federalist congressman from Boston that "the democrats are pretty equally divided, on many important questions, which gives our little phalanx no inconsiderable weight."[5]

Macon's reelection meant that the most powerful of the House committees, Ways and Means, would continue to have as its chairman the brilliant and bilious John Randolph of Roanoke, the ideological mentor of the Quids and a cousin of Jefferson. Randolph had first acquired his chairmanship in 1801 while serving as Jefferson's spokesman in the House. Since then, however, the two Virginians had parted political company. Although insiders had seen it coming earlier, the first public indication of a split occurred during the 1804 Yazoo land debates, when Randolph opposed an Administration-sponsored compromise as an intrusion by the federal government into state affairs. Naturally, such a charge embarrassed Jefferson, author of the Kentucky Resolutions. When Randolph then proceeded to botch the Administration's carefully prepared impeachment case against the Federalist Supreme Court justice, Samuel Chase, the President decided to forego his cousin's services.[6]

Randolph welcomed the break, indeed he may have intentionally provoked it. His principled fears of executive tyranny and his personal pique combined to make the clash with Jefferson almost inevitable. By the fall of 1805 he had committed himself to the idea of testing his strength and that of his Quids in the House against the President and his Northern minions. "Randolph has crossed the Rubicon" was how many reported his decision. While few expected that his moving into open opposition would break Jefferson's immediate hold on the House, no one was prepared to dismiss the possibility that his quixotic adventure would encourage other defections and thus gradually erode the party unity upon which the President depended. At the very least, the Quid schism would put that unity to its first serious test.[7]

Understandably, the imminent Randolph-Jefferson confrontation elicited interest from all but the most moribund Federalists; even Fisher Ames, hardly a Pollyanna, thought "the symptoms of discord among the bad deserve notice." But no one in Washington took more notice than the newly-arrived Quincy. Soliciting for funds to install a Federalist stenographer in the capital, he wrote excitedly early in the session to party leaders in Boston and New York: "the democratic party is splitting, obviously in all directions, and declarations will probably be made before the end of the present session very necessary to be seized and presented and published." On New Year's Day, 1806, he promised his friend William S. Shaw, a young and aspiring Boston Federalist, "hereafter you shall hear of things strange and amusing, gratifying to your political prejudices and *not unfriend-ly to your political hopes*."[8]

Quincy's initial impulse was to help the Quids along by joining in their attacks upon the Administration. "For my own part," he wrote Oliver Wolcott, "I have no worry or apprehension at engaging the enemy at close quarters. If our little band be beaten for the present, it is no matter. It will show our spirit. . . ." Party elders, however, disagreed. Having earlier persuaded themselves that Federalist partici-pation in floor debates only served "to consolidate the majority," Samuel Dana and John Cotton Smith of Connecticut opposed Quincy's getting involved. Though still "anxious to get upon the stage," the young congressman deferred to those he called "remnants of the ancient stock" who presumed to set party policy.[9]

By February he was defending that policy as his own. "I do not think the people should come forward at present," he told constitu-ents who complained of Federalist inactivity; "it is a great point to make these prostrate leaders show themselves and their utter in-capacity. If left to their own ignorance they will render themselves ridiculous, if not odious." Thus he too acknowledged that the Federalists, however desirous of humbling Jefferson and wrecking the Republican party, could only "wait the event," leaving responsi-bility for precipitating it with Randolph.[10]

Quincy, because of his assignment to the Ways and Means Committee, found himself in daily company with its redoubtable chairman. He had previously known Randolph only by his reputa-tion: arch-maligner of New England and its "excrescent carrying trade"; inveterate foe of Federalists and Federalism; the most scathing orator in Congress. His falsetto voice, scarred but childlike features, emaciated frame and spindly limbs, his sartorial eccentrici-ties and his ever-present hounds had long made him a favorite subject of Federalist satirists. Many found particularly titillating the doubts about the Virginian's virility, Quincy's own speculation as to "Mr. Randolph's puberty" in the *Port Folio* in 1804 being a mild example.[11]

Comparing his father and Randolph, Quincy's son Josiah Jr. concluded, after meeting the Virginian in 1826, "two men more utterly dissimilar in temperament and opinions can scarcely be imagined." Superficially, the judgment is apt. What could be more dissimilar than a blasphemous Southerner and a proper Bostonian, an unbelieving Anglican and a devout Unitarian, a physically repulsive bachelor and a handsome paterfamilias? Randolph regularly gave himself over to violent excesses with an abandon Henry Adams thought endemic to the slaveholding South, while Quincy, with puritanical fervor, maintained a close check on his passions. One dueled and drank too much; the other eschewed the pistol as immoral and the bottle as unhealthy.[12]

Politically, their differences were equally distinct. Whereas Randolph traced his political ancestry to the Virginia Anti-Federalists, to George Mason and Patrick Henry, Quincy identified with the Founding Fathers, Washington, Hamilton, and Adams. All through their public careers the one defended the institution of slavery while the other condemned it. By inclination and constituency the Bostonian was an economic internationalist, the Virginian an isolationist. In one of their first exchanges in the House, Randolph argued that "the United States is a great land animal, a great mammoth, which ought to cleave to the land," to which Quincy countered, citing his own national symbol: "the cod—enterprising, active, skilful . . . spread-[ing] himself over every ocean."[13]

These very real differences notwithstanding, during the opening weeks of the Ninth Congress Randolph and Quincy reached a political understanding which was to remain intact as long as Quincy served in Congress. They discovered that they were more often in agreement with each other than either was with the Administration, proving the political spectrum of Jefferson's Washington less linear than circular. An instance of this concurrence of views is to be seen in their respective responses to a House resolution introduced on January 24, 1806, by a Pennsylvania Republican and Administration supporter, William Gregg. Gregg's Resolution called for a ban on all English imports until that country relaxed its restrictions on neutral trade. Randolph attempted to dismiss the resolution by insisting that the government ought not concern itself over "a few mercantile megrims." Though Quincy dissented from the Virginian's implication that "the carrying trade is not worth support," he too opposed the resolution, on the grounds that it protected American ships from harassment at sea by obliging them to rot in port.[14]

Political expediency brought the two men together, but personal affinities sustained the relationship and eventually transformed it into a lifelong friendship. One such bond was common animosities.

Neither, for example, could abide Thomas Jefferson and both regularly said so. While Quincy's early dislike of the President was the product of sectional and partisan biases, three years of personal exposure in Washington confirmed him in his belief that the Sage of Monticello was an intellectual fraud. His description of Jefferson offered to John Adams in 1808 was meant to be definitive: "A dish of skim milk curdling at the head of our nation." Randolph's final estimate of "that prince of projectors, St. Thomas of Cantingbury," was, of course, so damning as to make Quincy's sound eulogistic.[15]

New England Republicans in the House evoked their combined wrath even more than the President did. "If there is any one being in nature," Samuel Taggart averred, whom Randolph hated "more than any other it is a New England Democrat [i.e., Republican]." The same could be said of Quincy who thought the Joseph Varnums and the Orchard Cooks and the Barnabas Bidwells, all Massachusetts Republicans, social no less than political bounders. Such men, he and Randolph believed, spoke neither for the old ruling order of New England nor for the states' rights principles of Southern Republicanism, but for themselves and other unlettered, ambitious men who used Jefferson's party as the means to challenge their betters at home and in Congress.[16]

"I am exceedingly disappointed with Randolph," Quincy reported after their first meeting. "I expected to find a cynic and a boor—and a coarse, careless brutality. On the contrary, his conduct *to me* has been remarkably gentlemanly, yet not obtrusively so." Three weeks later, he confirmed his initial estimate: "It is impossible for any man to be more gentlemanly. . . . He has more aristocratic pride than vanity." Here then was the vital source of their friendship, one that transcended politics and temperament. Each acknowledged the other's claims as an aristocrat amidst Washington's hoi polloi, or, as Randolph might have phrased it, as a pearl amidst the swine.[17]

More important than the fact that Randolph's ancestral roots went deep into the Virginia countryside and Quincy's into the rocky South Shore of Massachusetts was the common fact of rootedness. A sense of place and family tradition brought them together, just as it served to set them apart from the bulk of their fellow legislators. Their opposition to territorial expansion can be explained largely in terms of their dread of the social dislocation that would inevitably attend it. Precisely because their own loyalties remained fixed and provincial, they distrusted Americans-on-the-move. Even more, they distrusted those like Henry Clay who came forward to represent this essentially rootless constituency.[18]

Both were political no less than social elitists. Neither ever accepted the view that an elected representative ought to mirror the views of those who elected him. Accordingly, both were regularly charged during their congressional careers with ignoring their constituents. But popularity at home, like success achieved in Washington by compromise and accommodation, they willingly sacrificed in the pursuit of the moral distinction that usually came with intransigence. However often they engaged in legislative machinations, neither was ever so much in character as when he stood alone. The notion that political effectiveness and personal integrity were antithetical drew them together, just as it distinguished them from the Clays and Websters and the Douglases who were to come after them. Remnants of the eighteenth century, they confirmed their alienation from the post-Revolutionary political order taking shape under Jefferson by seeking refuge from it in each other's exclusive company.[19]

Whatever his virtues as a friend, Randolph soon proved inept as Jefferson's nemesis. His efforts throughout the spring of 1806 to split the Republican party, though bringing him to the point of physical collapse, were unproductive. Except for exposing and thereby terminating secret Administration negotiations with France relating to the purchase of West Florida, and the tabling of Gregg's Resolution, Randolph's oratorical fireworks and parliamentary legerdemain did little more than enliven the session. His efforts on behalf of the presidential candidacy of James Monroe, intended to thwart Jefferson's efforts to secure the nomination for James Madison, proved abortive. Despite one Federalist's announcement in March that "the Administration are trembling for their very existence," and Mrs. Quincy's assurances in April that "Randolph carries all before him . . . the Administration were certainly in a very unpleasant situation," by May the Quid revolt had been quashed.[20]

Never more the consummate politician, Jefferson had moved quickly to contain the insurgency and isolate its leader. Some Quids, like Joseph Nicholson of Maryland, were bought off, while other Southerners, like Speaker Macon, were cajoled back into line. Randolph actually made the President's task easier by his rhetorical excesses. "He has brought some in favour of the measure, who, I believe, would otherwise have been opposed to it," Senator Plumer noted from the House gallery after hearing Randolph attack an Administration proposal. His violent attacks on Madison and other members of the Cabinet raised doubts whether he was conducting a political crusade or a personal vendetta. As Samuel Taggart concluded after watching him perform: "Randolph is an excellent fellow to pull down, although I have no great opinion of his talents for building up."[21]

By the end of the session all but the most obdurate Southern Republicans had responded to the President's call to close party ranks. Many retained their states' rights views and their misgivings about Northern influence within the Administration, but only a handful were willing to follow Randolph into political oblivion. When Congress reconvened the following December, Jefferson's control over his party was more absolute than ever.[22]

That Quincy ever believed Randolph capable of destroying the Republican party is a testament, of sorts, to his powers of positive thinking. It also reveals less about the vulnerability of the President's party than about the marginality of his own. He came to Washington to do more than watch the Republicans run the government; throughout his first year he tried to convince himself and his friends that there was more to do—or soon would be. When not predicting Randolph's imminent success in the House, he occupied himself with delusions of a national Federalist revival. The most ambiguous election returns provided him with evidence that "there are many in the ranks of democracy [Republicans] who are not prepared to sacrifice all principle and character to party projects." On the eve of the Massachusetts spring elections he told Fisher Ames, "I have little doubt of the federal success. I have always thought last year was the turning point. I think so still." The Republicans then proceeded to win both houses of the legislature and only narrowly missed electing a governor.[23]

Having invested so heavily in his fantasy of a crumbling Republican party, Quincy was unwilling to abandon it. Upon his return to Washington for the second session of the Ninth Congress, however, certain facts were irrefutable. Randolph had been reduced to his eccentricities by the events of the previous session; never again would he constitute more than a mild irritation to the Administration. Fall congressional elections had cost the Federalists another eight seats, leaving the twenty-four that were left more isolated than ever. Quincy, whose own seat on the Ways and Means Committee had been reassigned to a Republican, was left without even a good vantage point from which to observe what he could do nothing about.

Finally, on February 10, 1807, the whistling stopped. "I should have written you before," Quincy apologized to the same William Shaw whom a year earlier he had promised to apprise of "things strange and amusing," "but it is difficult to lift oneself, without any external motive, out of the Lethean wave, in which I am sunk, in this morbid and unnerving state to which I am doomed."[24]

That Cemetery of All Comfort

Quincy's opinion of life in Washington followed the same downward curve as his political prospects. What had been in 1805 a situation in which he "delighted" became in the aftermath of the Randolph debacle "that cemetery of all comfort." Four decades later, when other memories of his eight years as a congressman had faded, he could still recall vividly the capital's "comfortlessness and desolation."[25]

Early Washington was characterized by nothing so much as social discontinuity. One of its first hostesses aptly called it "a land of strangers." Although the 1810 census recorded the respectable figure of 8208 permanent residents, this included 1437 slaves, 867 free blacks, and what one observer described as "a disproportionate number of needy people." The entire governmental establishment consisted of fewer than four hundred people, nearly half of whom held seats in Congress. A motley collection, drawn from all parts of the country and all social strata, they had little in common beyond a determination not to remain in the capital any longer than their official responsibilities required. Every spring, with the President leading the exodus, they deserted the town immediately upon the adjournment of Congress, not to be seen again until the late fall, if then. With the biennial turnover in the House more than one-third, and with mid-term resignations commonplace, it appears that many congressmen, having experienced a season in Washington, decided that one was enough.[26]

Many believed the capital's location to be unhealthy. Complaints about the "suffocating air," raised when the government first moved there, were still being heard years later. Rather than appropriate funds for draining the swamps bordering the western edge of the clearing and cutting back the underbrush which threatened to reclaim Pennsylvania Avenue as part of Virginia-Maryland wilderness, Congress began having serious second thoughts about remaining in Washington. In February 1808 the House approved a preliminary proposal to move back to Philadelphia.[27]

Although White House intervention brought about reconsideration and ultimate rejection of the proposal (by two votes), the episode served to underline how tenuous were the claims of Washington as the permanent capital. And until these claims were certified, the private developers and professionals who had been expected to flock there stayed away. "Unfortunately," as one New England Republican delicately characterized the situation in 1807, "commerce has not fixed here her abode." A Federalist senator the same year put it more bluntly: "Little progress has been made the last year in building up the city. . . . There are many buildings whose brick walls are mouldering in ruins. It looks like a deserted city."[28]

The capital's economic marginality paled before its cultural deprivation. For those "too long used to drink at the fountains of good principles, society, literature, and religion," Mrs. Quincy concluded after four months' residence, "this wilderness city affords little to amuse, less to interest, and nothing to gratify." Her husband's judgment, though slower in coming, was equally negative. "You have heard of 'an Iliad in a nutshell,'" he remarked to Boston friends in 1810, "and although Swift says it has been his fate 'more often to find a nutshell in an Iliad,' yet Swift was never in Washington."[29]

The nation's capital was perforce a man's town. With housing scarce and expensive, and schools nonexistent, few officeholders brought their families with them. Although Mrs. Quincy accompanied her husband during his first two winters in Washington, a succession of pregnancies and her distaste for the capital kept her in Boston during all but one of his subsequent six sessions. When alone, Quincy usually rented a room at Coyle's, one of the dozen boardinghouses scattered about Capitol Hill and catering to congressmen. Although one of the better establishments of its kind, taking pride in its fastidious New England clientele, Coyle's proved a sad substitute for the comforts of home. Life in such "a gloomy cockloft in the wilderness, without any but boardinghouse comforts," he wrote, was unavoidably "solitary, stupid, and jaded."[30]

Drinking, gambling, and an occasional cockfight constituted the capital's principal diversions, prompting Mrs. Quincy to despair at "what a state of manners and morals exists here!" Her husband, rather than partake of these primitive pleasures, generally kept to his room. This was largely, though not entirely, of his own choice. Having supported the return of the government to Philadelphia, he had rendered himself unwelcome at the tables of those few permanent residents, all engaged in local land speculation, who occasionally entertained Federalist congressmen. But his habit of declining invitations from the White House, the only other respectable respite from the boardinghouse, was a matter of personal taste.[31]

"Party spirit," he later recalled, "greatly qualified social intercourse. Men of the same party generally boarded together. Among these social intercourse chiefly took place." These constraints notwithstanding, Quincy's failure to make a single lasting acquaintance other than Randolph among the hundreds of Republicans filing in and out of Washington during his eight years there must be attributed largely to his lack of interest. The same may be said of his dealings with fellow Federalists. Though by all social indices they represented a considerable improvement over the Republicans, they were for the most part country lawyers or small-town merchants. "Some of us have seats in Congress at six dollars a day," one Federalist acknowledged, "for the pleasure of seeing the name honourable attached to our names, which otherwise would be simple John, James, Joseph." Quincy, the only Federalist during all but two of his years in Congress to represent an urban constituency, and probably, as Henry Adams thought him, the best educated, found little in these simple Johns, Jameses, and Josephs worth cultivating.[32]

Almost by elimination he discovered that those with whom he felt most at home in Washington were not fellow Americans, Republicans or Federalists, but the Britsh envoys periodically assigned to what one of them called "America's raw and rude court." First David M. Erskine, then Francis J. Jackson, and finally Augustus John Foster provided him with a measure of companionship otherwise unavailable. With Foster particularly he developed a cordial relationship. Like Quincy, the dapper stepson of the Duke of Devonshire regularly despaired of Washington's primitive conditions. "There are no clubs established and no theatres except ropedancers," he complained upon arrival; his subsequent discovery that "excellent snipeshooting and even partridge shooting was to be had on each side of the main avenue and even close under the Capitol" failed to put things right.[33]

Not only did Foster agree with Quincy that Washington was unlivable, he shared his American friend's belief that it was intentionally so. "Mr. Jefferson knew all too well what he was about," the English diplomat concluded from the President's successful efforts to keep the government from being removed to Philadelphia or some other sizable city. By retaining the capital in "a mere swamp," Foster inferred, Jefferson hoped to dissuade "the richer and more respectable [Federalist] deputies" from keeping their seats in Congress, at the same time providing his "rough and unfashioned" Republicans with a setting not unlike "the forests and morasses" they called home.[34]

Quincy went further in impugning the President's motives, by insisting that he kept the government quarantined off in the woods of Virginia to avoid contact between it and the Federalist commercial and cultural elites of Philadelphia and New York. Alexander Hamilton had argued in *Federalist* "Number 27" that "a government continually at a distance and out of sight can hardly be expected to interest the sensations of the people"; Jefferson, or so Quincy came to believe, had decided for that reason to keep his government "at a distance." "What can we know, in this wilderness, of the effects of our measures upon civilized and commercial life?" he complained from the floor of the House in 1808. "We see nothing, we feel nothing."[35]

Conspiratorial theorizing of this sort was not the exclusive franchise of lonely Federalists and homesick Englishmen, nor were such explanations invoked only to explain the matter of the capital's location. On the contrary, suspected plots and suspicious counterplotters were a regular feature of early Washington life; never have they flourished as during those first years. One explanation for this phenomenon, presented by Richard Hofstadter, stresses the novelty of the governmental arrangements. Because most early national legislators lacked practical experience with either a two-party system or the idea of a "legitimate opposition," they regularly fell back on the familiar anti-party ideological premises and conspiratorial pre-occupations of the eighteenth century.[36]

The unavoidable emphasis by the government on foreign relations also heightened suspicion. With Europe almost continuously at war during the Jeffersonian era, each party feared that the interests of the country might be sacrificed by the other in a deal with one of the foreign combatants. Thus the Republicans, with less reason than they imagined, suspected all Federalists of wanting to destroy the Union and to reunite New England with Old. Concurrently, most Federalists, with still less reason but more fervor, believed the Republicans to be "legislating under an imperial decree of the Emperor of France."[37]

Aside from these essentially political considerations, however, early Washington's addiction to rumors can also be seen as a by-product of its untoward social circumstances. Like dueling, that other popular pastime of the nation's first lawmakers, divining plots and hatching counterplots helped relieve the tedium hanging heavy over the capital. Living "like bears, brutalized and stupefied . . . from hearing nothing but politics from morning to night," as one congressman described his fellows' condition, they easily lapsed into fantasy. Federalists dining at Coyle's night after night, having exhausted all other topics, found themselves speculating about what the Republicans over at McNunn's or Conrad's were up to. Was it a secret alliance with Napoleon? A scheme to destroy what was left of the Federalist party? The more outrageous the speculation, the livelier the ensuing debate over appropriate countermeasures, the quicker time passed.[38]

The size of the parties and their tendency to resort to conspiracy-mongering appear to have been inversely related. Republicans occasionally engaged in such activities, but the bulk of their time was given over to running the government. They were also better informed. The Federalists, excluded from the decision-making process, seldom had any idea of what, if anything, was happening. "This House," Quincy complained bitterly in 1809, "is a political non-descript. It acts and reasons, and votes and performs all the operations of an animated being, and yet . . . all the great questions are settled elsewhere." Reduced to scavenging for rumors as to the Administration's intentions, what they could not find out the Federalists often made up.[39]

Some Federalists tried giving their presence in Washington meaning by imagining themselves as the last line of defense against the extra-legislative machinations of the Republicans. "I do feel a pang in separating from that noble band of chevaliers," the Connecticut Federalist John Cotton Smith confessed after resigning his seat in the House in 1806. "Small as their number is, [they] have become the only depositories of their country's honor; and but for these the American Sodom must ere now have suffered the vengeance of heaven." For Federalists to have viewed the situation in less apocalyptic terms would have been to confront the futility of their position and the irresistible logic of resigning.[40]

Many, like Smith, did resign. Only the even less attractive prospect of returning to a country parsonage kept the Reverend Samuel Taggart at his congressional post for seven terms. For all he accomplished, however, he might have been back tending to his congregation. "Here I am silent, and sometimes perhaps almost a sullen spectator of what is going on," he once confessed. "[I] can do little else than vote against almost every measure which is brought into view."[41]

Unfortunately, Smith's solution to the Federalist dilemma was not available to Quincy. Having assured party leaders back in 1805 that he would serve in Congress at their pleasure, he felt bound to his office long after its novelty had faded. With the Boston electorate's flirtation with the Republicans over, the Federalists experienced little difficulty in securing his reelection in 1806. Two years later, he stood virtually unopposed; and in 1810, despite his request to be relieved, he again headed the Federalist ticket, easily winning a fourth term. "So," he had written that fall, "I shall be made for another term a political packhorse to travail to Washington, with the burdens of this part of the country without hope of relief for either it or myself."[42]

If his stubborn rectitude prevented him from resigning, his temperament precluded his adopting the role of "sullen spectator." Another way had to be found for coping not only with the political exasperation that was the lot of all Federalists in Republican Washington, but also with the social isolation and personal malaise that were peculiarly his own. Eventually he found it. By elevating conspiratorial theorizing from an occasional diversion to a full-time occupation, indeed to an all-encompassing obsession, Quincy was to learn how to make even "that cemetery of all comfort" endurable.

I Live, However, Happy

During his second winter in the capital Quincy took little part in House business, subscribing to the prevailing policy, "to do nothing." Depressed and apathetic, he wrote not a little cynically to William Shaw that "there seem to be no instant reasons for action except general ones, resulting from the conditions of the country and the state of our foreign affairs."[43]

By the spring of 1807 his torpor had become a matter of concern among friends. Fisher Ames urged him to take the floor more often, if only "to cry 'fire' or 'stop thief' when Jacobinism attempts to burn and rob." "Federalism is not a sword, nor a gun; it is not wings, but a parachute," he counseled. "In this sense the good men of Congress should be on the alert." When such gentle proddings produced no effect, Ames switched metaphors. "It is better to suffer the fatigue of pumping," he bluntly informed his dispirited congressman, "than to sit sullen until the ship sinks."[44]

The Tenth Congress had convened by the time Quincy received Ames's last stricture, and his depression had already hit bottom. After a summer in Braintree with his family, he had returned to the capital somewhat revived. "Pumping," he was prepared to concede, could have its value. It might, for one thing, provide an outlet for the unexpended energy that had built up during the previous session and probably caused the "nervous headaches" he had been complaining of. For reasons of personal therapy more than from any continuing illusion that his efforts would be politically productive, Quincy decided he would take the floor whenever an opportunity presented itself. It would be, as he later admitted, "useful as an exercise, and if nothing else, at least keeps me out of mischief."[45]

The decision to engage actively in House debates was more than non-political; it represented an abandonment of political considerations altogether. Though he never acknowledged it, his partial psychic recovery in the fall of 1807 was achieved at the cost of repudiating the role he had come to Washington to play—to be what Burke called "a non-metaphysical barterer." Direct evidence for this is lacking, perhaps inevitably so, given the likelihood that Quincy himself was not fully conscious of it. Nonetheless, such a break can be inferred by examining his relations with three groups both before and after the first session of the Tenth Congress: the Republican majority in the House; the Federalist minority; and several leading Boston constituents.[46]

Quincy's relations with the Republicans during the Ninth Congress had been cool but civil. His first formal address, delivered on April 15, 1806, in support of a bill for fortifying seaboard cities, was reasoned, restrained, and altogether respectful of the sensibilities of his predominantly Republican and back-country audience. While acknowledging the existence of differing opinions on the subject, he stressed the nation's interest in securing for its commercial centers adequate protection. It was, in short, a most politic speech. Even Henry Adams, no admirer of Quincy's later oratory, thought it "far superior to the ordinary level of Congressional harangues."[47]

Beginning with the Tenth Congress, his speeches took on a radically different tone. No longer were they conceived as political instruments, designed to persuade and disarm, but as personal apologias wherein the speaker registered his dissent from the majority in the most uncompromising terms possible. Rather than seek out areas where consensus was likely, he chose to dramatize those where discord was inevitable. One does not, after all, go about seeking support from an already critically disposed audience by announcing beforehand that one's political differences with it are attributable to the fact that "I never schooled in the school of the scavenger; I never took degrees at the oyster bench; I never sat at the feet of fishwomen. . . ."[48]

Filled with personal attacks upon the most choleric Republicans, sectional aspersions, and, perhaps most infuriating of all, abstruse classical allusions his fellow congressmen neither understood nor appreciated, Quincy's speeches were calculatedly abusive. They were designed to provoke, and they succeeded. No other congressman, not even Randolph, had his remarks interrupted with such regularity as did Quincy during his last three terms in the House. "It is not the fact intimated . . . which startles gentlemen from their seats," he informed a Republican who sought to have him ruled out of order, "but the force of the argument stated." Quincy's arguments were nothing if not forceful.[49]

Rumors reached Boston in early 1809 that their congressman had been killed in a duel with George W. Campbell, a Tennessee Republican with a reputation for resorting to pistols whenever words failed him, as they frequently did. The rumor was unfounded, though Campbell had extended a challenge to Quincy after taking umbrage at a reference to him as "Aeneas . . . posting away into the

woods." "Do not be alarmed at any harshness the papers may convey
to you," he assured Mrs. Quincy, who found such rumors unsettling.
"I shall live down calumnies; and as to *tongue fighting*, if anyone has
a longer weapon or a sharper, I must be content to contend at a
disadvantage."[50]

Denied power, Quincy learned to make notoriety suffice. How else
can one explain the obvious pleasure he took in being attacked by his
colleagues and the Republican press? "I was first told I deserved *a
halter*!" he informed William Shaw after delivering a typically
inflammatory speech in 1811:

> Now my landlord tells me he heard a gentleman say that a member from
> Massachusetts said I must be '*deranged*' and that '*my family were subject to it*!' I
> desired him to ask the person to read what I had said—and that he would be
> satisfied, at least there was 'method in my madness.'

When, later in the same session, Felix Grundy told him that "except
Tim Pickering, there is not a man in the United States so perfectly
hated by the people of my district as yourself," Quincy thanked the
Tennessee Republican and promptly reported the compliment to his
wife.[51]

Along with this new policy of baiting the Republicans went a loss
of interest in his fellow Federalists. The pronouncement of Burke's
that had figured most prominently in Quincy's preparations for
Congress in 1805 was "to be useful a man must belong to a party."
Throughout his first year in Washington he had adhered to this
admonition, subordinating his own impulsive inclinations to the
cautious policy prescribed by the party elders. Beginning with the
Tenth Congress, however, party needs became subordinated to his
own.[52]

Many historians have accepted Quincy's first biographer's description of him as leader of the Federalists in the House during his later
years in Congress. To do so is to confound the frequency of his
pronouncements and the authority with which he made them.
Unquestionably the most outspoken Federalist in Congress, he spoke
for himself and not his party. After the Ninth Congress he appears
never to have bothered discussing his speeches with other Federalists
before delivery, nor to have solicited their responses following
delivery. At least one Federalist believed that his reputation, not
only for inciting Republicans but for ignoring Federalists, was such

that any gesture he made in behalf of a particular position "had little or no effect."[53]

The Federalists had no leader during Quincy's years in Congress. Less a party in the modern sense of an organization collectively engaged in the legislative process than a wailing chorus off on the edge of the political stage, they lacked a positive program around which a leader might rally them. There is little to indicate, for example, that Federalists living in different boardinghouses regularly came together to discuss strategy. Before 1812 there seems to have been no formal party caucus. As Samuel Taggart concluded, after observing his colleagues in the Eleventh Congress, "a more completely divided, bewildered, disorganized set of men hardly exists."[54]

Even if the Federalists would have responded to vigorous leadership, Quincy was not the man to provide it. Incapable of restraining his own impulses in the interest of political expediency, he could hardly impose constraints upon others. Moreover, he simply was not interested in assuming the responsibilities incumbent upon a party leader. As he told John Adams in 1811, he much preferred "breaking new ground . . . as little anticipated by anyone of my own [party] as by any of the opposite."[55]

The most flagrant instance of Quincy's political contrariness occurred during the closing days of Jefferson's second term. On January 25, 1809, after detailing at great length the personnel problems besetting the Boston Customs House, he startled the House awake by calling for an immediate inquiry into the President's appointment policies as a preliminary to impeaching him! "Notwithstanding gentlemen near him had asked him to withdraw his resolution," the *Annals of Congress* relate, he remained "convinced that it was proper that an inquiry should be made." Someone, most likely a Republican, seconded the motion and brought it to a vote. It failed 117 to 1.[56]

However else such gestures can be explained, they clearly were not in keeping with the political holding action Ames had suggested in his "parachute" metaphor. They seem more appropriately part of what Joseph Gusfield has characterized as a "symbolic crusade." Quincy's activities in Congress can most accurately be understood as a series of individual, often spectacular, but essentially ceremonial joustings against forces privately conceded to be overwhelming.

"Democracy is, as you will find," he told Federalist congressman Jabez Upham in 1809, "inveterate." It was this recognition that his views would not prevail, either in Congress or out, that determined his strategy and choice of weapons. Like a lawyer confronting a hopelessly hostile jury, while going through the motions of arguing his case, Quincy seems already to have been preparing his appeal to the higher courts—posterity.[57]

The same personal considerations which led him to outrage Republicans and ignore Federalists in Washington rendered him indifferent to the views and concerns of his most prominent constituents. Any current discussion of Quincy's relations as a congressman with the Federalist leadership in Massachusetts can easily become entangled in the recent debate over what David Hackett Fischer has called "the myth of the Essex Junto." But even if Fischer's suspicions—that the "Junto" was a figment of John Hancock's imagination perpetuated by four generations of Adamses and by Samuel Eliot Morison—are ignored in favor of the traditional view of the Junto as an exclusive group of North Shore and Boston Federalists who controlled Massachusetts politics from the late 1770's to the 1820's, Quincy was not, as Morison has contended, "their political chanteyman."[58]

The Essex Junto's politics have usually been described as intermittently secessionist and unremittingly pro-British. Quincy differed on both counts. He had nothing to do with the "Northern Confederacy" schemes of either 1803-1804 or 1808, orchestrated by Timothy Pickering. His relations with Pickering, the most insistent secessionist among those thought to have constituted the Junto's inner circle, were friendly but limited. Their surviving correspondence explicitly avoided politics, focusing instead on such subjects as "the history of the silk worm." As for his friend Fisher Ames's senescent despair over the prospects of the union, Quincy thought it unwarranted. "Each member will bear much," he wrote in 1810, "before it will entertain the idea of disunion and severance."[59]

It is equally clear that he dissented from the view that the British could do no wrong. Unlike George Cabot, John Lowell, Christopher Gore, and other reputed Junto members, Quincy had neither commercial connections with nor personal affection for England. Too much his father's son ever to forget the Revolutionary generation's distrust of the English, he faulted many of his constituents for their "foolish leaning upon [Great Britain] . . . which, at the same time that it does little credit to their patriotism, does infinitely less to their judgment." Although Republicans at the time, and historians since, have lumped him with what Albert Gallatin called "the Tory party of Boston," the Reverend John Thornton Kirkland, who knew that party as well as anyone, easily distinguished between Cabot and Lowell, "who should be thought Englishmen," and Quincy, "a true American."[60]

Finally, it is inconceivable that John Adams could remain on friendly terms with Quincy if he was in fact the henchman of those whom Adams held responsible for his forced retirement from the presidency. During Quincy's years in Congress, Adams regularly questioned his opinions and tactics, but never his independence. Thus one is obliged to concur in Eliza Susan's choice of her father's most distinguishing trait as a congressman: "an inveterate habit of thinking for himself." One need not agree that it was a virtue.[61]

"I keep my place," Quincy wrote in 1810, "by not thinking about anything but business into which I plunge, headlong, and in which I am wholly absorbed." "The malign spirits of democracy have shot after me in storm all the terrors of their quivers," he informed the Reverend Joseph McLean of Cambridge a year later. "I live, however, happy; laugh some; labour much; lounge little. My rule is to fill up my time. . . ." Unfortunately, no other business open to him in Republican Washington proved as absorbing or equal to his need to fill up time as that of witch-hunting.[62]

Although he did not give himself over to this occupation prior to the Tenth Congress, he had earlier demonstrated proclivities toward it. In preparing for Congress in 1805, he had conducted researches "among the filth of party newspapers and pamphlets" in hopes of "extracting the slight thread of a [word obliterated] policy." By his own admission he also spent "an enormous amount of time" during his first two winters in Washington sifting through the accounts of Jefferson's Secretary of the Treasury, Albert Gallatin, in order to "detect some of his artifices." When he discovered nothing wrong, he conceded Gallatin to be craftier than he had imagined, but no less a crook.[63]

Specific suspicions later gave way to general and operative convictions. Once he started pursuing Republican witches in earnest, he found them everywhere. Each move by the Administration was assigned a secret motive; the only explanations discounted were the obvious. One conspiracy unmasked always led to another until by 1811 Quincy saw them where the "conspirators" themselves did not. "What would you say," he asked McLean, "could you witness all the mean, all the interested, all the vindictive motives which often constitute the cause of actions, and are hidden from the world, and often concealed, by their self-love, from the agents themselves?" Washington had become, as he later recalled it, like Solomon's Tadmor, "where creeping things had possession of the palace and foxes looked out of the windows." That such creatures were imaginary—the product of his psychic needs rather than a reflection of the mundane reality of the capital—made the fervor with which he came to pursue them no less real.[64]

4 / Escape into War

We shall never be comfortable until we have 'a round' or 'a rough and tumble' with some nation or another. And I believe the sooner it comes the better.
— Josiah Quincy, December 21, 1810

Within this context of political exasperation and personal belligerency, Quincy's curious role in the proceedings leading up to that most problematical of all American wars—the War of 1812—becomes more intelligible, if less commendable. Of sufficient moment to warrant examination for its causal implications, it also constitutes a case study in the benumbing effects of political paranoia.

The Great Transgression

During Quincy's long public career he was never more categorical than in his later condemnation of the War of 1812 and his disavowal of any complicity in it. Less than a week after Madison declared war on Great Britain Quincy informed his constituents that "it is an event awful, unexpected, hostile to your interests, menacing to your liberties, and revolting to your feelings." On January 5, 1813, with the war then in its seventh month and going badly for the United States, he announced to his fellow congressmen, "I am clear of the great transgression." Twenty-one years later, while still impugning the motives of those who supported the war, he insisted that neither partisan nor personal considerations influenced his own actions during the spring of 1812. Later still, in the 1850's, he prepared memoranda which again presented the case that war had come in 1812 in spite of his heroic efforts to avert it.[1]

These protestations lack neither plausibility nor documentation. Like all Federalists, Quincy had been excluded from the White House conferences and the Republican caucus out of which came the decision of war. When Madison brought his War Message before the House on the first of June, Quincy opposed its acceptance, "uttering, I trust," he wrote to his wife during the debate, "piercing truths, which were felt deeply enough, though they produced no conviction." Four days later he joined forty-eight other congressmen and voted against declaring war on Great Britain. After the Senate approved Madison's recommendation and war was declared, he drafted the dissenting statement eventually signed by thirty-four Federalists. During his last session in Congress, and thereafter in the Massachusetts Senate, he was acknowledged by supporters as well as critics of the war, as its most outspoken opponent.[2]

His own opposition to the war part of the public record, Quincy freely attributed the blame for it to others. The initial impulse, he argued, came from Western and Southern Republicans in the House, men like Henry Clay of Kentucky and Felix Grundy of Tennessee, John Calhoun and Langdon Cheves of South Carolina. These "War Hawks," a term Quincy had coined in the fall of 1811, sought war with England as an excuse to seize Canada and perhaps the Floridas as well. Patriotic sensibilities and concern with national honor informed their rhetoric, he allowed, but territorial greed determined their policies.[3]

Quincy's indictment did not stop the War Hawks. As he acknowledged, they constituted a small minority in the Twelfth Congress and, accordingly, could not be burdened with all the guilt for plunging the United States into a war it had avoided for thirty years and was woefully unprepared to fight. Belligerent talk had been heard before in Congress, and in the face of provocations greater than those in 1812, without a war ensuing. What made 1812 different, he argued, was not the presence of congressional jingoes but presidential deference to them.[4]

According to Quincy, Madison decided to follow the War Hawks only after meeting secretly in March with Speaker of the House Henry Clay, who informed the President that his renomination by the Republican caucus would be dependent upon his acquiescence to their war policy. Madison agreed to comply, thus proving that "a country may be ruined in making an administration happy."[5]

For his own part in this "combination of violence with individual interest" which produced the War of 1812, Quincy admitted only his failure to detect it in time to do anything about it. "When war against Great Britain was proposed at the last session," he stated on January 5, 1813, "I confess to you, I . . . believed not one word of the matter. I put my trust in the old-fashioned notions of common-sense and common prudence. . . . the idea seemd so absurd that I never once entertained it as possible." In explaining his critical lapse, he reminded his colleagues "that I am not one of those who worship in that temple where Condorcet is the high priest, and Machiavel the God."[6]

However appealing, this modest self-characterization will not stand scrutiny. It both distorts the nature of the Administration's decision for war and neglects the Machiavellian component in Quincy's own actions. The President had been clumsy but not intentionally devious or conspiratorial. Nor is there any solid evidence to back up the claim of a Madison-Clay deal. Moreover, Quincy's failure to discern the drift of events should be attributed less to naïveté, as he would have it, than to his cynical refusal to consider the possibility that the Republicans meant what they said. And finally, his indictment of the President and the War Hawks for acting from sectional and personal motives retains moral force only if his actions were differently motivated. They were not. Indeed, it is one of the ironies surrounding the decision of the United States to initiate hostilities with Great Britain that the most outspoken dissenter from that decision was an accomplice in it.[7]

The historiographical debates over the origins of the War of 1812 share at least one element in common with the military events of that war: inconclusiveness. Throughout the nineteenth century most American historians accepted at face value Madison's explanation that the war had been entered into for the defense of national honor and the protection of neutral maritime rights. Richard Hildreth, a New Englander with marked Federalist sympathies writing in the 1850's, was virtually alone in citing Randolph's charge of western designs on Canada and Quincy's allegations of a Clay-Madison deal. Henry Adams, though conceding in the sixth volume of his *History of the United States* that interest in Canada was a back-country consideration, basically subscribed to the traditional maritime interpretation.[8]

Adams' acceptance of the traditional view, rather than confirming it, only served to direct attention to an inconsistency which neither he nor his predecessors had faced: that support for the war came from those sections of the country least concerned with maritime trade. How could the defense of neutral maritime rights be the leading cause for a war which maritime interests opposed? In order to find a more satisfactory explanation, historians after Adams shifted their focus from the Northeast, where the war had been patently unpopular, to where it had received its most enthusiastic support, the West and the South. Resurrecting Randolph's explanation, Louis M. Hacker announced in 1924 that the War of 1812 had been fought not over maritime questions at all, but because the West coveted the agricultural land reserves of Canada. Julius W. Pratt insisted that the West's interest in Canada was less territorial than a defensive response to Indian violence along the border; yet he cited Southern interest in the Floridas as a contributing cause. A few years later George Rogers Taylor restored British trade policies to their old status in the debate by arguing that, whatever their impact on the Northeast, they had so depressed the price of export staples in the Mississippi Valley as to encourage Americans living there to think of war with England as the only means to secure economic relief.[9]

However conclusive such explanations seemed to a generation preoccupied with economic questions, they have failed to persuade recent students of the subject. Bradford Perkins, Norman K. Risjord, and Roger H. Brown have all noted that those who cited "western" or material motives in explaining the War of 1812 suffered from their own variety of sectional myopia as well as from too great a willingness to view history as economically determined. Revealing their own generation's very different preoccupations, they fault their elders for assuming that the causes of this or any other war were essentially rational. Like Von Holst, McMaster, and Mahan earlier, these more recent historians stress the Orders in Council, impressment, and the harassment of American shipping by the British navy. But unlike their predecessors, they are at pains to distinguish between the economic effects of such British policies, which they argue are inconsequential, and their psychological impact, which they see as "determinative." "All the insults suffered by the United States," Bradford Perkins writes in his exemplary *Prologue to War*, "posed a greater threat in the realm of the spirit than in the realm of the merchant and accountant, the seaman and the frontiersman."[10]

But even these insults, felt though they were, did not constitute an unanswerable case for war. Americans, frustrated by the failure of their government's policy of economic coercion and indignant at the British government's rebuff of its diplomatic efforts, were also militarily unprepared to do battle with the most powerful nation in the world and they knew it. Jingo sentiments, high in the fall of

1811, had ebbed by the following spring. *Niles' Weekly Register*, after describing "an almost universal disposition of war" in January, noted no such disposition in April. After an exhaustive examination of American public opinion during the spring of 1812, Perkins has concluded that "the nation did not want war." Nevertheless, on June 19, 1812, the United States found itself entering into what Samuel Eliot Morison, writing in the shadow of Vietnam, has called "the most unpopular war in our history."[11]

Clearly the War of 1812 was no prototype of the Spanish-American War, where a rabid public impressed its will upon Congress which in turn forced a reluctant President's hand. The question remains: why did Madison slide over rather than draw back from the brink like his predecessors in 1798 and 1807?

A different and potentially more productive approach to the question why the war sentiment prevailed in Washington in 1812 is to turn it around and ask why the peace sentiment did not. The problem thus becomes to understand why the forty-nine congressmen and thirteen senators who ultimately opposed the war failed to convince Madison beforehand that, as Jefferson phrased it in 1811, "peace had not become more losing than war." Given the ebbing popular enthusiasm for war, the Administration's gloomy cost projections in January, the wretched state of the navy and the unwillingness of many Southern Republicans to do anything to improve it, and finally the long history of waffling by the White House on the issue of peace and war, the failure of the peace advocates ought not to have been a foregone conclusion.[12]

A cursory glance at the recorded debates of the first session of the Twelfth Congress, in the fall of 1811, provides one explanation for the ineffectiveness of the anti-war argument: it was never articulated until *after* the Administration had made its decision. Throughout the session talk of war was exclusively Republican talk, nearly all of it originating in the House. Logically then, it should have been responded to by the thirty-seven Federalists holding seats in the House, none of whom later voted for war. Though in the minority, they had ample opportunity during the first four months of the session to state the reasons which later prompted their dissenting votes. At the very least they could have confronted the Administration with evidence attesting to the country's growing wariness of war with England.[13]

They did neither. Except for Randolph and Richard Stanford, a North Carolina Quid, nobody in the House openly disputed the War Hawks. Only after Madison announced a sixty-day embargo on April 1, an act which most observers interpreted as the prelude to war, did the Federalists sound the alarm. By then it was too late; the country had already begun its irreversible slide into armed conflict. The War Hawks had won, not by the logic of their arguments, not by their numbers in Congress, and not by their popular backing; they won by default.[14]

Dull Times

On November 25, 1808, John Adams had offered his "dear friend," Josiah Quincy, some thoughts on the times:

You are greatly to be pitied, I mean all of you, of all parties, for I see you must labour very hard and with much anxiety without the smallest hope that I can discern of preserving yourselves and us from very dull times. If you institute a total non-intercourse the times will not be more cheerful. If you repeal the Embargo, circumstances will occur of more animation, but perhaps not more profit or more comfort. If you arm our merchantmen there will be war. The blood will not stagnate it is true; but it may run too freely for our health and comfort.

Such were the options, some having only the promise of "more animation" to commend them. But when "dull times" persisted for three more years, many Americans, including Quincy, were to view even that as no insignificant commendation.[15]

Quincy's recovery from his depression coincided with a critical juncture in Anglo-American relations. The diplomatic rapprochement painfully fashioned during the Adams administration and sustained through Jefferson's first term, began coming apart early in his second. With the resumption of the Napoleonic War in 1804, the British navy reactivated its impressment crews and the practice of halting American ships to search for deserters. Parliament, through a series of Orders in Council, and the admiralty courts, most notably in the *Essex* decision (1805), meanwhile extended the definition of "unneutral activity" to include virtually all American trade with Europe. Amicable relations with the United States, the British government had decided, were a peacetime luxury.[16]

Though Jefferson at first minimized the implications of this decision, he could hardly do so after the events of June 22, 1807. That afternoon, a few hours off Norfolk, Virginia, the British line-of-battle ship *Leopard* hailed the American frigate *Chesapeake* and demanded the right to search for deserters. When the *Chesapeake* refused, the smaller *Leopard* opened fire. Fifteen minutes and three broadsides later, the American ship struck its flag, an impressment team came aboard, and four members of its crew were removed. The *Leopard* then sailed off, leaving the bloody and battered *Chesapeake* to make its hapless way back to Norfolk.[17]

American reaction was both swift and indignant as the anglophobia of the early 1790's resurfaced with all its old virulence. In Virginia the militia was called out and a coastal watch established; in Boston protest meetings were held in Faneuil Hall, attended by Federalists as well as Republicans; in Washington Secretary of the Treasury Gallatin, fearing that war with England was imminent, began planning how to finance it. Whether despite the clamor or, more likely, because of it, Jefferson resisted public pressure to call Congress into emergency session, citing the unhealthiness of the capital in July. He did agree, however, to advance by a month the convening date of the Tenth Congress and assured his aroused countrymen that the crisis would then be attended to.[18]

When Congress convened on October 26, more than four months after the *Chesapeake's* humiliation, public tempers had cooled. Republican congressmen who had earlier feared that the Administration would be obliged to declare war, now felt free to join in the cry for retaliatory action. Similarly, Jefferson, having decided against a military response in favor of some form of economic coercion, grew more bellicose as the likelihood of war grew more remote. But if Republicans intended to do little more than talk, circumstances seemed to deny the Federalists even that modest activity. Unhappy over British restrictions on neutral trade and disinclined to defend the *Leopard's* precipitate actions, yet unwilling to exacerbate Anglo-American relations still further by joining in the Republican saber rattling, they again appeared consigned to the role of silent observers.[19]

As the session moved along, however, and his own spirits continued to revive, Quincy began faulting his fellow Federalists for what he thought was their too ready acceptance of this passive role. "I confess myself incapable of perceiving the policy of that course," Harrison Gray Otis concurred in mid-November, "which gives to our adversaries the exclusive possession of the public ear, and exhibits the Federal minority as a browbeaten and desponding cabal." Finding Federalist silence personally untenable, he pronounced it politically unsound.[20]

Although his own first response to the *Chesapeake* affair had been to play it down in the hope that it would be quickly forgotten, he decided shortly after returning to Washington to turn it to his own purposes. The *Chesapeake*'s dismal performance (it had sustained twenty-two hullings and twenty-one casualties without getting off a volley) soon became his favorite subject and proof for his contention that the Republicans were criminally negligent in their disregard for the needs of the splendid navy bequeathed to them by the Federalists in 1801. Tentatively at first, and then more assertively as the session progressed, Quincy pointed to the disparity between the Administration's verbal militancy and its unwillingness to bring forward serious proposals for military preparedness.[21]

Quincy was discovering that the preparedness theme fitted his needs nicely. Politically, it exempted him from the charge of being a British apologist and certified his patriotism; personally, it allowed him to seize the offensive in debating the Republicans. The fact that military preparedness had been one of the essential elements in the Federalist program in the 1790's gave it an added legitimacy. And finally, given his suspicion that the Administration was bluffing and had as little taste for war with England as he did, it was perfectly harmless.[22]

The announcement of Jefferson's Embargo plans only confirmed his suspicion. Unable to stop its implementation, Quincy soon distinguished himself as the Embargo's most vociferous congressional critic. For once he found himself on the popular side of a national issue. Whatever the long-range diplomatic potential of the President's experiment in economic coercion, its political impact was almost immediately evident. Twice as many Federalists won seats in the Eleventh Congress as had served in the Tenth. The Administration's efforts to enforce the Embargo had proved so unpopular in New England that Republican congressmen like Joseph Story and Ezekiel Bacon came out in favor of its repeal. Thus, by the fall of 1808 the *Columbian Centinel*'s January headline, "The Embargo — A great Blessing — The Revival of Federalism," seemed on its way to being borne out.[23]

Northern Republicans filed back to Washington prepared to

abandon the Embargo as well-intentioned but unworkable; but Quincy returned in a far less magnanimous mood. During the course of the summer he came to suspect the Embargo to be more than the Administration professed it to be. Far from being a temporary measure forced upon the United States by the exigencies of the international situation, it was, he persuaded himself, a permanent part of a Republican scheme to bankrupt New England and destroy the Federalist Party. When Administration supporters opened the session by defending the continuation of the Embargo as the only alternative to war or complete submission, his worst suspicions seemed to be confirmed.[24]

Jefferson's request in December for fifty thousand additional troops, ostensibly for use in the event of hostilities with Great Britain, fitted all too well into Quincy's conviction that a conspiracy existed. The Embargo would be permanent and the troops would be used to force compliance with it, especially in New England where some citizens were still not sufficiently frightened by the specter of war to surrender their livelihoods without fuss. It was all too transparent.[25]

On January 19, 1809, in his fourth speech in as many weeks, Quincy called the Administration's bluff:

Sir, I am sick, sick to loathing, of this eternal clamor of 'war, war, war,' which has been kept up almost incessantly on this floor, now for more than two years, sir. If I can help it, the old women of this country shall not be frightened in this way any longer. I have been a long time a close observer of what has been done and said by the majority of this House; and, for one, I am satisfied that no insult, however gross, offered to us by either France or Great Britain, could force this majority into the declaration of war. To use a strong but common expression, it could not be kicked into such a declaration. . . .

Having convinced himself that there were no attendant risks, he intended to take full advantage of the oratorical possibilities of this new strategy.[26]

Not all critics of Administration policy shared his belief in the existence of a conspiracy or his fascination with Republican tail-pulling. Of the House Federalists, Jabez Upham of Massachusetts came closest to agreeing with him when he stated that the Embargo's "real object was neither precaution nor coercion, in my belief. It was to destroy our active commerce—to form this country into a China." Most of Quincy's other colleagues enjoyed hearing him attack the

Embargo "in front and rear" but refused to join him in calling for military preparations; the last thing they intended to do was arm the Republicans. As he admitted, having "thrown off certain shackles of other men's opinions," he had become "the object of attack to every one who has spoken, and with not a single Federal aid."[2 7]

His strategy fared little better at home. "Though you seem to deride [the Administration's] pretense of war," John Thornton Kirkland wrote Quincy on February 10, 1809, "yet your friends here are not so much at ease." John Adams, who had earlier advised him not to "teaze the President," thought he was being unnecessarily provocative. Far more disturbed were George Cabot, John Lowell, and Boston's other leading anglophiles, who shared what Cabot called "a just dread" of war with England and believed that the United States had "no cause for war with that nation." They were appalled to hear Quincy announce from the floor of the House that "the idea that nothing on earth is so dreadful as war is inculcated too studiously among us."[2 8]

Behind "the apparent difference between our friends at Washington and ourselves here" were two different views of the Embargo. Cabot and others in the Boston mercantile community saw it as a temporary commercial restraint, while Quincy was certain it was a politically inspired thrust at the economic heart of New England. The Embargo had unquestionably hurt business, but less than Quincy imagined and not seriously enough to make his constituents look upon war with England as a more attractive alternative. No businessman himself, and probably unaware of the amount of illicit trade moving in and out of Boston despite the Embargo, he failed to appreciate such prudence.[2 9]

All the anxiety generated by his outspokenness notwithstanding, Quincy was proved by the events of 1809 to be an accurate judge of the temper of the Administration. There was no war in the offing and none had been seriously contemplated by the Republican leadership. On February 27 Congress responded to Northern pressure, from Republicans and Federalists alike, and passed a Non-Intercourse bill to replace the more stringent Embargo. Two days later, in one of his last official acts, Jefferson reluctantly signed it into law. Because he had insisted throughout the session that all commercial restrictions be lifted, Quincy voted against the bill. Nevertheless, after three months of almost non-stop speech-making, he took the occasion of the enactment of the Non-Intercourse Act to resume his seat and let the dull times set in again.[30]

President Madison, still operating within Jefferson's orbit, occupied himself during his first two years in office with a series of unsuccessful negotiations with Great Britain and France, while his Cabinet tinkered with the motley system of commercial restrictions inherited from the previous Administration. Uncertain of his control over congressional Republicans and faced with a sizable Federalist contingent in the House, he appeared willing to let the government come to a standstill. As for the prevailing attitude of the Republican leaders in the House, Henry Adams wrote that "no course would have pleased them so much as to do nothing at all."[31]

Meanwhile, Quincy's personal situation in Washington grew more and more intolerable. His wife and two oldest children had accompanied him to the first session of the Eleventh Congress, but not the second. "O mamma! I wish we were in Quincy," twelve-year old Eliza Susan complained during her second winter in the capital. "Don't you think it must be very pleasant there now?" The following winter her father endured Washington alone. And, as before, he let his personal discomfort manifest itself in public irascibility.[32]

For want of diversion, he fell to provoking his colleagues. On January 14, 1811, without prior warning, he predicted the demise of the Union. If the pending Louisiana statehood bill, then under discussion and certain of passage, became law, he said, "the bonds of this Union are virtually dissolved." When called to order, he repeated his blasphemy, adding that Louisiana's admission into the Union would render the original states "free from their moral obligations; and that as it will be the right of all, so it will be the duty of some to prepare definitely for a separation—amicably, if they can; violently, if they must." While consistent with his long-held views on Louisiana and the procedures adopted for the territory's inclusion in the Union, his remarks served no positive purpose. Instead they embarrassed members of his own party by lending credibility to the Republicans' charges that all Federalists were disunionists. They had, however, caused a considerable stir, and they accomplished what Quincy had intended.[33]

Far more serious than these petulant outbursts was the increasingly cavalier attitude he began to take toward the question of war with

England. Whereas earlier he dismissed all talk on the subject as saber rattling, he now tried to provoke it. Like many others in Washington, Quincy had found the protracted international impasse in which the United States found itself unnerving. Jefferson's economic alternatives to war had proved as psychologically unsatisfying as diplomatically ineffective. Nor was there much reason to expect a more vigorous policy to be supported by Jefferson's successor. "As to Jemmy Madison," Washington Irving wrote, expressing a not uncommon view of the President, "he is nothing but a withered little apple-john." Quincy's need to have the country act, to do something, *anything*, grew more intense precisely as did his belief that the government had lost all capacity for action.[34]

When the second session of the Eleventh Congress convened, he was prepared to favor virtually any governmental policy that promised, to recall Adams' phrase, "to make the blood flow more freely." As the *status quo* became more intolerable, the idea of war as an escape became more acceptable. He hoped, of course, that if it came it would be blamed on the Republicans and redound to the Federalists' benefit, but partisan considerations were secondary to personal. Politics rationalized what otherwise could not be articulated. Nor did he manage to sublimate these inner drives. In a disconsolate Christmas letter written to friends back in Boston almost a year before the War Hawks were fledged, he said it all: "I feel ready to fight anybody, or anything. . . . We shall never be comfortable until we have 'a round' or 'a rough and tumble' with some nation or another. And . . . the sooner it comes the better.[35]

A Worthy Experiment

President Madison's third annual message, delivered at the opening of the Twelfth Congress, reflected the Administration's own irritation with the diplomatic impasse. Although Napoleon had been devious, it was "the unfriendly spirit" of the British which offended Madison more. Their refusal to modify the Orders in Council after the French announced the cancellation of the Berlin and Milan Decrees persuaded the President that stronger measures than a restatement of the nation's disapprobation were in order. Accordingly, his message called upon Congress to increase military appropriations, enlarge the army, and construct additional naval fortifications; it closed with an expression of his "deep sense of the crisis" and an assurance to the nation that he would do whatever was required in "vindicating its rights and advancing its welfare."[36]

While Clay and the War Hawks cheered the message, inferring that the President intended to fight, most House Federalists remained unimpressed. "I have nothing new to write," the Massachusetts Federalist Abijah Bigelow informed his wife in early December, "except the old story of war, and rumors of war. By the speeches of many of the members you would suppose that the enemy were already at our heels, but alas, we federalists are so heedless that we pay no attention to it." Three days later Samuel Taggart told a constituent that the Federalists had taken no part in any debates "and intend to take none."[37]

Such insouciance only partially cloaked the despair permeating their ranks. Gains registered in the 1808 elections had been almost completely erased in 1810, leaving the Federalists in the Twelfth Congress as they were in the Tenth—a hopelessly outnumbered and dispirited silent minority. Recent state elections indicated that the worst was yet to come. Why bother then tangling with the likes of Clay or Calhoun?[38]

Quincy shared his colleagues' skepticism about Madison's militant message, probably their despair over party prospects, but not their public resignation. Temperamentally unable to sit back with Bigelow and Taggart to await the inevitable, he felt compelled to force it. Moreover, since the last session he had added yet another twist to his already labyrinthine interpretation of Republican policy, one that predictably required immediate counter-measures of the Federalists.

Trade restrictions were designed not only to impoverish commercially oriented Federalists, as he had long assumed, but also to stimulate domestic manufacture. The purpose, Quincy believed, was to create in the Northeast both a new economic elite which would owe its political loyalties to the Republicans and a new proletarian class of factory workers which would vote as that elite directed. Even in New England, Quincy warned his merchant constituents, "new interests are gradually rising . . . which are intended to become the rivals of the ancient ones, and to penalize their influence." There seemed no end to intrigue.[39]

Restrictions on maritime commerce had precipitated a shift of capital in the Northeast from international trade to domestic manufacturing. This occurred most dramatically in New England where cotton textile production had increased tenfold between 1808 and 1810. "Embargo has raised a spirit of factory enterprize in this country," a Massachusetts Republican proclaimed in 1811, "that will never be extinguished." It was also true that many of the entrepreneurs in the new manufacturing projects were not part of the old Federalist commercial elite; some were Republicans and all were appreciative of the domestic monopoly afforded by the Administration's trade policies. But to conclude from these facts that the economic transformation of New England was part of a Republican master plan to destroy the Federalist party by uprooting the social order which it represented required what Richard Hofstadter has called "a characteristic paranoid leap into fantasy." Quincy was, by 1811, equal to the exertion.[40]

On November 8, 1811, three days after the President's message, Quincy set out his own battle plan in an eleven-page letter to the head of the Federalist party in Massachusetts. It was his intention, he informed Harrison Gray Otis, to support all calls for military appropriations. Not only would he not argue with the War Hawks, he would spur them on whenever their martial spirits flagged. If other Federalists adopted this strategy, they would force Madison into making a choice: either give in to the demands of the militant wing of his party and declare war, or publicly disavow his War Hawks and admit that his own verbal militancy had been "vaporings."

Anticipating objections to such brinkmanship, Quincy rebuked his Boston constituents for their "absurd and palsying fear of a war with Great Britain." It was their "vanity as commercial men," he told Otis, whom he exempted from the indictment, which blinded them to the "meanness and pusillanimity" of the Administration—and their own expendability. "War with Great Britain," he lectured, "is the machinery by which they induce one set of men to acquiesce in, through fear, a system of commercial annihilation, *in the continuance of which all their policy terminates*."

His plan took into full account the exigencies of Massachusetts politics. By 1811 Republican successes at the polls were no longer dismissed as aberrations as Elbridge Gerry's election to the governorship had been the year before. With Gerry reelected and both houses of the General Court Republican, the situation suddenly looked desperate. Quincy attributed the decline of Federalism in Massachu-

setts to the success Republicans had in picturing it as a party of
British lackeys. But by pursuing his strategy of supporting all
proposals for preparedness his party could refute such a charge. With
Republican redistricting already under way, the approaching elections were crucial. "They will either elevate to state power," Quincy
warned, "or throw, for a long time into the shade, men, whose
talents and virtues are the best inheritance of their country."

But what if Madison, forced to choose between repudiating a
segment of his own party or declaring war, chose war? Quincy,
minimizing its likelihood, refused to be intimidated by the possibility. "The present situation of the commercial parts of the
country," he flatly stated, *is worse than any war, even a British.*"
Moreover, Federalists should not overlook the "fair consequences"
to be derived from such a war, not the least being the elimination of
"the political influence who should induce it." He then capped his
argument by averring that even if war came between the United
States and Great Britain, it would be brief and bloodless. "If we dare
not attack her by land, and will not meet her by water," he wrote, "I
pray all 'nervous gentlemen' to consider what sort of war that must
be. . . ."[41]

By almost any standard, Quincy's was a most comprehensive
counter-strategy, a Machiavellian mixture of political audacity, economic determinism, and covered bets, all premised on his belief that
the commercial annihilation of New England constituted the great
and persistent goal of the Administration. His assumption that a
military confrontation with England was unlikely turned in large part
on his cynical view of the War Hawks. "They cry 'war' in public," he
told Otis in a follow-up letter; "in secret they say 'we cannot
undertake it.' Clay our speaker told me yesterday with some naiveté,
'the truth is I am in favour of war and so are some others but some
of them fear that if we get into war you will get our places.' " "If
you only consider their natures," he concluded in a classic instance
of the pot calling the kettle black, "it must be obvious that concern
for their seats and their power is and will be the leading motive; and
in this consists their leading passion."[42]

The Quincy plan, however imaginative, found little support among
Boston's "nervous gentlemen." Otis expressed some initial interest
but made no effort to proselytize on its behalf. Some Federalists,
notably ex-governor Christopher Gore, thought Quincy was courting

Republican support by exposing anglophiles like himself to "vulgar abuse." Timothy Pickering thought the whole scheme "flighty" and would have nothing to do with it. Still others refused to accept the idea that the economic situation was so desperate that war would constitute relief. Smuggling, the coastal trade, and increasingly, investments in manufacturing had kept most members of the old commercial elite of Massachusetts comfortably solvent. And they knew it, if Quincy did not.[43]

Nor did his plan generate much enthusiasm in Washington. Veteran Federalists like John Davenport and Lewis Sturgis of Connecticut, and Richard Jackson of Rhode Island, while accustomed to conceding the floor to the Republicans, balked at the prospect of voting with them. Samuel Taggart and Abijah Bigelow of Massachusetts expressed early interest in Quincy's scheme but neither could bring himself to support Republican-sponsored military appropriations bills. Of his thirty-six Federalist colleagues in the Twelfth Congress only six agreed to undertake what he, James Emmot, and Thomas Gold, both second-term congressmen from upstate New York, described on January 1, 1812, as his "worthy experiment" to prove the Administration "time-serving, self-oppressive, and hypocritical." The remaining four recruits, Harmanus Bleecker of New York, James Milnor of Pennsylvania, George Sullivan of New Hampshire, and William Reed of Massachusetts, were all serving their first term in the House. The experiment clearly did not constitute Federalist party policy.[44]

Despite his failure to convince others, Quincy himself remained convinced throughout the winter of 1811-1812 that Madison and the Twelfth Congress had no more taste for war than had Jefferson and the Tenth. His technique was simply to apply the "lessons" he had learned four years earlier. Interpreting the President's silence since November and Gallatin's gloomy financial report in January as proof that the Administration had already lost its nerve, he pressed on with greater confidence and less reason.[45]

On January 25, 1812, at the specific request of South Carolina's leading War Hawk, John Calhoun, Quincy delivered an address in support of the navy bill then before Congress. The speech, a dispassionate defense of maritime commerce and the need to protect it, elicited considerable national comment, mostly favorable. "Quincy is acknowledged by all parties to have made a most able and excellent speech and has given no offense," Abijah Bigelow reported. John Adams called it, with "neither hyperbole nor flattery . . . the most important speech ever uttered in that House since 1789." Yet the fact that it was enthusiastically received by the Republican press, and applauded by the War Hawks, served only to confirm Boston's "nervous gentlemen" in their opposition to Quincy's contrived militancy and to erode further what little support it had previously claimed in Congress. When the House voted during the last week of February and the first of March on new taxes to finance the military build-up, only three Federalists joined him in voting with the Republicans.[46]

Quincy appears to have extended his efforts beyond his constituents and Federalist colleagues in the House. Although no names are mentioned in the relevant documents, circumstantial evidence suggests that he with other Federalists tried to persuade the British to resist American diplomatic pressure for repeal of the Orders in Council and so to eliminate that possible escape for Madison. The intermediary in this undertaking was Quincy's personal friend and political confidant, the British envoy, Augustus John Foster. "The opposition know the embarrassment of the President," Foster reported to the Foreign Office on January 16, 1812, "and endeavors to take advantage of it by pushing for measures so decisive as to leave him no retreat." But opposition strategy did not stop there. "Some individuals," he went on incredulously, "have even gone so far as to reproach us for not concocting measures with them for that purpose."[47]

But Foster remained unconvinced. While several times alluding to the plan his friend espoused, the envoy carefully dissociated himself from it, pointing out that it was a position on which "the Federalists are by no means united." Thus Parliament's tardiness in repealing the Orders in Council is hardly to be attributed to Quincy's efforts. The lengths—one could say seditious lengths—to which he went are an indication not only of his desperation to prove his strategy correct, but of the degree to which he had become its captive.[48]

"However respectable Federalists may be as upright and downright politicians," Samuel Taggart wrote apropos of Quincy's maneuverings, "whenever they have attempted anything like intrigue they have proved themselves to be mere bunglers at the business. Intrigues are now in hands who understand the business better." And so it seemed on March 9 when President Madison presented Congress with the letters of a British agent, Captain John Henry, who had circulated among New England Federalists in 1809 and reportedly found them ripe for secession. When first publicized, the Henry Letters caused no little embarrassment among the Federalists.[49]

Upon closer inspection, however, they proved surprisingly innocuous, indicating that whatever secessionist sentiment had existed in New England in 1809 was so half-hearted and unorganized as to be inconsequential. And when Quincy revealed that the Administration had paid a French poseur, the "Compte de Crillon," $50,000 for the letters sight unseen, the entire affair proved so embarrassing that the White House dropped it. Yet for all his detective work in unraveling the story of how the Administration acquired the Henry Letters, Quincy failed to grasp their significance: Madison had begun his pre-war countdown. Publication of the letters was intended to increase American resentment toward the British and to prepare the country psychologically to accept a declaration of war, while discrediting beforehand those most likely to oppose such a declaration.[50]

"My fate is odd," Quincy wrote to his wife during a moment of introspection late in March:

By some I am thought such a raving Federalist as to be shrewdly suspected of being one of Henry's confidants; by others that I am so strongly hostile to the British that I am in danger of turning Democrat. The truth is, that there is an intermediate ground for an American politician to stand upon. That I seek, and when I think I have found it I shall not hesitate to defend it, let who will shake or wonder, condemn or applaud.

The truth was, however, that such intermediate ground no longer existed. His diplomatic options exhausted and his party growing daily more rebellious, Madison had already screwed up his nerve and decided on war. Ironically, Quincy's plan, by its refusal to articulate a dissent from the War Hawks' cry, had made the decision easier.[51]

On April 1, 1812, the Administration announced a sixty-day Embargo. Still Quincy held firm, refusing to see it as anything but a "refuge from war." "Can any man believe," he asked Oliver Wolcott, "that such an Embargo, accompanied by such a state of things is preparatory to war?" Apparently many did. "Mr. Davis and Mr. Perkins were here last evening," Mrs. Quincy informed her husband on April 27. "Both were very dull at the prospect of war; and said, if you saw any light or hope, you were the only man in the country who did so."[52]

Quincy had broken with the War Hawks in opposing the Embargo; he also voted against them on April 25 in support of an unsuccessful motion for adjournment. Both came too late. "I observe," Samuel Taggart informed Timothy Pickering on April 3, "that the aspect of affairs more strongly indicates war approaching than at any other period during the session." Much of the responsibility for this he placed with Quincy and his "scarecrow plan of warfare":

It has entirely failed in its effect and has on the contrary produced in ruin, so that now our government has no choice left but either to secede from the ground they have taken or proceed to the last resort. I have all along been fearful that a series of blunders and mismanagements, to give them no harsher epithet, would lead to that result. My fears are I believe like to be realized.[53]

The Declaration of War against Great Britain on June 18, 1812, ended Quincy's national political career. Returning to Boston, he informed party leaders that he would not stand for a fifth term. Although he attended the second session of the Twelfth Congress that winter, he arrived late and left early. A speech opposing the enlistment of minors, another against the invasion of Canada, a personal attack on Gallatin's patriotism, several bitter exchanges with Speaker Clay: and that was that.[54]

Quincy had been badly miscast as a national legislator, particularly as a member of a hopeless minority in a period of sharp ideological conflict. His self-righteousness rendered him ineffective as a politician and his intense sectional loyalties restricted his capacity for statesmanship. Denied an opportunity to put his talents to use in shaping national policy, he frittered away his eight years in Congress chasing bogeymen of his own creation. In this his fate was not unlike that of his friend Randolph who characterized his own tenure in Washington as "time misspent and faculties misemployed." Fortunately for Quincy his opportunities for public service did not end with his departure from the nation's capital, though for a while it was to look that way.[55]

5 / Between Jobs

Time, now a days, spins along without noise or apparent motion. . . . Nothing to find fault with, and yet nothing to make happy. If we yankees were Englishmen, I take it for granted, we should hang, drown, or shoot ourselves out of life through mere wearisomeness.
— Josiah Quincy, 1820

Now that their father was at home more, the seven Quincy children made the necessary adjustments. "This winter," sixteen-year old Eliza Susan recorded in 1814, "we gave up the front drawing room during the day as much as possible" to him. There the forty-two year old ex-congressman could be found mornings, squirming at his desk. About midday he left his Oliver Street town house and trudged down Water and School Streets to Tremont and the Athenaeum where "he passed much of his time." Although his daughter never put it so baldly, Father was out of work.[1]

On the Homefront

As long as the war with England lasted, Quincy managed to appear busy. Elected to the Massachusetts Senate as part of the Federalist sweep in April, he found throughout 1813 a most receptive audience for his anti-war sentiments and obstructionist proposals. The opening of the General Court on May 28, with a fulsome speech by Governor Caleb Strong *On the Present Unhappy War* in which he announced that the Massachusetts militia would not serve outside New England, was followed a week later by Quincy's sponsoring a joint resolution opposing the further extension of the United States and demanding revocation of Louisiana's statehood. Unless the South agreed "to give up the trophies of her intrigue," he warned, "a dissolution of the Union will ensue." On June 19 the General Court forwarded a *Remonstrance* to Congress in which the war was called "impolitic, improper, and unjust," sentiments coinciding so completely with Quincy's that Timothy Pickering ascribed the phrasing to him.[2]

Quincy's most memorable action, however, occurred later in the session. The capture of the British sloop *Peacock* by the *Hornet* in

February, one of the few bright moments in an otherwise gloomy
year of war, had prompted the Massachusetts House to pass a resolution commending the *Hornet*'s Captain James Lawrence and his
crew. When it reached the Senate, Quincy introduced an alternate
resolution:

Resolved, That in a war like the present, waged without justifiable cause, and
prosecuted in a manner indicating that conquest and ambition are its real motives,
it is not becoming a moral and religious people to express any approbation of
military and naval exploits not immediately connected with the defence of our
sea-coast and soil.

Only days after the substitute resolution was adopted, news reached
Boston of Lawrence's heroic death and the taking of the *Hornet* by
the British ship *Shannon*. The phrase "a moral and religious people,"
like "can't be kicked into war" and "the bonds of this union are virtually dissolved," promptly became, as Otis charitably called them,
"catchwords to injure his popularity" which were hurled at Quincy
for the rest of his life. Though words may not be mightier than
swords, he had an uncanny propensity for impaling himself on
them.[3]

Aside from his legislative duties, Quincy involved himself in the
activities of the Washington Benevolent Society and the Boston
Hussars. The Benevolent Society, ostensibly devoted to charity and
honoring the memory of Washington, was a Federalist front organization designed to enlist the political sympathies of mechanics, artisans, and common laborers. Of the more than two hundred branches
established between 1810 and 1814, Boston's was the largest (over
1600 members) and most active. All of them, copying the Republican Tammany Societies with their sachems and wigwams, went in for
mummery and elaborate rituals, but the truly spectacular events
staged by the Boston Society seem to have been largely the product
of the élan, and the frustrations, of its president-impresario.[4]

On both April 30 (Washington's first inaugural date) and July 4
Boston streets were given over to the Benevolent Society for its
parades. Schoolchildren wearing copies of the Farewell Address
around their necks, assorted militia units in parade dress, members of
the clergy, representatives of the artisan trades dragging miniature
printing presses and anvils behind them, state legislators and town
officials all joined in the line of march. At its head, carrying the silver
gorget worn by Washington during the French and Indian War, rode
Quincy. At dawn he had supervised the artillery salute opening the

activities; later he would direct the State House illuminations mark-
ing their close.[5]

The Boston Hussars were the most sartorially elegant of the many
militia groups formed in New England during the War of 1812. Some
Republicans feared it had been organized for use against any troops
sent into Massachusetts by Madison. Its ranks did in fact consist
exclusively of wealthy Federalists, who wore expensive uniforms
modeled after those of the French Imperial Guard. Astride his white
stallion Bayard, Quincy, who had become company commander only
a year after joining in 1812, made a most impressive ceremonial
soldier. Although drill field exercises, formal parades, and an occasional bivouac on Boston Common constituted the sum total of the
Hussars' engagements, such activities permitted Quincy in some
measure to assert his masculinity and patriotism when his dissent
from the war brought these things in doubt.[6]

While Quincy enjoyed the support of the Federalist-dominated
state government, not everyone in Massachusetts approved of his
obstructionist policies. The *Independent Chronicle*, Boston's leading
Republican newspaper, supported the war while condemning as
seditious the activities of the Benevolent Society and the Hussars.
Quincy's reference, in a speech before the Society on April 30, 1813,
to the "conditional allegiance" owed by Massachusetts to "a certain,
extrinsic association, called the United States," was snapped up by
Republicans as proof of the Federalists' disloyalty. Both John Adams
and John Quincy Adams decried "the contumacious spirit" which he
personified, while the Reverend William Bentley, a Salem Republican
and staunch supporter of the war, reflected the opinion of many in
Massachusetts when he wrote that "Quincy's ghost, if not his son,
still calls us to duty."[7]

By the middle of 1814 a growing number of Federalists were finding Quincy's adamancy something of an embarrassment. In part this
reflected the altered complexion of the war; what most New
Englanders believed had begun as an obscene land grab and an excuse
for a marauding expedition into Canada had recently turned grimly
defensive. British troops occupied parts of Maine in July; a month
earlier Washington had been put to the torch. These events, combined with the continual taunts of disloyalty from the Republicans
may have roused the Federalists' slumbering patriotism, but other,
pecuniary, forces were also at work.[8]

The war hurt his own income, Quincy complained to John

Randolph; yet it proved a boon for the rest of the Commonwealth. Spared the British blockade that disrupted maritime commerce in states to the south, New England ports hummed with activity and Boston harbor was busier than it had ever been before. Not only shipowners and merchants but bankers and insurance underwriters experienced new levels of prosperity and even farmers enjoyed a steadily rising demand for their goods. Yet the most dramatic impact of the war on the Massachusetts economy was the added impetus it gave to the shift of capital and entrepreneurial energies from commerce to manufacturing. When, during the summer of 1814, the British navy finally included New England in its blockade, the shift became still more pronounced. "British tyranny drove us into manufacturing," a Massachusetts Republican announced, "factories, wool, etc., are here in irresistible progress."[9]

The political implications of this reorientation of the state's economy were not difficult to discern. Where maritime commerce depended on free trade and on maintaining links with foreign markets, the manufacturing interests were committed to expanding the domestic market and promoting protectionism. Accordingly, talk of secession, of states' rights, of limiting the growth of the United States and discouraging immigration was viewed as economically counterproductive. With nearly twenty million dollars already invested in New England textile mills at the beginning of 1814, much of it coming from Federalist pockets, continued opposition to the national government began to sound not only unpatriotic but imprudent.[10]

While many Federalists quickly adjusted to the changing economic situation in Massachusetts, Quincy did not and thus missed the crucial turn that led his more economically attuned brethren to adopt a nationalistic and conciliatory posture. "The spirit of our fathers will disown those as their children," he warned in 1813, "who stand by in apathy while the deep and ancient foundations of the prosperity of their state is upturning." "Upturning" it was, but apathetic its children were not. When the Boston Manufacturing Company received its charter that year, among the principal subscribers to the first stock issue were members of the Jackson, Lowell, Appleton, Gore, Cutting, and Lloyd families—Federalists all. And when surplus capital built up in Boston banks in 1814, Thomas Handasyd Perkins and Harrison Gray Otis both reconsidered their earlier opposition to buying government war bonds. Like his uncle William Phillips,

Quincy preferred to "sink every dollar he had to the bottom of the sea."[11]

Many of the arguments for reconciling New England with the national government, which Otis had been quietly circulating during the summer of 1814, were elaborated upon in a popular pamphlet published in Philadelphia that fall, Mathew Carey's *The Olive Branch, Or Faults on Both Sides.* In an otherwise mollifying essay, subtitled "On the Necessity of Mutual Forgiveness and Harmony," Carey repeatedly singled Quincy out for criticism, for his actions both in Congress where he had supported the war "in almost every stage but the last," and in the Massachusetts Senate where his opposition to it had been "conspicuous." By placing upon a single individual the blame for fomenting what remained an unpopular war and for obstructing its prosecution, Carey neatly absolved virtually everybody else, Republicans and Federalists alike, from responsibility for either.[12]

Quincy made an ideal scapegoat on yet another count. For Carey, soon to become the leading apologist for American industrialization, he was not only a nationally known practitioner of the older, more ideologically disputatious style of politics, but the onetime leading congressional spokesman for the older, commercially oriented economics, and could now be discredited with impunity. Unsympathetic to Carey's argument for reconciliation as also to the economics upon which it was based, Quincy remained fixed in his essentially pre-industrial loyalties. Long after New England's representatives in Washington adopted protectionism to aid industry, he continued to espouse the Federalists' free trade position. For economic as well as personal reasons, he refused to endorse Henry Clay's American System. In short, there was little of the Whig about Josiah Quincy.[13]

By 1814 his opposition to factories and his fears about their social implications were well established, having been voiced at least thirteen years earlier. Traveling through Rhode Island in 1801, he and his wife had visited Samuel Slater's textile mill in Pawtucket, the first to be built in the United States. After noting the ravaging of the Blackstone Valley countryside and the proprietor's hesitancy about revealing the mill's operations, Quincy recorded the following scene:

All the processes of turning cotton from its rough into every variety of marketable threat state . . . are here performed by machinery operating by Waterwheels, assisted only by children from four to ten years old, and one superin-

tendent. Above an hundred of the former are employed, at the rate of from 12
to 25 cents for a day's labor.

Then, in moral terms anticipating Dickens, he discussed the plight of
these children:

Our attendant was very eloquent on the usefulness of this manufacture, and the
employment it supplied for so many poor children. But an eloquence was ex-
erted on the other side of the question more commanding than his, which called
us to pity these little creatures, plying in a contracted room, among flyers and
coggs, at an age when nature requires for them air, space and sports. There was a
dull dejection in the countenances of all of them. This, united with the deafen-
ing roar of the falls and the rattling of the machinery, put us into a disposition
easily to satisfy our curiosity.

Quincy died in 1864 a rich man, leaving an estate of three quarters of
a million dollars, but none of this wealth came from investments in
manufacturing.[14]

His opposition to industrialization, as to expansion, transcended
economic considerations, focusing instead on its social and ideological implications. He saw powerful, centrifugal, dislocating forces with
consequences equally unpredictable for both. Just as he feared the
disruptions of community life attendant on the westward migrations,
he thought the draining of the countryside and the stimuli to immigration provided by labor-hungry mill owners threatening to New
England's social fabric. The political impact of an emergent property-
less proletariat he viewed as no less portentous. Though unable to
slow these transforming processes, Quincy refused to adopt the ploy
of assessing whatever is inevitable to be beneficial.[15]

Massachusetts chose its delegates to the Hartford Convention with
considerable care. Quincy was not among them. Political probity and
economic good sense, not contentious ardor, had been the criteria
for selection, thus disqualifying him and John Lowell. Those who
were chosen were men like Harrison Gray Otis, aptly described by his
biographer-descendant Samuel Eliot Morison as "not of the stuff
from which revolutionaries are made," and certain to keep the new
economic interests of Boston well in mind. By the fall of 1814 Massachusetts "men of substance and worth" were in a most conciliatory
mood and, as George Cabot acknowledged, they intended that the
Convention should "allay the ferment" generated by Quincy and
Lowell, who had talked of secession as if it were a viable option.
James H. Banner Jr., essentially concurring in Morison's earlier view,

has described the Hartford Convention as not a cabal of disunionists but a collection of cautious party captains anxious to bring New England back into closer accord with the rest of the nation. Quincy could not have agreed more; for him it was "a tub to a whale" out of which nothing came but "A GREAT PAMPHLET."[16]

News of the war's end reached Boston on February 17, 1815, and found Quincy at his desk in the drawing room of his new house on Summer Street. "The whole town was in an uproar, cannons firing, drums beating, bells ringing," Eliza Susan recorded in her diary. "It was a scene and a day never to be forgotten by anyone who enjoyed it." The following week, on Washington's Birthday, Boston formally marked the occasion with a parade. "The whole celebration passed off without accident and was highly successful, and we were gratified it was so," Eliza Susan bubbled, "especially as my father had the chief direction."[17]

Peace meant, for a while at least, the end of Quincy's parades. The Boston Hussars immediately disbanded, obliging the company commander to put his uniform in storage and Bayard out to pasture. The Washington Benevolent Society lingered on a few years but as early as 1817 began omitting its annual celebrations; Washington's gorget was thereafter locked away "for safekeeping." With most Bostonians back at their professional offices, countinghouses, and new factories, Quincy found himself embarrasingly underemployed.[18]

Busy with Nothing to Do

As an old man looking back on the years immediately after the War of 1812, Quincy attributed his minor role in Massachusetts politics during its "Indian Summer of Federalism" to lack of interest. "I had formed myself for a public man on a large and national scale," he wrote in 1859. "For the sphere of State politics I had neither taste nor adaptation of mind." Without doubting his memory, it should be noted that his withdrawal from Federalist politics during the years following the Peace of Ghent was neither altogether voluntary nor wholly amicable.[19]

Quincy's failure to become part of the inner circle of Boston politicians that determined Federalist party policy in Massachusetts can be partially explained by the fact that he had spent most of his time between 1805 and 1813 in Washington. But his continued proscription from the Central Committee after his resignation from Congress was prompted by other factors. Many Boston Federalists refused to forgive his behavior in the first session of the Twelfth Congress. Christopher Gore, ex-governor and soon-to-be United States Senator, characterized Quincy in the fall of 1812 as one of "the middle aged and ardent politicians . . . who have become tired of waiting for Place and Distinction," while even those who believed his actions had been honorable faulted him for his obstinacy. The reputation he brought back to Boston in the spring of 1813 was that of an outspoken politician whose judgment was dubious and whose penchant in the past for going his own way made it unlikely that he would submit to party discipline in the future.[20]

Though he produced a campaign tract for the 1815 state elections in which he commended Federalists for their "virtuous efforts and patriotic energies" during the war, and retained his own seat in the Senate for another five years, his heart was not in it. The party, now under the leadership of Otis, one of the architects of "the Era of Good Feelings," was able to hold power in Massachusetts only by supporting President Monroe nationally and working with prominent Republicans at home. In such a delicate situation, Quincy's idiosyncrasies were not readily tolerated. Some Federalists thought him motivated by nothing more than contrariness and he did little to confute them.[21]

Quincy's most serious breach of party discipline occurred during the 1816 legislative session. Otis and other leading Federalists in the Senate, well aware that the District of Maine sent a preponderance of Republicans to the General Court and anxious to protect the slim Federalist majority in both houses, agreed to support a Republican proposal calling for Maine's separate statehood. They thought by doing so to insure that Massachusetts would remain "a snug little Federalist state" indefinitely. On June 15 the bill authorizing the separation came to a vote in the Massachusetts Senate; it carried thirty-five to one, Quincy casting the lone dissenting vote.[22]

After Maine voters in the fall of 1816 failed to give the necessary two-thirds approval for separation, the question was again brought before the Massachusetts Senate in 1819. Again Quincy sided with those Maine Federalists who believed, with good reason, that they were being deserted. "I am not ambitious of that sort of distinction which arises from mere singularity," he explained while preparing to cast his "solitary negative" against separation. "I have accordingly, and sedulously too, endeavored to raise a doubt upon this question; but I cannot. . . . he who cannot doubt, cannot compromise." By the standards of his contemporaries Quincy suffered from what William Tudor called the "confusion of totally different eras and events in his mind." "He is a worthy man and might be a useful one," Tudor conceded, "if there was any syphon to draw him off but before he pours out his wine he always shakes the bottle, so that the liquor is commonly turbid."[23]

It became obvious soon after his return from Congress that state politics alone would not keep him occupied. Yet he had no profession to return to. Though he later bemoaned the fact, he never seriously considered taking up the law again. The Boston bar was no longer what it had been when he had set up his office in the 1790's. Once a respectable refuge for cultured gentlemen, it now attracted young and hungry men from the provinces, men like Daniel Webster and Rufus Choate, who transformed the profession into a fiercely competitive business. Quincy was too old and too well fed to want any part of that.[24]

Nor did he give much thought to going into business. His real estate holdings, though considerable, and his investments in the Middlesex Canal, Neponset Turnpike, and Massachusetts Hospital Trust Company required little personal attention. Anti-speculative by nature and consistently opposed to industrialization, he restricted his business dealings to attending an occasional investors' meeting, collecting his rents, and verifying dividends, hardly enough to qualify as "specific employment."[25]

While visiting Boston in 1831, Alexis de Tocqueville discovered to his surprise that "there are already a certain number of people who, having nothing to do, seek out the pleasures of the mind." Actually the young Frenchman exaggerated the novelty of his finding; gainfully unemployed, culturally preoccupied gentlemen were to be found in Boston fifteen years earlier. One, Richard Dana Sr., rather prided himself on being "an Idle Man," while others, like Daniel Appleton White, Samuel Pickering Gardner, the two Gray brothers, Francis Calley and John Chipman, and James Bowdoin Jr., all survived without an office to go to each morning.[26]

Nonetheless, as Tocqueville recognized, "the prejudice against people who do nothing is strong," and it was a prejudice Quincy shared. Although John Lothrop Motley, the historian-diplomat, later memorialized him as "the type and the head of the Brahmins in America," he ought not be considered more than a provisional and skittish member of that fraternity. Proud of his historical, classical, and scientific interests, as well as his efforts on behalf of local institutions fostering cultural activities, he always regarded this facet of his life as secondary to his official duties. It was said of Francis Calley Gray, a far more representative Brahmin in the sense that Oliver Wendell Holmes had in mind, that "he never tired of repeating that intellectual and moral culture was the object worthiest of highest ambition." Though Quincy respected such an opinion coming from a man like Gray, he never subscribed to it, for unlike the Brahmins he rejected the idea that Private Culture might serve as an alternative to Public Labors.[27]

His personal antidote for "that fastidiousness of fancy, which is called refinement," was mucking about on his Braintree farm. Agriculture had always been at least a subsidiary concern of his family and experimental farming was one of his earliest scientific undertakings. During his years in Congress he maintained friendly relations with both John Adams and Timothy Pickering—no mean feat—by virtue of their common interest in such matters as the uses of manure. By 1818 farming had acquired for him an additional function: it offered, he wrote, "the political gladiator . . . other labors than those of spurning the sand of the Arena."[28]

Unlike John Lowell's Bromley Vale in Roxbury, with its stone castle and five greenhouses filled with orchids, Quincy's farm was expected to yield a profit. When he took over its management in 1814, he immediately set about introducing methods of farming that he hoped would increase its productivity while providing a model for others. When championing the hawthorn hedge and merino sheep, it was not his intention to transform the Massachusetts countryside into a replica of rural England but to reduce fence-maintenance costs and find a profitable use for non-arable land. His frequent articles in the *Massachusetts Agricultural Repository and Journal*, praising the humble carrot and lowly rutabaga, were similarly meant to encourage his fellow farmers to adopt the intensive methods of agriculture used in Europe.[29]

Yet like Lowell and the other gentlemen of the Massachusetts

Agricultural Society, Quincy was interested in more than just making New England farmers efficient. The great desideratum was to keep them farmers. "The natural effect of peace and of the resulting competition of the commerical nations," he wrote in the *North American Review* in 1818, "must necessarily be to limit the sphere of commercial industry." Capital that was leaving commerce, he argued, might well "seek employment upon the land." With the crumbling of one of the two economic bases of eighteenth-century New England society—maritime commerce—he and the Agricultural Society tried buttressing the other. By so doing, they hoped to stem the flow of capital and human energies from the countryside to the factory towns like Lowell, Waltham, and Lawrence already encircling Boston.[30]

"Whatever carries happiness to the home, and content to the bosoms of our yeomanry," Quincy told those gathered at the 1819 Brighton Cattle Show, "tends, more than anything else, to lay the foundations of our republic deep and strong, and to give the assurance of immortality to our liberties." Upbraiding the farmer who "repined at his lot" and looked wistfully to the city, he advised him to "consider his, as among the highest and happiest of human destinies, since in relation to the earth, he is the instrument of Heaven's bounty; and in relation to the inferior orders of Creation, the almoner of Providence." The Jeffersonian resonances were not coincidental; Quincy credited John Taylor of Caroline's *The Arator*, to which he had been introduced by John Randolph, for "the general turn of thought" informing his remarks. Thus, his advocacy of scientific farming constituted still another ideological rear-guard action to slow the movement away from that earlier, essentially agrarian America, with which both he and his old political antagonists identified.[31]

Unfortunately Quincy's hopes of becoming the evangel of "a new era of Agriculture" in New England were soon shattered. Eliza Susan's opening entry in her 1820 journal revealed this bucolic dream's denouement: "My father on settling his accounts the first of January found that his expenses were exceeding his income." The economic slump in 1819 had undoubtedly cut into his investment income, but Eliza Susan reported, "his farming experiments were the cause of this difficulty." "And this," she added superfluously, "made him very unhappy." How could he ever hope to instruct "these ten, fifteen or twenty acre men who will become the most important element in preserving and perpetuating conservative principles," when he could not make his own one hundred and seventy acres pay? Even nature seemed to be conspiring against him.[32]

His financial situation that winter was no small concern and caused him, his daughter recalled, "anxiety with regard to future independence." After a general accounting, a policy of rigid retrenchment was put into effect. At one point it was decided that the lease on the Summer Street house would not be renewed in April, and the family would remove itself permanently to Braintree. No one relished this prospect; it "would take my father out of the sphere of public affairs and the rest of us," Eliza Susan remembered, "from Boston society which we enjoyed very highly. However, we decided upon it."[33]

Thanks to William Phillips, Quincy's uncle and the principal heir of his maternal grandfather, the brush with "going into the middle class" proved brief. Upon hearing of his nephew's decision to give up the Summer Street house, Phillips offered No. 1 Hamilton Place for the permanent use of the Quincy family. So rather than being banished to Braintree, in April they moved one block closer to Boston Common.[34]

Still, he confessed that summer to his old congressional colleague, Harmanus Bleecker, "the globe seems to run upon a very level surface. . . . we go on trading at a loss, busy with nothing to do, sharpening our wits, with no prospect of anything to cut with; and some chance, in case nothing else occur, of cutting one another." His temper had in fact grown shorter. During the previous year he became involved in a dispute between Eliza Susan and Eliza Lee Cabot; before extricating himself he was no longer on speaking terms with the Cabot family. In January, as President of the Boston Athenaeum, he flew into a rage upon discovering that, in violation of the rules, five of the twenty thousand volumes in the collection had been removed by members from the reading room. Labeling it "petty plunder," he vowed "sooner or later to detect the guilty and bring them to well deserved disgrace and punishment." "We yankees are never at ease," he confided to Bleecker, and "are ready to split with vexation when the turning of things oblige us to sit still a while."[35]

Among the Whores and Rogues

John Adams chose a singularly inappropriate moment, the summer of 1820, to announce that "in all my life, I have never known such a fortunate man as Mr. Quincy . . . in his ancestors, his rank in society, independence in regard to property, his pursuits, his wife, his children, his excellent health, and firm constitution—in short, fortunate in everything." "If Mr. Quincy is only sensible of his own happiness," the old President added as a caveat, "he is the happiest man in the world." But rather than wallowing in his good fortune, Quincy had been growing increasingly despondent. The tonic used during his Washington years—"work, work, work!"—had lost its potency. A feeling of listlessness, first acknowledged in the spring of 1819, had become a constant companion. Though he "would not willingly be thought worse than any neighbors in this respect," he confessed to exerting himself less and sleeping more.[36]

No sooner had he escaped a financial reversal than he was confronted with a political crisis. On March 28, 1820, the Federalist Central Committee submitted its slate of senatorial candidates for the April elections; Quincy's name was conspicuously absent. The fact that since 1815 he had trailed the other five Boston senators and the fear that his continued presence on the Federalist ticket would weaken all their chances for reelection were the ostensible reasons for the committee's action. Most political observers agreed, however, that it was his stand on the Maine statehood issue the year before which led to his being dumped.[37]

After much coaxing from his family, Quincy decided to make the best of the humiliating situation by attending the Federalist public caucus on April 2 in support of the ticket. This expression of loyalty earned him the warm applause of the gathering, but nothing more. Not until six weeks later, after John Lowell's public blast against the Central Committee's "fickle and ungrateful" action and John Phillips' insistence that his cousin be provided for, did Federalist party leaders agree that he might run for one of Boston's fifteen seats in the lower house of the General Court. On May 12, 1820, trailing the entire Federalist ticket, Quincy narrowly won a seat in the House.[38]

His uncle William Phillips appears to have been even more visibly distressed by the Central Committee's actions than he. Had such an insult been directed at him, Phillips told his nephew, "I would go out of Boston and shake its dust from my feet." Though badly hurt by the personal rebuff, Quincy declined the advice. At forty-eight, there was no place to go.[39]

Disappointment with his agricultural experiments, combined with the prospect of permanent removal to Braintree, had only confirmed Quincy's essential Boston identity. Although he retained management of the farm for another year and remained a member of the Agricultural Society, his interests during the course of 1820 took a decided urban turn. "The pride of the farmer should be out in his fields," he had advised his Brighton audience a year earlier; "in their beauty, in their product, he should place the gratification of his humble and honorable ambitions." These sentiments notwithstanding, it became clear to him that his own ambitions could be gratified only in town.[40]

On May 21, 1820, Quincy entered the State House, no longer as one of Boston's six senators in an upper house of thirty-six members, but as one of Boston's fifteen representatives in a lower house of nearly two hundred. These reduced circumstances, to say nothing of the maneuverings required of his friends to provide him with any public status at all, had a chastening effect upon him. Complete political oblivion loomed as a distinct possibility. With no substantial popular backing and no party influence, and without standing in the House, he entered into its business with a positive enthusiasm which suggests he realized this might be his last chance.[41]

The 1820 spring session of the General Court was the first in Massachusetts legislative history to begin grappling with the social implications of industrialization and urbanization. Governor John Brooks opened the session with a speech emphasizing the growing problems of crime and pauperism, the expenses involved in maintaining such crowded state institutions as the Charlestown Prison and the General Hospital, and the rising cost of public relief. These were all matters in which Boston's new representative, as a critic of industrialization and a worried observer of the exodus from the countryside to the city, had more than a passing interest.[42]

Quincy's views in these essentially non-partisan areas immediately impressed his colleagues, Federalists and Republicans alike. When he presented a bill for creating a legislative committee to canvass the towns of the Commonwealth to determine how they dealt with the problem of poor relief, it was promptly approved and he was made chairman. This decision to commit himself to the study of new social problems attending industrialization and urbanization gave him a new lease on public life. At the same time it opened up to him the possibility of acquiring responsibilities far more suited to his peculiar talents and reviving energies than any he had previously undertaken. If Quincy's subsequent public life can be said to have turned on any one decision, this was it.[43]

The separation of Maine in 1820 made necessary the updating of the Massachusetts Constitution, and on August 15 the voters of the Commonwealth authorized the holding of a constitutional convention in November. Despite his opposition to the idea of a convention when it was first broached in the House, Quincy wanted very much to be one of Boston's forty-five delegates. When the election was held in Boston on October 18, he just made it, placing forty-fourth among those chosen. Narrow as his election was, and however indicative of his almost exhausted popular backing, it represented another crucial step in his return to public favor.[44]

The Massachusetts Constitutional Convention, which ran from November 15, 1820, to January 9, 1821, proved to be a very amiable affair. Moderate Republicans like Levi Lincoln, Joseph Story, and James Trecothick Austin joined Federalists Leverett Saltonstall and Lemuel Shaw to assure that little violence was done to the 1780 Constitution. Quincy served as chairman of a committee examining Article V of the old constitution, which dealt with the relationship of Harvard College and the state. Cambridge had nothing to fear from him. After a brief committee meeting, its chairman announced that "the unexampled prosperity of Harvard College furnished the most satisfactory proof that no provision in relation to that institution was necessary."[45]

Throughout the rest of the convention he opposed virtually all changes recommended, including one which would have eliminated ownership of property as a qualification for voting. His argument against unrestricted male suffrage, which reflected both his persistent Federalist sentiments and his continued fears about industrialization, took on a proto-Marxist cast. Conceding that in the past the property requirement had made little difference, since the preponderance of citizens engaged in farming and owned the land they worked, he thought it would be essential in the future. "There is nothing in the condition of our country," he warned, "to prevent manufacturers [workers] from being absolutely dependent upon their employers, here as they are everywhere else." When such a situation develops,

the whole body of every manufacturing establishment therefore, are dead votes counted by the head, by their employer . . . and in time there probably will be, one, two, or three manufacturing establishments, each sending, as the case may be, from one to eight hundred votes to the polls depending on the will of one employer, one great capitalist. . . .

While such gloomy views were not shared by the incipient Whigs and their young spokesman Daniel Webster, who dominated the convention, neither did they seem to offend anyone. On the contrary, many of the more moderate Republican delegates who were also members of the House were impressed with their colleague's dispassionate, albeit conservative, argument.[46]

During the Christmas recess, Quincy further helped his own cause by delivering a speech before the Massachusetts Peace Society. "He spoke admirably well with great eloquence and effect," Eliza Susan reported, "to the surprise of everyone as people thought he could not find anything to say on the topic." The guarded optimism of the speech about the prospects for international peace as well as for social and political harmony in the United States elicited widespread comment. The *Columbian Centinel* flattered Quincy by stating that "his most happy and elaborate address in style and description was scarcely inferior to Burke," while his old friend Oliver Wolcott was so startled by its hopeful tone that he wrote from Connecticut to ask whether he really meant all he had said.[47]

On January 10, 1821, the day after the Massachusetts Constitutional Convention concluded its modest business, the General Court reconvened with the election of a new Speaker as the first order of business in the House. After two inconclusive ballots, a sufficient number of Republicans and Federalists combined to elect Quincy! While it is not clear precisely how this happened, an entry in Eliza Susan's diary two weeks later is suggestive:

I never expected to see Mr. Levi Lincoln and Mr. J. T. Austin dining here, but violence of party spirit has died away. . . . Conversation chiefly political. Mr. Quincy said he did not think it proper to call gentlemen, members of the House, by their military titles, Gen., Col., etc. Mr. Lincoln laughed and said, 'Well Mr. Quincy, I did not expect to find that I was *more aristocratic* than you,' on which Mr. Quincy replied, 'I always told you Mr. Lincoln that I was most of a *Republican*,' at which the company laughed loudly.

Further on, Eliza Susan transcribed some additional remarks and concluded with her own assessment of her father's altered circumstances:

Mr. Lincoln said that nothing had given him greater pleasure than to see gentlemen of different opinions voting together without reference to party, that no one was more happy to see Mr. Quincy in the Speaker's Chair than himself. Mr. Quincy had never been so well understood as since the Convention. At the beginning of that assembly no one would have thought Mr. Quincy would be appointed Speaker.

However belatedly, and only on a local level with little cost to his ideological principles, Quincy had entered into his own "Era of Good Feelings."[48]

During the second week of the 1821 legislative session Quincy filed his *Report of the Committee for Consideration of Pauper Laws of the Commonwealth of Massachusetts.* It represented the first comprehensive survey of the various methods in which Massachusetts towns met, or evaded, their responsibilities for the poor. Besides informing the legislators of the dimensions of the problem, Quincy intended the *Report* to have a shock value as well. After referring to the "desperate and malignant" growth of pauperism in England, he argued statistically that the number of paupers in Massachusetts (7000 in 1820) was increasing at a still faster rate (60 percent in twenty years). Some towns, he reported, did nothing and intended to do nothing with the poor in their midst. "The more and better provisions is made for Paupers," the Selectmen of Richmond told the committee, "the more the numbers of Paupers will increase." But even in Boston it was found that the "able poor" were promiscuously mingled with the truly incapacitated in the town's single almshouse. "The pernicious consequences of this system are palpable," Quincy concluded, "that they are increasing, and that they imperiously call for interference of the legislature."[49]

Quincy's report immediately established its author as the state's leading authority on poor relief and related subjects. Accordingly, in May the Boston Selectmen asked him to head a town committee to study the feasibility of establishing a House of Industry in South Boston where able-bodied paupers would be put to work. During the following months he filed a series of reports recommending such a project and in 1822 was appointed by the town to oversee construction of the proposed building. These activities and the publication in the spring of 1822 of his *Remarks . . . affecting Poverty, Vice and Crime* testified that in two years he had become, if not the first, then one of the most knowledgeable experts on the social problems that were, even in America, the inevitable concomitants of the Industrial Revolution.[50]

When the spring session of the 1821 General Court convened on May 30, Quincy easily won reelection to the Speakership. He enjoyed his duties and was gratified by the distinction of his office, but he began to feel that his new interests directed him elsewhere. Meeting only two months a year and already starting to adopt what Oscar Handlin has called "the policy of state acquiescence," the General Court seemed increasingly remote from the essentially municipal problems now engaging Quincy's mind. Involvement with Boston's House of Industry project had introduced him to still another social problem, the local administration of criminal justice. Thus when the judgeship of the Municipal Court of Boston fell vacant during the winter of 1821-1822, he expressed interest in the position. On January 16, 1822, he announced his intention to resign from the House at the end of the session; two months later Speaker Quincy had become Judge Quincy.[51]

To be Judge of the Municipal Court, with jurisdiction over all non-capital crimes committed in Boston and Suffolk County, was considered neither a sinecure nor a particularly prestigious office. Quincy's acceptance of it therefore generated considerable comment among his former Federalist associates. "You may be surprised at the nomination of Mr. Quincy," William Sullivan remarked to Harrison Gray Otis. "He goes into the municipal courts with the most honorable intentions, and as I think, with the ability to be useful, and acceptable at least, as much as any man who would go there." "I feel assured he will render important public service," Sullivan added, "though it is impossible to honor his *taste*."[52]

Otis, then in Washington finishing a term in the Senate, concurred in this patronizing appraisal.

It is a sort of practical bathos, to jump from the Speaker's Chair into that of the Boston old Bailey. . . . As his zeal for his friends and party have hurt his popularity, he probably expects the reward of neglect, which his friends and party are least apt to show towards those who are too zealous in their favor—as he gets nothing by being a great man among gentlemen, he will try his hand by showing himself a good one among whores and rogues—Good luck to him say I. . . .[53]

A few weeks later Sullivan and Otis were obliged to reconsider their condescending estimate of Quincy's "zeal for his friends and party." For when still another public office came up that spring, the newly created Boston mayoralty, the fact that the Federalists immediately claimed it for Otis did not prevent Quincy from joining in the scramble. In such matters, after so many years between jobs, he was less disposed than ever to stick at questions of either "taste" or party proprieties.

6 / Back to Work

Sunday, . . . Wrote Report on Fire Department. . . . Plutarch devoted himself at once to the service of the Gods and the duties of Society. He did not think that the pursuit of Philosophy or Letters exempted a man from personal service in the community to which he belonged.

—Josiah Quincy, September 19, 1825

"I should like to answer your letter," Quincy wrote hastily to Harmanus Bleecker in the summer of 1823, "but I have nothing but drains, highways, streets, dirt and nuisances *et id genus omni* in my head." This was the same Bleecker to whom three years earlier he had complained bitterly of ennui. Obviously, during the interim, the world had come alive again, and he with it.[1]

A Very Hazardous Thing for a People to Do

Few ideas appealed less to colonial Bostonians than incorporation. By 1800, seven separate proposals to replace the town meeting with a mayor and city council had been rejected, and all for the reason offered by one conservative Bostonian in 1714:

A People can hardly be guilty of greater folly than to change a Government under which, not only they, but their Fathers also, for a long time have Lived, Flourished and Prospered; it having been ever looked on as a very hazardous, perilous and dangerous thing for a People to do.

On October 16, 1815, the Boston Town Meeting heard a report on the *Expediency of Making an Alteration in the Municipal Government*, the fourth such since 1784. Disclaiming any desire "to alter forms that are settled and familiar to our citizens . . . in conformity to some chosen or theoretic form of city government," the report recommended only modest changes in the prevailing arrangements. Nevertheless, four weeks later a majority of Bostonians voted against making any alterations in the way they governed themselves. "Where the spirit of liberty is on so high a key," Timothy Dwight had observed the year before while visiting Boston, "necessity only, and that little less than absolute, will persuade most men to admit cheerfully the unpleasant change from a smaller to a great number of restrictions."[2]

But more than loyalty continued to commend ancestral forms to Bostonians at a time when more than fifty other American municipalities had already opted for incorporation. During its long history, town government had proved both responsive to community needs and effective in meeting them. Although ultimate power resided in the meeting, the administrative details of governance were left to a board of selectmen. As Boston grew and its problems became more readily differentiated, special boards were established by the town meeting to deal with them. In 1679, following a fire that gutted much of the town, a board of firewards was created and charged with directing all fire-fighting operations. Thirteen years later a board of overseers of the poor was formed, ostensibly to manage the almshouse, but also to discourage vagrants from taking up residence in the town. A century later a school committee was created to administer the town's growing educational system; and nine years later, in the wake of a yellow fever epidemic, a board of health was established. The members of these boards were elected annually in a general meeting of all freeholding townsmen and, except for the senior selectman who was usually superintendent of police as well, served without salary. Yet, because these positions reflected standing in the community, they did not lack for volunteers.[3]

In theory, a more democratic, decentralized arrangement would be difficult to imagine. In practice, however, it was controlled by an oligarchy. In the 1770's, according to James A. Henretta, all the important offices of Boston "were lodged firmly in the hands of a broad elite, entry into which was conditioned by commercial achievement and family background." Educated, propertied, and politically conservative—which by the 1790's meant Federalist—this elite retained into the early 1800's that indispensable trait of a dominant group, which Robert Dahl has defined as "the sense, shared not only by themselves but by the populace, that their claim to govern was legitimate." So long as this sense prevailed, town government worked.[4]

But by 1820 it was no longer working well. Of several factors contributing to the declining effectiveness of town government, the overriding one was demographic. After having reached a population of 16,000 in the 1740's, Boston had remained at that level throughout the 1760's. During the Revolution the town experienced a net loss in population, in part due to the Loyalist exodus and in part due to the growth in New England of secondary ports. Then, in the late 1780's, Boston's population began to grow again. The 18,000 recorded in the 1790 census grew to more than 43,000 by 1820, an increase of nearly 150 percent in thirty years. (A city census in 1825 reported a population in excess of 58,000, indicating that the annual growth rate had accelerated to 7 percent.) Although the increase during this period was chiefly among the native-born—unlike the situation in the 1840's—it nevertheless rendered the town's almost familial governing arrangements suddenly obsolete.[5]

Coinciding with this rapid growth, and accelerating the resultant impersonalization of public life, was a redistribution of Boston's population. Beginning in the 1790's, hills were cut down and coves filled in—a process which at the same time that it provided more usable land, helped destroy the relatively stable residential patterns of the eighteenth-century town. The North End, for example, during the Revolutionary era a mixed neighborhood of the well-to-do and of artisans, by the early 1800's was well on the way to becoming a slum. Similarly, Fort Hill was subject to an exodus of wealthy residents, who either went to Beacon Hill or left town altogether. Profits from the War of 1812 and new revenues from manufacturing enterprises widened the economic gap between Boston's rich and poor and underwrote their residential segregation. The result was a discernible loosening of those civic ties that had earlier transcended class differences and bound one member of the community to another.[6]

Another factor contributing to the decline of Boston's cohesiveness was the blurring of town boundaries. As late as 1784, Boston could be approached by land only from the southwest. Physical isolation reinforced social solidarity. During the following thirty-seven years, however, Boston was connected by bridges to Cambridge, Charlestown, Dorchester, and Roxbury. "Our town resembled a hand," a speaker recalled at the opening of the Western Avenue Bridge in 1821, "but it was a closed one. It is now open and well spread." Whatever benefits Bostonians derived from their greater mobility were purchased at the cost of their earlier common identity.[7]

By 1820, nearly eight thousand people were eligible to participate

in town meeting—a statistic which of itself made unattainable the
ideal of such meetings as deliberative assemblies. "The time is rapidly
approaching," one Bostonian complained hoarsely in 1821, "when
the dictates of reason can find no human voices strong enough to
carry them through the whole extent of the assembled citizens and
when deliberations will be wholly impossible." Others believed that
the point had already been reached. Some meetings were crowded
and unruly, but most were so poorly attended that often a majority
of those present were elected officials. The town budget, which by
1820 amounted to $150,000, was regularly approved at meetings
attracting fewer than fifty citizens.[8]

Another casualty of Boston's rapid growth was its deferential
pattern of politics. The presence of so many new voters either
unfamiliar with or hostile to the town's governing elite certainly
helped to undermine it, as did a growing fragmentation within the
elite itself. During the first two decades of the nineteenth century,
Boston's upper class was divided into Calvinists and Unitarians, into
those whose wealth derived from foreign commerce and those whose
interests had shifted to manufacturing, and into proto Whigs, those
Federalists who joined in "the Era of Good Feelings" after the War
of 1812, and the intransigents. No longer able to agree among
themselves, they all found it increasingly difficult, as one of them
delicately phrased it, "to manage that class which is acted upon."[9]

The rebuff Charles Bulfinch suffered at the polls in 1815, after
having served the town as chairman of the selectmen for sixteen
years, marked the point at which many prominent Bostonians ceased
regarding town offices as their prerogative or public service as a
responsibility incumbent upon them. Rather than vie with "the
wickedly aspiring," they voluntarily withdrew from public life and
permitted less disinterested and more politically aggressive Bostonians to gain office by default.[10]

Thus, as the town's problems grew more complex, those elected to
deal with them were increasingly less able to do so. Generally
inexperienced and often inept, the new officeholders seemed more
intent on shirking than on meeting their public responsibilities.
Jurisdictional disputes among the various boards became commonplace as each tried to shift the blame for the decline in the quality of
municipal services. The board of health, for example, which had
performed heroically earlier in the century, by 1816 was a way-sta-

tion for politicians hoping to become selectmen. Such men were more concerned with their own careers than with keeping the streets clear of animal waste or checking on clogged sewer vaults. Boston, as a result, literally stank.[11]

By 1820 even the most conservative Bostonians acknowledged the shortcomings of the governmental arrangements they had inherited and agreed with Lemuel Shaw that they should be replaced by a system "more suited to the needs of a numerous people." That same year the Massachusetts Constitutional Convention, in clarifying the provisions relating to incorporation, cleared the way for reform. On December 21, 1821, after rejecting an earlier proposal "for not going far enough," the Boston Town Meeting elected a committee to devise a new system of government.[12]

The committee's report, presented eight days later, called for sweeping changes, including replacing the "Town of Boston" with the "City of Boston." During the ensuing three-day session, the meeting discussed and accepted the committee's proposed charter, which contained provisions for a popularly elected mayor with broad if ill-defined powers, an eight-man board of aldermen elected at large, and a common council, composed of forty-eight members, four from each of the twelve wards. On January 7, 1822, Boston voters by a seven-to-five margin approved the charter and directed that it be sent to the General Court for its endorsement. An era, begun 192 years earlier, had ended.[13]

The Darling of the Boston Democracy

At first it seemed obvious who would be selected mayor. William Sullivan, a member of the Federalist Central Committee and a Boston representative, had already made his selection by January 6, 1822, the day before the town voted whether to submit a city charter to the General Court. "If we should arrive at the point of having the right to choose a mayor," he wrote to the party chief Harrison Gray Otis, then serving in the United States Senate, "you are that one of my fellow citizens, whom I expect to see engaged in the labor of putting the executive machinery in motion." Thomas Handasyd Perkins shared Sullivan's sentiments, assuring Otis that he also had the backing of "Webster, Lowell, Tudor, all the Judges and those whom I know you feel a high respect for."[14]

The fifty-six year old Otis had not enjoyed his four years in Washington. In addition to lacking the gastronomical amenities he was accustomed to, the capital had proved intractable on the matter that most occupied his time in the Senate, Massachusetts' war claims. Otis went to Washington in 1818 very likely expecting a substantial office in Monroe's administration, possibly even a Cabinet post. Unfortunately his own conciliatory spirit and willingness to forget party labels were not reciprocated by the White House. Earlier that spring he had decided to resign his seat in the Senate and return home where "I can help train the young leaders of my own breed." Thus the prospect of becoming Boston's first mayor was appealing; he might respectably serve in that position for a year while waiting for John Brooks to step down from the governorship, the office Otis really wanted.[15]

Once having "consented to the solicitation of my friends," Otis began writing to Federalists back in Boston as if not only the nomination but the office were already his. And with some reason. On March 19 the *Boston Evening Gazette* started the Otis bandwagon rolling; the following day the *Daily Advertiser* climbed aboard with its endorsement of his candidacy. The Federalists had known better days but few doubted their capacity to determine yet another Boston election.[16]

Federalists looked forward confidently to the mayoral election despite the fact that balloting would be conducted not at Faneuil Hall, as they wanted, but in the wards as the Republicans had insisted as the price for their support of the city charter. Long opposed to such a reform, Federalists realized that much of their past success in Boston elections was attributable to the personal influence they exercised at the polls. With voting for state and federal offices limited to Faneuil Hall, as Otis fondly recalled, he and his Federalist friends, by handing out ballots, had obliged the voters "to shew their colors." Intimidation might be another way of describing it. If voting were to be done in the wards, however, "the influence and example of the most respectable persons" would be dissipated and the town "revolutionized."[17]

It was precisely this possible revision in voting procedures that prompted Boston Republicans to back incorporation in 1822, after both the *Independent Chronicle* and the *Boston Patriot* had opposed it in 1815 as a Federalist plot. But, as they had learned during the interim, retention of old forms had only perpetuated the old ruling order. Thus when the provision for ward-voting for city offices carried in the referendum by a margin far greater than did the charter itself, Republicans and political independents alike began to think that they might have a voice in determining the city's first mayor. Boston's days as a Federalist "rotten borough" were over.[18]

"The chief reason for our friendship towards the city bill," the *Independent Chronicle* editorialized two days before the town referendum, "is that it will introduce into power the *Middling Interest*, an interest among our citizens, which if it had assumed to its due weight, would long ago have swayed the government of our town." A phenomenon of Federalism's last days, the Middling Interest represented a new and ultimately short-lived force in Boston politics. Although backed by the Republican press, it drew most of its support from disaffected Federalists. Political mavericks like William Sturgis, a riding academy proprietor named Roulstone, and the newly arrived Baptist minister Francis Wayland, later President of Brown University, figured among its leaders. While they insisted that the Middling Interest was not "an array of the POOR against the RICH," but represented "men of property and men of business," there existed some dispute on this point. Young Ralph Waldo Emerson, just out of Harvard and very much a political elitist, dismissed them as "a band of murmurers . . . a parcel of demagogues, ambitious, I suppose, of being known, or hoping for places as *partisans* which they could not achieve as citizens."[19]

Many of Boston's small businessmen identified with the Middling Interest in protest against a recently reimposed ordinance forbidding the construction of wooden buildings more than ten feet high anywhere in town. These "ten footers," as Emerson disparaged them, believed the ordinance was intended not as a fire prevention measure but to thwart the legitimate aspirations of undercapitalized business-men. Otis' identification of the ordinance with other measures "to prevent the triumph of the revolutionary movement" suggests that their charges of a conspiracy may not have been entirely spurious. Whether legitimate or not, the Middling Interest's position was overwhelmingly confirmed on March 7, when the wooden building ordinance was rejected by a town vote of 2837 to 547. Such a huge turnout, coming only three days after the ward-voting victory, prompted the *Independent Chronicle* to announce that "Aristocracy is in a tremble."[20]

On March 29, less than two weeks before the municipal elections, the politically independent *Boston Galaxy* reviewed the credentials of those mentioned as possible mayoral candidates. After judging Otis, John Phillips, and William Tudor all "fit" for the office, the *Galaxy* proceeded to make clear its own choice:

If a public life of the most undeviating adherence to principle—if the course of honest and independent conduct through good and evil report—if experience in the deliberative assemblies of the state and nation—if courtesy to political opponents, and the exercise of gentlemanly deportment to all, then Mr. Quincy is pre-eminently entitled to be the first mayor of Boston.[21]

At first glance Quincy seemed a most improbable choice. Long despised by the Republicans, he had not of late been a particularly strong vote-getter even among Boston's Federalists. Moreover, his attitude toward the new city charter was less than enthusiastic. As a member of both the 1815 and 1821 town committees as well as of the Constitutional Convention, he had opposed incorporation. In January 1822, when it became clear that Boston would adopt a charter, he went along with William Sullivan and William Tudor in their attempt to fashion one that comported with Federalist interests. Describing Quincy as "one of my fellow laborers" on the House committee examining the charter, Sullivan assured Otis that "I am not aware that any on the committee has any sinister view." Like everyone else, he assumed Quincy to be content with his own immediate prospects as Judge of the Municipal Court.[22]

He *was* content in January. But sometime "early in March," as Eliza Susan later dated it, when a group of Boston voters, led by a carpenter, came to his house and asked him to run for mayor, the situation changed. Momentarily taken aback by the proposition, Quincy reminded them of his public opposition to incorporation, joking coyly that choosing him "would be like nominating Guy Fawkes for Mayor, for he had done all in his power to blow up their city." When the delegation persisted, he accepted.[23]

His family later insisted that Quincy knew nothing of Otis' plans at the time he was approached and expressed interest in the nomination. They also contended that he believed it was a delegation of loyal Federalists that visited him, not a splinter group representing the Middling Interest. As proof of this, Eliza Susan pointed to a condition her father imposed before agreeing to run: that he be "regularly nominated" at the Federalist party's public caucus. "Of course the nomination of Mr. Quincy was a great surprise," she wrote many years later, "and he was requested to withdraw his name, but as he had given his word he would stand under certain conditions, he would not consent."[24]

Quincy may perhaps have thought the delegation that first approached him represented an insurgent though not disloyal wing of the Federalist party. The assertion that he was ignorant of Otis' own designs on the mayoral office, however, is more difficult to accept, particularly in view of his cordial relations with Sullivan back in January. More likely, he suspected Otis wanted the office for himself and decided to go ahead with his own candidacy anyway. He may also have believed that the Middling Interest's strength within the party was sufficient to secure him the regular nomination at the open caucus irrespective of Otis' plans. With the Federalist ship breaking up, he decided, rather than to remain aboard with its officers, to take his chances with the fleeing crew.[25]

The Middling Interest had selected its weapon to challenge the entrenched Federalist leadership with a perceptiveness which was political and not a little psychological. To add legitimacy to its cause, it needed a well-known figure, but one neither politically beholden to the Otises, Sullivans, Tudors, and Perkinses, nor terrified by the social consequences of crossing them. Ideally, such a candidate should be a Federalist whose loyalties were tenuous enough to allow him to bolt the party if the need arose. Quincy qualified on all counts. One would like to believe that his personal involvement with urban problems, which unquestionably made him the most qualified candidate for the office of mayor, also entered into the selection. More crucial, however, seems to have been the fact that, as the *Galaxy* duly noted in its endorsement, he "was not a favored child of a junto."[26]

"A man of forty is a fool to wonder at anything," Daniel Webster conceded, "and yet one is in danger of committing this folly when he sees Mr. Quincy the very darling of the Boston Democracy!" His exasperation had been prompted by the events on April 4 at a large meeting " *called* a Federal caucus." The Middling Interest had appeared in force and came within five votes (175 to 170) of denying the party's mayoral nomination to the absent Otis and securing it for Quincy. When the results were announced, the Middling Interest charged fraud, refused to abide by them, and stormed out. Rather than immediately disown his unruly supporters, Quincy permitted his name to be brought before the Middling Interest's rump caucus the following evening and accepted its unanimous endorsement, his stipulation about being "regularly nominated" apparently forgotten.[27]

So nonplussed by this turn of events were Otis' supporters that they considered withdrawing his name from "the unworthy controversy." "We are in a deplorable state here," Webster acknowledged on election eve. "Nothing seems practicable but to go forward and support Mr. O. and probably be beaten." Thomas Handasyd Perkins, informing Otis of the unanticipated complications, voiced the betrayal many Boston Federalists felt at one of their own "having thrown himself into the hands of the 'Middling or Meddling Interest.' " "Quincy has done himself up, by the course he has pursued," Perkins concluded, "he will have the high gratification of having split up the federal party."[28]

Quincy, however, seems to have taken his divisive role in stride, perhaps seeing the irony in his applying the *coup de grace* to the party he had so long identified with and whose principles, if not its recent politics, he continued to espouse. "I gave him my mind fully on the subject," Perkins assured Otis, "we are of course at sword's point." Nevertheless, Perkins acknowledged, "he met me yesterday in the street and gave me a formal bow and a stately 'good morning.' "[29]

As it turned out, neither Quincy nor Otis won the honor of becoming Boston's first mayor. A number of North End Republicans balked at the idea of supporting Quincy, "whose whole political life," one of them explained, "has rendered him obnoxious," and scattered their votes. Quincy outpolled Otis by more than three hundred and fifty votes (1736 to 1384) but fell sixty-nine short of a majority. Otis, clearly hurt by his defeat, declined to allow his name to be entered in the run-off; Quincy similarly withdrew although he tried to influence the choice of a compromise candidate. His statement of withdrawal is classic: "It is a station which I never sought or coveted. My permitting myself to stand as a candidate was the result of circumstances, indicating a plain and unequivocal path of duty; concerning which I had, and have no question." Eliza Susan remembered her father's feelings somewhat differently: "He rejoiced at his own defeat—as he feared going in by a small majority."[30]

On April 16, 1822, running unopposed, John Phillips was elected

the first Mayor of Boston. He made an ideal compromise, acceptable
to the Federalists as one of their own, to the Middling Interest which
had endorsed his senatorial candidacy in March, and to most
Republicans as "a moderate, intelligent, independent man." Halfway
through his one-year term, however, Phillips fell seriously ill (he died
in May 1823) and announced that he would not stand for reelection.[31]

For once Quincy was in a position to benefit from Federalist
exigencies. Although no one forgot what John Lowell referred to as
his "memorable treachery of March last," most Federalists recognized that as a successor to his cousin Quincy was the only
alternative to having Phillips succeeded by a Republican; for Otis had
eliminated himself by deciding to make what proved to be a futile
try for the governorship. Nevertheless, Otis was far from enthusiastic
about the idea of endorsing the man he thought had betrayed him and
the party. It took Lowell to remind him that unless all Federalist
office-seekers closed ranks "they will eat no more corporation
dinners, nor be regaled any longer with the odoriferous praise upon
which they have subsisted heretofore." Otis got the message and
Quincy received the Federalist endorsement.[32]

"None of the men in our circle of society were active in his
election," Eliza Susan recalled; her father did not need them. On
April 14, 1823, with formal Federalist backing and the support of
the already disintegrating Middling Interest, he easily defeated the
Republican candidate George Blake by a vote of 2505 to 2180 and
became Boston's second mayor. The path to that office had been
neither straight nor narrow, but what awaited him at its end proved
redemptive. For there his talents and energies found the opportunities and responsibilities that were to bring him the public approbation and personal fulfillment he sought.[33]

Its First Public Officer

Josiah Quincy was seldom given to understatement. A rare
instance, however, occurred during his first inaugural address in his
description of his predecessor's administration: "Their labors have
been, indeed, in a measure, unobtrusive." Temperamentally disinclined to assert the powers given him by the charter and physically
unequal to the job of divesting the heretofore autonomous boards of

theirs, Phillips had allowed the town forms to persist. Although the charter specifically abolished the elected Board of Health and assigned its responsibilities to the mayor and aldermen, he simply reappointed the board members and delegated to them all their old powers. Similarly, the suzerainty of the Board of Overseers of the Poor, the School Committee, and the Firewards over their special fiefdoms remained unchallenged.[34]

"It was apparently wise to shape the course of the first administration," Quincy conceded, "rather by the spirit of the long-experienced constitution of the town, than by that of the unsettled charter of the city." Having made this gesture to Phillips, the new mayor announced that such caution was no longer warranted. "One great defect in the ancient organization of town government," he reminded his inauguration audience, "was, the division of the executive power among many," which produced jurisdictional squabbling among the boards and often resulted in failure to provide needed services. This he intended to avoid by taking at face value the charter's description of his powers as the "general superintendence over all the boards and public institutions." Though he still expressed doubts about the wisdom of incorporation, Quincy assured his fellow citizens that the experiment would not fail for want of executive exertions during his tenure as mayor.[35]

An hour after the morning's ceremonies at Faneuil Hall were completed, the City Council found itself called into session to receive a report from the mayor on "the state of the streets in the city" and a plan "for making and keeping them clean." Under the town government the streets had been the concern of the selectmen, acting in their capacity as Surveyors of the Highways. They supervised the laying out, widening, and repairing of the streets, but the Board of Health was charged with cleaning them. Ordinarily, the board depended on local farmers who occasionally collected street-sweepings for fertilizer, thereby keeping the streets at least passable. In 1819 the board tried to auction off scavenging rights to private contractors, a common practice in European cities, but found no buyers, and those farmers who assumed the rights, *gratis*, became somewhat selective in what they collected.[36]

Phillips had failed in his referendum to have the old powers of the Surveyors of Highways vested in the mayor and the aldermen. Quincy, however, simply assumed them as part of his program to provide Boston with "that surest pledge of health, a pure atmos-phere." A Superintendent of Streets was appointed to represent the mayor in all matters relating to street-maintenance and cleaning; teams of laborers hired by the city were set to work, producing one of the more impressive statistics of Quincy's first year in office, that of the amount of street dirt collected: six thousand tons.[37]

This burst of executive activity was an intentional encroachment upon the powers of the Board of Health. The board had unquestion-ably rendered valuable service to the town since its establishment in 1799, particularly in its efforts to quarantine contagious diseases. But like other elective town boards, it had become entangled in political buck-passing and was inadequate for the public health needs of a city of nearly 50,000 inhabitants.[38] Quincy wanted a full-time professional to oversee these matters, appointed by and reporting directly to the mayor. On May 13, 1823, after creating the office of "Marshall of the City," he placed in it a young lawyer, Benjamin Pollard, whom he charged with the duties not only of Boston's principal law enforcement officer but of its health officer as well. "If there be any advantage in the form of a city over that of a town government," Quincy reminded his fellow citizens a year later, in his second inaugural address, "it lies in one single word,—*efficiency*," which he defined as the "*capacity to carry into effect*." On May 31, 1824, in the interests of efficiency and with little fanfare, the Board of Health was abolished.[39]

The mayor and his marshal accomplished what the board had not. So conspicuous was their success in street-cleaning that some Bos-tonians complained it was being practiced "to a needless and pernicious extreme." While the Board of Health had left the sewers to private enterprise and tolerated the lucrative but "noxious" practice of church-vault burials, the sewers were now brought under public control and church-vault burials outlawed. Throughout Quincy's tenure as mayor, Boston's death-rate declined steadily, as it had not done before and would not again for several decades. "Cleanliness," he reminded Bostonians, "has reference to morals as well as comfort," implying that all three could best be maintained by his taking personal supervision of them.[40]

Quincy approached more cautiously the Board of Firewards, the most hidebound and politically intrenched of the town agencies. Organized in the 1670's, the firewards during the eighteenth century were drawn from many of the town's leading citizens; Paul Revere, Samuel Adams, John Phillips, and John Winthrop had all served in that capacity in the 1770's. As late as 1818, Lemuel Shaw, later Chief Justice of the Massachusetts Supreme Court, took charge at fires in his neighborhood by establishing fire lanes and conscripting onlookers. By this time, however, the prestige of the board had been gradually eroded by the breakdown of community ties and the declining social status of the firewards themselves. Nevertheless, the thirty-six elected members remained a potent political force in Boston and a serious obstacle to reforming a fire-fighting system which many, including the new mayor, believed to be badly outdated.[41]

Still more committed to the old system were the nearly four hundred members of the city's sixteen volunteer engine companies. Well organized and fiercely competitive, they possessed an *esprit de corps* unmatched by other civic organizations. When called out, each company raced to the fire, hoping to claim the cash premium that went to the first on the scene. Off duty the competition consisted of trying to outdo each other in the elaborateness of their premium financed banquets. In addition to the social camaraderie which it offered, membership in one of the engine companies also provided exemption from military and jury duty. More important in making membership sought after was the personal gratification that came with serving the community in a conspicuous capacity. It was this which prompted Boston's engine-men to disdain the use of hoses, standard equipment in New York and Philadelphia. For those who believed "the nearer the fire the higher the honor," tending a length of hose would be nothing less than a humiliation. If such reforms were to be made, they would have to be imposed.[42]

The mayor's first confrontation with the engine companies involved the question of premiums. During Phillips' term a fifteen-dollar premium had been established, but it failed to satisfy the engine-men. On June 16, 1823, they demanded of Quincy a premium of fifty dollars and threatened to resign "at the proper season" if their figure was not met. The mayor tried to have the chairman of the Board of Firewards, Thomas Melville, reason with them, but Melville refused, leaving little doubt that he and the other firewards supported the engine companies' demand. On November 24, 1823, Quincy rejected the ultimatum; a week later the engine-men acted on their threat by resigning. Replacements were quickly found, but the problems inherent in an antiquated volunteer system outside the mayor's control persisted.[43]

Fate intervened on the side of reform on April 7, 1825, in the guise of a fire begun in a chowder pot. Before burning itself out, more than fifty stores along State and Broad Streets had been destroyed at an estimated loss of $1,000,000. Efforts to combat the blaze had proved wholly unsuccessful, at times so futile as to be ludicrous. Quincy, capitalizing on the public clamor, presented the city council on June 7 with a comprehensive plan for the creation of a fire department modeled after New York City's. Although the proposed department would continue to draw upon volunteers, the firewards were to be abolished and a chief engineer, answerable to the mayor, was to be assigned to each of the engine companies. The plan also called for the construction of water reservoirs throughout the city and the immediate introduction of hoses. Two weeks later these reforms, incorporated in an "act establishing a fire department in the city of Boston," were approved by the General Court. A city referendum was scheduled for July 7.[44]

The proposal generated considerable controversy in the press. The *Boston Patriot*—Republican, friendly to the engine-men, and consistently critical of Quincy's administration—condemned it as a usurpation of power properly belonging to the firewards, while the *Daily Advertiser* and the *Columbian Centinel*, generally sympathetic to the mayor and to Boston's propertied interests, warmly endorsed it. But it was Quincy himself who made the best case for the need for reform. "Our present system," he argued in his *Public Letter to the Citizens of Boston*, "presupposes either a *will* in the surrounding multitude at fires, to aid in forming lanes to pass water to the engines, or a *power* in the firewards to compel them to form such lanes." When both suppositions were operative, Boston's volunteer system was a source of civic pride. But now neither was operative. It no longer sufficed for a fireward to point out a laggard; social obloquy had force only in a community small enough that everyone knew everyone else and each believed in the effectiveness of his personal contribution to the collective effort. Boston, its mayor insisted, with a trace of sadness, had long since outgrown that primitive state.[45]

The introduction of insurance, he argued further, vitiated the communal spirit by causing fires to be viewed less as public calamities than private risks. "I ask no protection from others," retorted a Bostonian who had been reproached for not joining in a fire lane, "and I mean not to incur the risk of health and life in protecting them." However much Quincy might deplore "such cold, selfish, calculating language," as mayor he could not ignore it. "In all cities, after they have obtained a certain amount of greatness," he pointed out, "the system of depending upon the aid of all the citizens has been abandoned, and a system, self-dependent and which so far from requiring the aid of all the citizens, excludes that aid, has been adopted." Such were the realities of nineteenth-century urban life.[46]

Quincy got his fire department, though just barely. Of the more than twenty-five hundred votes cast, the plan received a majority of less than two hundred. Nonetheless, under the mayor's personal supervision, the reforms were quickly implemented. Over the next few years insurance rates on city property were substantially lowered, a testament to the efficiency of the new department, though hardly to the mayor's popularity among the ousted firewards and hose-toting engine-men.[47]

The Board of Health and the Firewards were not alone in feeling the effects of Quincy's consolidating zeal. At the close of his first inaugural address he had assured the city council that he intended, "by executing every duty and taking every responsibility which belongs to his office, to shorten and lighten your disinterested and patriotic labors." In practice this meant his assuming the chairmanship of all important council committees, the writing of most reports, and the supervision of the members' most insignificant activities. While he kept on reasonably good terms with the aldermen, the complete turnover in their membership during his first two years in office probably came about because they found themselves with too little to do. Members of the larger Common Council were openly critical of the mayor, frequently complaining of being left uninformed, and not a few wished he might take a bit less literally the charter's designation of him as the city's "first public officer."[48]

Nowhere was Quincy's executive vigor more dramatically evidenced than in the construction of the New Faneuil Hall Market, Boston's first publicly financed urban renewal project. Since its construction in 1742, Faneuil Hall had served Boston as meeting place, polling station, and public market. Despite its enlargement in 1804, under the direction of Charles Bulfinch, it was by 1820 again unequal to the multiple demands placed on it. On market days the adjoining streets were clogged with produce carts, which created epic traffic jams in the center of town. Nonetheless, neither the selectmen, worried about the expense and complicated condemnation proceedings that would be involved, nor Mayor Phillips showed any interest in expanding Boston's clearly inadequate market facilities.[49]

Instead of avoiding it, Quincy seized upon the problem during his first weeks in office. By July 31, 1823, he and the Boston architect Alexander Parris had drawn up a preliminary plan for constructing a building adjoining Faneuil Hall as well as several new access lanes and docking arrangements. A council committee chaired by the mayor worked out a plan that fall which was more elaborate. The project could not be undertaken before a public referendum, but in anticipation Quincy began buying up land around Faneuil Hall for the city.[50]

The following January he presented to a public meeting the plans for a two-story, classically styled, 535-foot long granite market house covering some 27,000 square feet. In addition to the building, six new approach streets and a new wharf were proposed, all to be built with public funds. Opposition to a project of this magnitude was inevitable. Republican papers had earlier denounced "the mammoth project" as prodigal; the *Patriot* protested that it would radically alter prevailing land values and was contrary to the city's "spreading out tendency." Quincy's enthusiasm proved overwhelming to all these objections, and the entire project received the meeting's endorsement.[51]

Having conceived of the project in the spring of 1823, helped draw up plans for it during the summer and fall, and sold them to a skeptical public the following winter, Quincy as chairman of the building committee proceeded to devote much of his time over the next two years to seeing it through to completion. It was he who selected the granite and he who decided what was to be contained in the cornerstone. By the time the New Faneuil Hall Market opened in 1826, downtown Boston had been totally transformed and $1,000,000 in public funds expended. As stall rentals easily serviced the debt and the city made a substantial profit from the sale of the adjoining land Quincy had quietly bought up in 1823, it proved a wise investment. By 1848 the market complex had paid for itself and has since yielded the city over $3,000,000. "Quincy Market," as it immediately came to be called, still operates, though looking a bit tattered and woebegone tucked in midst the architectural finery of the New Boston. In its day, however, it was a source of considerable civic pride. "Boston has long enjoyed the reputation of a neat city," the Boston *News-Letter* editorialized at the market's opening, "it bids fair indeed to gain the additional reputation of being a handsome one." When the current renovation is completed, Quincy Market should again contribute to that reputation.[52]

7 / Quincy's Boston

The true glory of a city consists ... in a happy, secure, and contented people; feeling the advantage of a vigorous and faithful administration, ... The poorest and humblest citizen should be made instinctively to bless that paternal government, which he daily perceives watching over his comfort and convenience.

—Josiah Quincy, 1823

The mayoral years were for Josiah Quincy his happiest. Dependent as he was upon access to power and public recognition for personal fulfillment—"the great and distinguished opportunity of usefulness"—he found presiding over a growing city, still responsive to vigorous executive direction, a completely satisfying experience. Promptly after taking office he announced that "everyday (Sundays excepted), between nine and ten o'clock A.M., he would attend at his office to receive communications of individual or public interest." The *Columbian Centinel* reported that the Mayor was regularly "seen before sunrise, riding like Jehu, his sorrel about the city, examining, exploring and reconnoitering." On one such excursion the night watch apprehended him for speeding. When Lafayette visited Boston in 1824, Quincy escorted him about with the proprietary pride of one who regarded the city's clean streets, its handsome new buildings, its salubrious atmosphere as not only the collective possession of all Bostonians, but in a real way his own. Indeed, some were ready to acknowledge his special claims. "It is a general time of health and prosperity in the city," Dr. George Shattuck wrote to his son away at school in 1825, "I could send you a map of the progress of Mr. Quincy's new improvements." And until Bostonians rebelled against his benevolent paternalism, as they eventually had to if only to prove the right to do so, he made the most of their indulgence.[1]

To Make Vice Less Obtrusive

Quincy was perhaps the most successful urban reformer in early nineteenth-century America. Contemporaries cited him as an exemplar of "this age of improvement" while historians have pointed to his activities as proof of the era's unbounded belief in progress, if not in "the perfectibility of man." Yet his reforms were infused less with hope than with a sense of impending loss, profound and irretrievable. His arguments in favor of overhauling Boston's firefighting system, for example, reflected an almost fatalistic determination to adapt civic institutions to the rapidly changing, basically uncontrollable conditions with which he had no sympathy. Though he occasionally took unto himself the obligatory role of city-booster, expressing satisfaction in Boston's growth and diversity, his loyalties remained with the older, smaller, more homogeneous town.[2]

Accordingly, his most characteristic reforms are best understood as attempts to retrieve some of Boston's earlier organic unity. He sought to make it a more attractive, healthier, and safer place to live, and so to foster the civic pride of all its citizens. His preference for public undertakings over private developments reflects this determination to restore to Bostonians a collective identity. Similarly, centralizing municipal powers in the office of the mayor, and his own conspicuousness in that office, can be seen less as self-aggrandizement than as an attempt to give Boston's government a focus that it had lost through the proliferation of boards and resultant dispersion of authority. By administrative consolidation he accomplished what he set out to do, to bring order and efficiency to a heretofore chaotic governmental structure, yet beneath all his strenuous efforts can be sensed his own belief that here too he was engaged in a holding action. His was never more than a conditional faith in the prospects of urban life.[3]

The conservative nature of Quincy's reform impulse is clearly discernible in his response as mayor to the triad of social problems that had engaged his attention since 1820: poverty, vice, and crime. All constituted for him inevitable features of any society, but most conspicuously of industrialized societies. "The poor, the vicious, and the criminal," he had declared as municipal judge in 1822, "are necessary parts of the social system." They might be contained, ought to be institutionally isolated, but would never be eradicated. The most any society could hope to do, or should attempt to do, was to deal with these problems in such manner as not needlessly to aggravate them. It was precisely this, he had come to believe, that was the error of Boston's Overseers of the Poor, and that he as mayor was determined to correct.[4]

Quincy's argument with the Overseers of the Poor began well

before his election. As a representative investigating pauper laws, as municipal judge, and as chairman of the town committee looking into the feasibility of a House of Industry, he had often condemned the town board for its lax management of the Leverett Street almshouse. After inspecting the facility in 1822 he called it a public disgrace. "In this collection of persons," he informed the city council, "are to be found all ages and colors; every stage of poverty and disease whether produced by misfortune or vice." Declaring the almshouse miserably adapted to the multiple uses to which it was being put by the overseers, he recommended that it be sold.[5]

The overseers responded by attacking Quincy's pet project for dealing with the pauper problem, a House of Industry, as a waste of money. Not to be silenced so easily, he countered that the overseers' increasing reliance upon "out-of-doors relief," placing public charges with private parties rather than employing them in productive work under restrictive scrutiny, was actually far more costly. "It is axiomatic," he informed the city council, citing Henry Brougham's researches in England, "that of all modes of providing for the poor, that of supplying their own families, is the most wasteful and expensive." Further, it indulged the poor, encouraging them to remain dependent upon the community for support. Quincy's institutional alternative, "House of Industry" being a euphemism for workhouse, would not be, like the almshouses, "abodes of idleness," but establishments where the indolent poor would be made to earn their keep.[6]

A month after taking office, Quincy ordered the Overseers of the Poor to transfer nearly three hundred able-bodied poor residing in the almshouse and the seven hundred receiving out-of-door relief to the just completed House of Industry in South Boston. The overseers refused to send any except those poor who specifically requested it. Needless to say, few volunteered for the mayor's new "Botany Bay." The $35,000 House of Industry sat vacant throughout 1823 and most of 1824, while charges and counter-charges were exchanged by Quincy and Redford Webster, chairman of the overseers.[7]

The mayor attempted to break the deadlock in the fall of 1824 by calling upon the overseers to make a public accounting of how they spent their $30,000 annual appropriation. When they refused, insisting that they had to account to no one but themselves, Quincy asked the voters of Boston to resolve the dispute by means of a referendum to alter the city charter in such a way that the overseers would be put directly under the mayor's control. Unfortunately, he underestimated popular support for the overseers and overestimated the city's disenchantment with the old elective boards generally. On December 16, 1824, his proposal was rejected.[8]

Having failed to dislodge the overseers by way of public referendum, Quincy simply sold the almshouse out from under them the following March. He then appointed a board of arbitrators who sanctioned his actions after the fact by declaring that the mayor had primary jurisdiction over all public charges. Three weeks later the city council, miffed by the overseers' refusal to provide an accounting of their expenditures, enjoined them from extending any additional out-of-door relief. Although their existence had been guaranteed by the vote in December, the overseers proved unable to check the mayor's systematic emasculation of their powers. Nor could they prevent him from putting those on public relief to "hammering stone and like material" in the House of Industry. Quincy did not make Boston a city without poverty, but he did make it a city without beggars.[9]

Equally indicative of the limited objectives of Quincy's social reforms was his approach to the problems he linked with poverty and "so often found together," those of vice and crime. Again, he had become familiar with the seamier aspects of his native city long before becoming mayor and carried into that office no illusions about eliminating them. His determination to combat vice and criminality, as he acknowledged in 1824,

did not originate in any theories or visions of ideal purity, attainable in the existing state of human society, but in a single sense of duty and respect for the character of the city; proceeding upon the principle, that if in great cities the existence of vice is inevitable, that its course should be in secret, like other filth, in drains and in darkness; not obtrusive, not powerful, not prowling publicly in the streets for the innocent and unwary.[10]

No one denied Boston its vice problem; alcoholism and prostitution were generally conceded to be its most common manifestations. The Society for the Moral and Religious Instruction of the Poor (later the City Missionary Society), had been founded in 1816 to dispense Bibles and conduct Sunday schools among Boston's poor. Along the way it had collected considerable data on the town's "licentious activity." The Society's Fourth Annual Report (1820), written by the Rev. William Jenks, examined the problem of prostitution and its place in the festering criminal subculture of Beacon Hill's western slope, generally referred to as "Nigger Hill." Of the estimated two thousand prostitutes thought to be operating in Boston, over four hundred lived on the Hill. There, hundreds of illegitimate children, abandoned by mothers either too indifferent or too disease-ridden to care for them, were left to their own devices. Jenks estimated that the mortality rate on the Hill approached fifteen percent, venereal-diseased prostitutes alone accounting for about four hundred of those each year "ushered into the presence of their creator." While they lived, however, they managed to keep a dozen brothels between Botolph and Charles Streets going long and loud into the night.[11]

On August 11, 1820, the town selectmen received a petition calling for the tearing down of "numerous, disorderly and lewd houses, filled with inhabitants devoted principally, in appearances, to vice of almost any kind." A similar petition was submitted six months later, but the selectmen were unwilling, or more likely, unable to do more than deplore conditions on the Hill. Even the town watch steered clear of the area after dark, having greater concern for their own safety than for the preservation of public morals. As Boston's population grew, the problem worsened. Reports of customers being assaulted by prostitutes on the Hill were common and residents of the fashionable eastern side of Beacon Hill regularly had "the quiet of the night . . . invaded by cries of distress and even of murder." But when whores began appearing on the Common during the day, disturbing the perambulations of the Park Street gentry, the situation could no longer be countenanced.[12]

Describing his tactics for dealing with the problem of the Hill, Quincy reported that "the evil was met in the face." Seizing upon his licensing power, he had drastically reduced the number of purveyors of alcohol throughout the city, making certain that the dance halls on the Hill felt the resultant drought. Boston's theaters, another favorite hangout for prostitutes and the scene of several public disturbances early in the 1820's, were brought under close surveillance. When it was discovered that many of the most notorious places on the Hill persisted in operating after their liquor licenses had been revoked, the mayor organized and led a posse of draymen up onto the Hill to shut them down and, acting in the capacity of a justice-of-the-peace, personally arrested the offending saloon-keepers.[13]

Public reveling declined markedly after that. By 1828 the City Missionary Society could report that "the great evil for which West Boston has long been noted is in a measure subdued—or dispersed." The Reverend Jenks had previously congratulated the mayor on the fact that "the number of wretched beings, 'whose nightly earnings are their daily bread,' is now comparatively few, and, we trust, continually diminishing." Though gratified by the city's improved moral appearance and the credit he received for it, Quincy never allowed himself to believe, as Jenks did, that "the time is at hand, when infamy and degradation will there be wholly exterminated." For him it sufficed that they were "less obtrusive."[14]

Unlike many of the humanitarian reformers who came after him, Quincy addressed himself as mayor almost exclusively to the consequences of poverty, vice and crime. While continuing to believe that the underlying causes for these social problems were beyond his or anybody else's control, and that industrialization, urbanization, and unlimited immigration exacerbated them, he operated as a reformer on the premise that they "must always exist." The outstanding exception to this fatalistic approach was in his dealing with juveniles. Here he acknowledged the role of environmental factors, especially the influence of elders upon the young, and saw some possibility for preventive action. "Their offenses," he argued, not only demanded punishment but "require restraint." He condemned the practice of confining children to jails like that "moral pest-house" in Cambridge, "in utter sloth and idleness . . . exposed to a perpetual influx and efflux of whatever is base, and vicious, and criminal." Rather than commit young offenders to the state prisons, "those well-endowed seminaries of crime," he believed they ought to be carefully segregated from older criminals and given special attention aimed at making them useful citizens. His establishment of a House of Juvenile Offenders in South Boston in 1826 was meant to serve both these functions.[15]

For "the vicious poor" or "the hardened criminal," he had little hope and less sympathy. His principal concern was protecting society, not rehabilitating the deviant, whom he wanted incarcerated and put at hard labor. Nathan Dane, a prominent Boston lawyer and early benefactor of the Harvard Law School, knew he would receive a sympathetic response when he wrote to Quincy in 1822 that "we must correct a modern notion, too prevalent, that punishment made almost no punishment, will answer a good purpose." His advocacy of a system of solitary confinement, as he acknowledged, was based on his discovery that most prisoners found it "almost absolutely, insupportable." "Can any fact more strikingly evidence the wisdom of the system or more clearly indicate the duty of society?" he asked rhetorically. "In the deep silence of the cell, it is God who speaks. It is He, who punishes. . . . In whose hands can hardened criminals be better left than in His, who alone knows, when to break and when to bind. . . ." Perhaps it was the Puritan in Quincy that caused him to stress the limitations to ameliorating the human condition, and made his reforms unduly modest. But it also spared him the disillusionment of later nineteenth-century reformers who, in their romantic and millenarian fervor, denied the existence of such limitations.[16]

Might As Well Be Fitted at the Publick Expense

Bostonians soon discovered that reforms cost money. Their mayor's scrupulous attention to cleaning and widening the city's streets, for example, meant an expenditure of more than $250,000 during his first three years in office, more than the total expenditure of the final year of town government. Fire department innovations cost nearly $50,000 while the sixty-acre complex in South Boston, which by 1826 consisted of Houses of Industry, Correction, and Juvenile Reform, required $100,000 to build and maintain. In addition to these, Quincy purchased downtown land for recreational use, including the rope-walks (at a cost of $54,000), that occupied the site of the present Public Gardens. But it was of course the new market which inflated the city debt to more than $1,000,000 and evoked "the most prodigious outcry."[17]

Quincy initially dismissed criticism of his spending as uninformed. "Abstractedly, a debt is no more an object of terror than a sword," he lectured his second inaugural audience. "Both are very dangerous in the hands of fools or madmen. Both are very safe, innocent, and useful in the hands of the wise and prudent." To the same forum, two years later, he repudiated the charge that his reforms had increased the city's tax burden by pointing out that the tax rate had actually dropped during his three years in office. It was the increase in property values, which he credited to his administration's progressive policies, not increased taxes, that had enabled him to match rising public expenditures. Having cleared up the confusion, the mayor concluded his 1826 inaugural address by recommending that the city undertake a new water-works project. "The introduction of an ample supply of pure water," he assured his audience, "would . . . contribute much to the health of the place." It would also cost $2,000,000.[18]

His 1827 inaugural address made no mention of a water-works project or, for that matter, any other costly projects under consideration. "Our chief duty," the mayor announced, "will be to finish what we have begun . . . the gradual extinction of the existing city debt." The sudden turnabout may have been prompted, as Quincy insisted, by realistic considerations of the magnitude of a debt Bostonians could be expected to service. But political factors also appear to have been taken into account. In response to the mounting criticism of his spending, he seems to have decided to cut back, eliminating the one issue capable of putting his tenure as mayor in jeopardy. He liked his job enough to make some accommodations to keep it. But whatever his motives for adopting a policy of retrenchment in 1826, it did him little good, political or otherwise, as his unhappy dealings with the school committee demonstrated.[19]

Compared with other American cities in the 1820's, Boston had an exemplary public-school system. In 1826 there were seventy-four public schools in the city, instructing more than seven thousand students at an annual cost of $60,000. In addition to fifty-one primary schools and nineteen grammar schools, there were an African School, two boys' high schools—Boston Latin and English— and an experimental High School for Girls, which was just completing its first year of operations.[20]

Quincy's relations with the school committee were initially very cordial. His early speeches as mayor lavished praise upon the city's schools and expressed satisfaction with the way they were being administered. It was not he but the aldermen who tried to divest the school committee of its former autonomy by insisting that the city charter place with them financial responsibility for the schools. When the city council appointed a committee to arbitrate the issue, Quincy declined to exercise his prerogative to act as its chairman. With the fire department reorganization just underway and the market project yet to be completed, he willingly kept out of this particular squabble.[21]

Himself a product of private schooling, as were his seven children, Quincy lacked, as his Republican critics later charged, either a real sympathy for or commitment to the concept of a publicly supported comprehensive school system. While not among those prominent Bostonians, including Harrison Gray Otis and John Lowell, who opposed the establishment of public primary schools in 1818, neither was he enamored of them as instruments of social control as Whigs like Horace Mann and Henry Barnard would later be. Still less did he share the Jeffersonian view of the public schools as nurseries for a "natural aristocracy" or springboards for the aspiring poor. In keeping with his Federalist loyalties, he believed that education was for those who could afford it, not an obligation upon the community for the benefit of those who wanted it. Thus when confronted with the question of whether to continue the year-old girls' high school, Quincy, underestimating its ideological implications, saw it merely as an opportunity to prove his commitment to his announced policy of fiscal austerity.[22]

During the spring of 1825 the school committee had taken under advisement a recommendation of one of its members, the Rev. John Pierpont, "to consider the expediency and practicality of establishing a publick school for the instruction of girls in the higher departments of science and literature." Nothing comparable then existed anywhere in the United States. In Boston only boys were permitted to attend the two high schools; girls who could not afford one of the private schools in the city had their formal education terminated at the grammar school level. The school committee thought it time to rectify this situation and informed the city council on June 22 that $2,000 would be needed to begin operations of an experimental girls' high school in the fall.[23]

The city council was already discussing what it regarded as a far more important but related subject, the introduction of the "Lancasterian" or monitorial system into the public schools. Devised in the 1790's by an English schoolmaster, Joseph Lancaster, the system utilized older students to instruct younger ones. Such monitors, its advocates contended, enabled a single professional teacher to handle as many as two hundred students. New York City had been experimenting with the system for several years before its obvious virtues caught the attention of Boston's economy-minded city council. When it approved the school committee's request for funds on August 22, 1825, the girls' high school was envisioned less as an experiment in female education than as a testing ground for monitorial instruction.[24]

Even before its doors opened in January 1826, the High School for Girls was viewed with enthusiasm. Headmaster Ebenezer Bailey found himself deluged with 300 applications for the 130 spaces available. It soon became clear that Boston girls had both more time and a greater desire to avail themselves of a high school education than the boys, as combined enrollment at Boston Latin and English was less than 300 and holding steady. By March Bailey had received 427 applications for the school's second year of operation.[25]

"The experiment has now been carried so far as to leave no doubt in the mind of your committee," reported the Rev. Pierpont on August 26, 1826. "The school has not only established itself in the confidence and affections of our fellow citizens, it has excited interest abroad." Accordingly, he moved that "further provisions for its enlargement" be made. Immediate approval of the motion was blocked by the mayor, who, acting as chairman, announced the formation of a new subcommittee to study the future of the High School for Girls and then promptly adjourned the meeting.[26]

Five weeks later the new subcommittee, with the mayor chairing it, submitted its own report. Two objections were raised to continuing the school, though both conceded its popular success. The first related to the stiff admission standards imposed by Bailey to cope with the large number of applicants. Such selectivity, the report contended, could only "provoke the inevitable discontent of the citizenry." The second objection, really only an insinuation, was that the success of the girls' high school came at the expense of "the character and prospects of the other schools in the metropolis." In order to prove this, the mayor announced his intention to poll the city's grammar-school headmasters as to their feelings on the subject.[27]

Quincy's own position was revealed in the questions he asked the headmasters. Did the girls' high school diminish the zeal of the girls in the lower schools? Did it hurt the lower schools by drawing off the ablest girls? Did it prevent the introduction of monitorial instruction in the lower schools? Did it cause the lower schools to feel reduced to a secondary rank? He obviously expected the headmasters to respond affirmatively to all four questions, thereby corroborating his own belief that the brightest girls in the grammar schools, rather than remaining until they were fifteen and monitoring the younger children, were moving over to the high school at twelve. Instead of a prelude to the introduction of the monitorial system, the girls' high school had proved an expensive obstacle to it.[28]

Unfortunately for the mayor's purposes, the headmasters were unaccommodating. While conceding that the girls' high school hindered the introduction of the monitorial system in their own schools, they judged this no great loss. Quincy should have anticipated that professional academics could hardly look with enthusiasm upon a reform aimed at reducing the need for teachers. Unlike the mayor or city council, they did not regard economizing on Boston's schools as in their best interest, and their enthusiasm for the girls' high school was virtually unanimous.[29]

Though not at all what he had hoped for, the headmasters' responses did nothing to allay Quincy's fear that the girls' high school would soon become an intolerable drain on the city treasury. It was apparent that the headmasters did not complain about losing older girls to the high school, because their loss was more than compensated for by greatly increased female enrollments in the lower grades. As Bowdoin Street's headmaster explained, many parents who had previously sent their daughters to private schools were now sending them to the city's grammar schools as preparation for the new high school. They had, he announced proudly, decided that "their daughters might as well be fitted at the publick expense."[30]

The very success of the girls' high school was the most compelling reason for the mayor to scuttle it. If a large number of the approximately three thousand girls attending Boston private schools in 1826 decided to transfer to the public schools, the city, he feared, would go bankrupt. Yet he could hardly state that he was opposed to the continuation of an institution supported by the taxpayers because too many taxpayers were about to avail themselves of it. Forthrightness, his favored approach, precluded by political exigencies, Quincy resorted to obfuscation.[31]

In announcing to the school committee the results of the questionnaire, the mayor did what editing he could. Rather than dwell on the fact that twelve of the fourteen headmasters endorsed the girls' high school and believed it had greatly increased the zeal of their own female students, he laid stress on their acknowledgment that it had prevented the introduction of the monitorial system in their schools and engendered some discontent among those girls denied admission. After painting as somber a picture as possible, given the headmasters' glowing reports, Quincy presented the committee with three alternatives: (1) abolish the girls' high school; (2) provide facilities in it equal to the demand; (3) reduce its scope. After admitting his own partiality for the first proposal but declining to recommend it to the committee, "considering the High School for Girls' apparent past success and general satisfaction of those who have enjoyed its benefits," he flatly dismissed the second as "objectionable in point of expense." That left the third.[32]

Pierpont and the other supporters of the girls' high school on the committee, while disappointed, were willing to compromise. At their behest, Headmaster Bailey volunteered to cut the length of attendance from three to two years and to raise the entrance age from twelve to thirteen, "so as not to deprive the Grammar Schools of high scholars who ought to remain in them." Quincy's demand, however, was for a one-year curriculum and an entrance age of fourteen, to which the committee deferred. On this restricted basis the school operated until the end of 1827 when its fate would again have to be decided.[33]

Despite these changes, the very existence of a public institution providing advanced instruction to females constituted a threat to his austerity program by encouraging other disadvantaged groups to seek equal consideration. In January 1827 the committee received a citizens' petition forwarded from the city council "Regarding the Establishment of a High School for the Education of Children of the Colored Citizens." Six weeks later a group of small businessmen called upon the committee to provide "French, Spanish and German Instruction in the Public Schools . . . to qualify our children for the pursuits of active life" and to "equalize the advantages of our schools among all classes of citizens." Quincy summarily dismissed the first petition as "inexpedient" while James Savage, his most consistent supporter on the school committee, rejected the second as "too expensive." But, clearly, additional assaults on the public treasury could be expected as long as the girls' high school continued to operate and attract attention.[34]

On December 10, 1827, in his sixth inaugural address, the mayor took note of the success of his administration in enforcing "a rigid system of economy," and immediately thereupon launched into an oblique attack on the girls' high school, without ever mentioning it by name. He again seized upon its stiff admission requirements and underlined his implicit charge of discrimination by pointing to the disproportionate number of successful applicants from private schools. "Every school, the admission to which is predicated upon the principles of requiring higher attainments . . . than the mass of children in the ordinary course of school instruction . . . can attain," he contended, "is in fact a school for the benefit of the few, and not for the benefit of the many." While there was an "undemocratic" aspect to the school's operation, it was disingenuous of Quincy to base his public opposition to its existence on this fact when it was his continued refusal to expand the school's facilities which made admission requirements necessary. However genuine his doubts about the city's capacity to finance open-admission female education, they were hardly ennobled by such demagoguery.[35]

Five weeks after the mayor's attack on the girls' high school, James Savage announced to his fellow school committeemen that he now opposed its continuation because of its adverse effect on monitorial instruction in the lower schools. With Pierpont no longer on the committee, Savage's motion to discontinue the girls' high school in June met with only token resistance. One committeeman did ask why the logic of the motion should not apply equally to the boys' high schools which ought accordingly to be closed. This impertinent line of argument was promptly closed off by the mayor who declared *ex cathedra* that the boys' high schools "*were* a distinct subject." Another member questioned the mayor's right to chair all school committee meetings, but was told by the chairman, "who disclaimed any *personal* motives," that it was his "by force of the City Charter." The committee then voted the High School for Girls out of existence. On June 3, 1828, its doors closed and Boston's pioneering effort in "placing women in respect to education, upon ground, if not equal, at least bearing a near and honorable relation, to that of men," was suspended. It would be another thirty-three years before the city reconsidered Quincy's judgment that it could not "provide fit wives for well-educated men"—at public expense.[36]

This Poor Exhausted Body Politic

Following his election in 1823, Boston's new mayor was reminded by one of his supporters "not to lose his popularity which gave such a power to be useful." Eliza Susan recorded her father's predictable response: "Mr. Quincy only laughed and told him Popularity was the last thing he should think of. He should do whatever he considered his duty, and the people might turn him out as soon as they pleased." This theme resonated through several of his inaugural addresses, "popularity . . . that evanescent splendor" always running a poor second to "the infinite consequence of possessing the consciousness of deserving it." Such protestations notwithstanding, Quincy managed as mayor of Boston to enjoy several years of both.[37]

When he ran against the Republican George Blake in 1823, his majority had been small, only 121 out of 4766 votes cast. A year later, however, implicit approval of his first year's performance was registered in an uncontested election. The shift of polling day in 1825 from April to December resulted in his gaining reelection on both occasions, still uncontested. In 1826, the Republicans again ran Blake, but he fell far behind his earlier showing, losing to Quincy by more than 1400 votes. In the following year, the incumbent undercut charges of fiscal extravagance by adopting a retrenchment policy. This strategy, combined with Amos Binney's half-hearted candidacy, assured him a six-to-one margin of victory. After five years in office, he seemed more secure than ever.[38]

Quincy's personal hold on Boston voters should not be exaggerated. Opposition to his reforms and to autocratic methods of implementing them had begun building up immediately upon his taking office. Certainly the dispossessed firewards, overseers of the poor, and health commissioners felt no more affection for him than did the harassed saloon-keepers on the Hill or the "lazy poor" cutting stone out in South Boston. In addition, special private-interest groups, notably North End property owners and investors in the Boylston Street Market felt that the mayor's urban renewal efforts had hurt them. And if Quincy's abrupt manner occasionally nettled members of the city council, one can imagine how it upset the recipient of this letter:

Sir—
I hereby give you notice that the Mayor and Aldermen intend to continue the widening of Hanover Street *through* the building you are altering. . . . you may govern yourself accordingly.

Josiah Quincy, Mayor of Boston[39]

It was not that there had been no opposition to his administration prior to 1828, but that it had been sporadic, unorganized, and lacked a focus. Quincy's decision to discontinue the High School for Girls changed all that. However defensible on financial grounds, it proved distinctly unpopular. Of all the Boston newspapers, only the *Columbian Centinel*, the most conservative and debt-conscious, endorsed his action, while even "the middling interest elements" in the press, those who had supported him consistently since 1822, were visibly distressed by it. Though opposed to higher taxes, they were still more opposed to what seemed to them the mayor's arbitrary contraction of their children's educational opportunities.[40]

Although Quincy had attempted to explain his opposition to the girls' high school in a *Report on the Subject of the Schools* published in February 1828, his efforts were thwarted by an immediate rejoinder from the school's first headmaster, Ebenezer Bailey. Bailey, who had resigned in November after a protracted dispute with Quincy and Savage, charged the mayor with educational quackery, political scheming, and personal dishonesty. "The *avowed* object of Mr. Quincy's report is to improve the system of instruction in the Grammar and Writing Schools," he wrote, but "the *real* object . . . is to discontinue the High School for Girls." As for the mayor's enthusiasm for the monitorial system, the headmaster contended it was based on his hope that it would "lead to dismissing half the present teachers."[41]

The most politically explosive charge in Bailey's *Review of the Mayor's Report* was leveled at Quincy's attitude toward public education generally. "Public schools," he was reported as feeling, "should be merely eleemosynary establishments where nothing but the lowest elements of learning should be doled out to the children of poverty." Such an attribution of elitist bias, consistent enough with Quincy's earlier politics and public manner, was promptly snapped up by Boston's Republican press, already doing some aristocracy-baiting on behalf of the presidential candidacy of Andrew Jackson.[42]

The *Columbian Centinel* found "fragments of the party feelings" of the national elections of November 1828 lingering on into the municipal elections of December. *The Jeffersonian Republican*, fresh from its battle against John Quincy Adams, simply shifted its attention from the defeated president to the vulnerable mayor. While on the one hand giving extensive coverage to Bailey's charge that Quincy had been unduly parsimonious in dealing with the city's schools, on the other the *Boston Patriot* characterized his administration as one of "Aggression and expense." Yet, as a contributor to the *Patriot* implied, it was not anger with the mayor's aggressions or his expenses but public weariness that gave his opponents the most hope; after nearly six years of witnessing his exertions, Quincy's Boston had become "this poor exhausted body politic."[43]

An election-day broadside circulated throughout Boston, entitled *Look to Your Interest*, clearly reflected the Jacksonian coat-tail aspect of the campaign against Quincy. Among other things, it charged the mayor with intentionally increasing the city debt "to furnish a safe and convenient investment for a few rich individuals . . . very agreeable to them, as the United States debt was to be paid off." More blatantly appealing to the Jacksonian animus was the manner in which the broadside exploited the school issue:

Has the conduct of the mayor in relation to Schools been such as to meet the public approbation? What think you of the expression used in relation to the High School for Girls? to wit: '*If this School is continued, by and by, the education of our servant girls will be equal to that of our daughters, and perhaps enable them to force connections with our sons!*'

Quincy's earlier use of demagoguery pales before this thoroughly professional performance.[44]

Yet even on election day the mayor's opponents lacked an acceptable alternative and were obliged to call upon the voters to support "any opposing candidate, with the fullest assurance, that almost any change will advance the best interests of the city." At two separate caucuses held that morning, the names of Thomas C. Amory, nominated by disgruntled elements in the fire department, and Charles Wells, described by the *Boston Patriot* as "a self-made man" and apparently the Republican party's candidate, were entered to challenge the incumbent. Between them they managed to poll enough of the more than 4,000 votes cast to deny Quincy a majority by 83 votes.[45]

A run-off election was scheduled for December 15. Quincy decided to await the results of the reballoting rather than resign as he had in 1822. His supporters assured him that additional votes would be forthcoming, while the *Columbian Centinel* and *Daily Advertiser*, silent before the first poll, now vigorously called for the mayor's reelection. On December 12 a public meeting of "Friends of Quincy," chaired by William Sturgis, was held, but young Charles Francis Adams found it to be "a tame affair." Dr. George Shattuck wrote to his son on the eve of the second balloting:

The people of this wise city who are always bustling about something are about gone half mad because the time has come that they must choose a mayor now though Mr. Quincy has served them most faithfully for five years. They have made the astonishing discovery that he is not perfect. At any rate they are determined to change, at least some of them such as never know when they are well off.[46]

The second balloting duplicated the first, even to the campaign literature circulated outside the polls. "Look at Mr. Quincy's overbearing and imperious manner," the broadside *Worse and Worse* !! admonished, "look at his haughty and anti-republican manners to Citizens generally; and then say whether you will vote for him." The mayor's critics, still without a candidate of their own, were out in force and again denied him a majority, this time by 66 votes. He then withdrew. A week later, Harrison Gray Otis, who had refused to stand as long as Quincy remained in the running, was elected mayor without opposition.[47]

Less surprising than the fact that Bostonians eventually turned Quincy out was the fact that they waited so long to do so. When William Sullivan defended the powers given to the mayor's office in the city charter as proposed in 1822, he assured those townsmen fearful of an overly vigorous executive that if any mayor "did his duty, he will not be reelected." Though Quincy was nothing if not vigorous, his forbearing electorate proved Sullivan wrong on five successive occasions. During those five and one-half years he guided Boston through the difficult transition from town to city, effected needed reforms in public health and public relief, fire prevention and vice control. Administrative procedures established by him remained essentially unchanged until the 1880's when a new city charter permitted, as he had advocated, still greater centralization of municipal powers.[48]

When his tenure ended, Boston was very likely the cleanest, most orderly, and best governed city in the United States. The defeat saddened him, but he accepted it gracefully, even proudly. "I know well that recent events have given rise, in some minds, to reflections on the fickleness of the popular will," he stated in his farewell remarks:

As if the right to change was not as inherent as the right to continue. . . . As if permission to serve a people at all, and the opportunity thus afforded to be useful to the community to which we belong and owe so many obligations, were not ample recompense for any labors or any sacrifices made or endured in its behalf.[49]

Quincy's opportunities "to be useful to the community" did not end with his mayoral career. At the age of fifty-six, more than a third of his life and many years of public service lay ahead. But never again would he feel the dissatisfaction with himself that had dogged him before becoming mayor. By his efforts in that office he had merited the grateful recognition both of his contemporaries and of later Bostonians who would look back on him as "the Great Mayor." He had achieved what he expected of a Quincy; whatever might follow could not detract from this.[50]

8 / The Making of a Schoolmaster

If we can ever have a university at Cambridge, which shall lead the intellectual character of the country, it can be I apprehend only when the present college shall have settled into a thorough and well disciplined high school.

— George Ticknor, 1821

Writing in the fall of 1829 to an English acquaintance, Boston's ex-mayor described his new circumstances:

I had not been free of the City employ a month, before I was invited to the office of President of Harvard University. . . . This offer I did not think myself at liberty to decline particularly as on many accounts it suited the general turn of my habits and mind.

Nor had four months in Cambridge caused him to doubt the wisdom of his decision.

The office . . . is altogether one of general superintendence, not involving me in the business of instruction, unless I voluntarily assume it, and leaving me at great leisure, hereafter, for general pursuits. It also being an office independent of the popular voice and held 'during good behavior,' it is perhaps, upon the whole, one of the most eligible as well as honorable situations in our country.

Sixteen years would provide ample time to compare these sanguine expectations with the realities of academic life in Jacksonian America.[1]

The Augustan Age

By virtually any criterion—financial solvency, student enrollment, faculty morale, educational offering, public reputation—Harvard during the 1820's was in serious trouble. Not since the late seventeenth century had friends more cause to fear for its future or enemies to exult about its imminent demise. The situation was made to seem gloomier still by contrast to the bright prospects which had been envisioned only a decade earlier.[2]

Writing in the *North American Review* in 1818, the Rev. John Thornton Kirkland proposed that the institution over which he had presided since 1810 should become nothing less than "a university upon the extended plan." Harvard would continue to prepare young men for the ministry, medicine, and the law, but beyond this he wished it to become the institutional locus for the "formation of the national character, and the elevation of the national spirit, the encouragement or rather gathering together,—the creating of the literary profession among us." After carefully distinguishing between the work of instructing undergraduates and contributing "to the intellectual wealth of the world," Kirkland concluded by implying that all Harvard lacked to transform itself into a university "after the most approved establishments of the kind in Europe" was the return of his academic emissaries from what one of them called "the holy land of the scholar."[3]

On April 16, 1815, George Ticknor and Edward Everett had sailed for Europe. There the twenty-four year old Dartmouth graduate whose literary inclinations had soured him on the law, and the twenty-one year old Harvard professor designate who had just resigned from the ministry, spent more than three years traveling, studying, and being lionized by salon society. Everett remained at Göttingen long enough to acquire a Ph.D., while Ticknor, after taking an early dislike to German universities and being notified in 1816 of his election as Harvard's Smith Professor of Modern Languages, transferred his studies to France, Italy, and Spain. In 1818 they were joined by two other aspiring scholars with Harvard connections: Joseph Green Cogswell, a former Latin tutor, and George Bancroft, an 1817 graduate of the college who came to Europe under the aegis of a Kirkland scholarship. All four viewed their undertaking with utmost seriousness and none was unduly modest about his probable impact, either on Harvard or on the country at large. When Ticknor and Everett prepared to leave Europe in 1818 to take up their professorial duties in Cambridge, Cogswell, who was to remain for another year, wrote that they should be welcomed back "as Plato was at Athens when he had finished his travels and began to impart the fruits of these to his countrymen in the groves of the academy."[4]

Scholarly pretensions were only one measure of Harvard's apparent vitality during the early Kirkland years. Financial solvency was another. A "public" institution in that its charter was an integral part of the Massachusetts Constitution and elected state officials dominated its Board of Overseers, Harvard had on several occasions been the recipient of legislative grants for specific projects. Although a coalition of Republicans and Calvinists had attempted to disrupt the comfortable relations which the Unitarian-controlled Harvard Corporation enjoyed with the state, by 1814 the General Court was again in the control of friendly Federalists. In that year the legislature passed "An Act for the encouragement of literature, piety, morality, and the useful arts and sciences," which made Harvard the principal beneficiary of a ten-year tax on state banks. When one considers that the total expenses of the college in 1812 were less than $63,000, this annual grant of $10,000 constituted a considerable windfall.[5]

The state money was quickly put to use. Holworthy and University Halls were completed and the Yard spruced up; faculty salaries were increased and a scholarship fund established. The heretofore nomadic medical school acquired permanent quarters in Boston while schools of law and of divinity opened in Cambridge. More importantly, the Commonwealth's generosity seems to have stimulated private endowments as Harvard alumni funneled an impressive portion of their wartime profits into new professorships. During Kirkland's first seven years as president fifteen chairs were established, nine of them in the college where previously there had been only four. Certainly contributing to the belief that Harvard was on the verge of becoming a genuine university was its apparent possession of the financial resources to do so.[6]

Enrollment statistics provide an important index of institutional health in an era when student fees were virtually the only source of operating income for American colleges. In the first eight years of Kirkland's administration, enrollments more than doubled; by 1818, with nearly three hundred students, Harvard again became the largest college in the country, a distinction it had lost to Yale in the 1790's. The student body grew not only larger but more cosmopolitan. Before 1810 ninety percent came from New England, the vast majority from within thirty miles of Cambridge; ten years later more than a quarter came from outside New England, most of them from the South.[7]

Kirkland's personality unquestionably contributed to the feeling of prosperity at Harvard during his early years as president. The son of an Indian missionary, he had attended Phillips Academy as a charity student before going on to Harvard in the same situation.

Following graduation in 1789 and a brief stint as a Latin tutor, he quickly moved into the upper reaches of Boston society as a spiritual counselor. In 1793, at twenty-three, he became minister of the theologically liberal, politically conservative, and socially prestigious New South Church. Affable and modest, the young bachelor got along well with the businessmen in his congregation and famously, Emerson later mischievously recalled, with their wives.[8]

When Harvard's President Joseph Willard died in 1804 and Fisher Ames declined the post, Kirkland became Boston's choice. The Corporation, fearful of exacerbating already strained relations with the Calvinist ministry by naming a Unitarian president, chose instead Samuel Webber, an ordained faculty member of indeterminate theological persuasion. Six years later, however, when Webber died in office, the Corporation overcame its earlier squeamishness and on August 10, 1810, unanimously elected the forty-year-old Kirkland Harvard's fourteenth president.[9]

Though officially residing in Cambridge, President Kirkland seldom permitted his duties to interfere with his thriving social life on the other side of the Charles River. Four days a week for seventeen years he could be seen crossing the West Boston Bridge about noon, arriving in the capital in time to dine with his patron and ex-parishioner, George Cabot, or with close friends and Corporation Fellows, Theophilus Parsons and John Lowell. These almost daily respites from the adolescent clamor of the Yard preserved his irenic disposition, though their effect on the college was less positive. When afternoon chapel back in Cambridge began to impinge on his increasingly protracted Boston visits he recommended that it be dispensed with.[10]

For a few years he was able by indulging the students to make up for what he lacked in attentiveness to the problems of the college. His tolerance of adolescent foibles and excesses was legend, his capacity for empathy was boundless. Many an overextended undergraduate found him generous with his own funds and prodigal with those of the college; all honored him for his "improvident virtues." "If not one of the greatest presidents of Harvard College," Samuel Eliot Morison has written of Kirkland, "he was certainly the best beloved." The Rev. John Pierce, Kirkland's eulogist, agreed that he "was very generally loved—even by the dissolute and unprincipled."[11]

That very adulation highlighted Kirkland's principal failing. It was one thing to be regularly toasted by the undergraduates and wished "a wife to tuck him up warm," another to maintain authority over the toasters. Increasingly during his tenure, hell-raising and the almost complete repudiation of parietal authority came to characterize student life in Cambridge. A typical Harvard undergraduate's existence was described in 1818 as one of indolence and dissipation.

The time not spent at the classes, is divided between eating and drinking, smoking and sleeping. Approach the door of one of their apartments at any hour of the day, you will be driven back from it, as you would from the cabin of a Dutch Smack, by the thick volume of stinking tobacco smoke which it sends forth; should you dare enter, you would find half a dozen loungers in a state of oriental lethargy, each stretched out upon two or three chairs, with scarce any other indication of life in them than the feeble effort they make to keep up the fire of their *cigarrs*.

Not all their time was spent smoking "cigarrs" in their rooms; during a six-month period in 1821 twenty-six cases of venereal disease among Harvard students were reported.[12]

During the Kirkland era social clubs like Porcellian and Hasty Pudding came into their own, their alcoholic and occasionally literary activities taking precedence over official college functions. Secret organizations committed to nothing nobler than disturbing the peace flourished, while the popularity of "blowing clubs" suggests that undergraduates thought more of their nightly entertainment than of scholarly pursuits. Students organized by class and, challenging the college authorities in "combinations," began exercising an authority of their own, blacklisting and ostracizing any classmate who informed on them. Tutors and even professors were routed out of their beds, their rooms destroyed, their persons threatened, but no one came forward to identify the culprits. Other colleges had their uncontrollable students, chapel explosions, and physical assaults on instructors, to such an extent that the situation at most pre-Civil War colleges has been described as one of "autocracy tempered by rebellion." At Harvard it was the reverse.[13]

Many factors, not peculiar to Harvard, contributed to the general rambunctiousness of early nineteenth-century college students. In part it was a function of the age at which they matriculated. Harvard, like other colleges, accepted students as young as twelve years old; given the competition among the proliferating institutions and the small, perhaps even declining number of boys interested in college, there was no alternative. In the absence of organized sports adolescent energies went into planning and executing the era's epic inter-class battles. Some observers thought student rebelliousness reflected the nation's traditional anti-authoritarianism. "The docility of an American youth," Joseph Cogswell wrote in 1818, "is not increased by the early and often wild notions of liberty he acquires. . . . College," he added, "is looked forward to by most of them as the time when the shackles of a master's and a parent's authority are thrown off, and that of freedom to commence." Still others, like George Ticknor, believed students rebelled because they were bored with a lock-step curriculum and daily recitations and pedantic instructors.[14]

Conceding all this, the responsibility for Harvard's disciplinary problems rested principally with Kirkland and his unwillingness to exercise his legitimate authority. Rarely did he expel a student. Occasionally he resorted to suspensions but more often he merely "rusticated" (suspended for six weeks under the authority of an appointed tutor away from Cambridge) or fined his unruly charges. Early in his tenure he successfully quelled an incipient rebellion by preaching to the students on the text, "O my son Absalom! would God I had died for thee!," but later, in a similar situation, his use of Matthew, "Do unto others as you would that others do unto you," proved ineffective.[15]

Evidence began accumulating early in his administration that Kirkland's failure to exercise control over the undergraduates was having an adverse effect on the reputation of the college. "Tis said that your Principal and Professors take a pride in the extravagance of the students and encourage it," John Randolph reported from Virginia in 1813, "whilst Yale zealously inculcates the sublime truths of Poor Richard's Almanac." New England Calvinist publications, particularly Jedidiah Morse's *Panoplist*, freely circulated reports of carousing in Cambridge as proof that Harvard's morals had deteriorated since it had cast off orthodoxy. Boys who earlier would have gone there were being advised by their ministers, many of them Harvard alumni, to go to places less costly, less scandalous, and doctrinally more sound: Bowdoin, Williams, and Yale. Midway through Kirkland's presidency enrollments began dropping; by 1820 Yale again forged ahead of Harvard, this time not to be headed for thirty years. "I regret to report that the general opinion in this part of the country is unfavorable to the college," a New Hampshire alumnus wrote in 1821, "on the score of morals and discipline. Such an opinion began to prevail five or six years ago, and has constantly been gaining ground."[16]

Yet another consequence of Kirkland's laxity was that the parietal burden fell wholly on the resident faculty, thereby reducing their effectiveness as teachers and the time available for their own pursuits. No wonder the Corporation found it impossible to induce the linguist John Pickering to give up his law practice and accept a professorship; he got far more scholarly work done in his Boston office than he would have in the riotous Harvard Yard. "Do not suffer these children so to monopolize your time and strength," one harried tutor admonished himself in 1815, "as to enfeeble the one, and deprive the other of enjoyment. It cannot, cannot be duty."[17]

Of the four European-trained scholars who returned to Harvard between 1819 and 1822, only Ticknor remained in 1824. Bancroft had lasted one year, a confessed failure in his efforts to inspire a love of Greek among his students. Instead, he so alienated them that he was the victim of almost daily classroom disruptions and nightly window-smashings. Cogswell lasted two years, complaining all the while that his assigned duties "might as well be performed by any shop boy." Everett stayed for five years, but from the first week of his return spent most of his time trying to get exempted from the faculty-residency requirement and seeking more "respectable" employment. "I have found College a sickening and wearisome place," Bancroft wrote in 1823, reflecting the sentiments of all three, "not one spring of comfort have I had to draw from. My state has been nothing but trouble, trouble, trouble, and I am heartily glad that the end of the year is coming so soon."[18]

Those faculty members who became permanent fixtures—Henry Ware, Sidney Willard, Levi Hedge, and John Snelling Popkin—were men of modest accomplishments. Edward Tyrrel Channing, Professor of Rhetoric and Oratory, stands virtually alone in the Kirkland era as a Harvard professor remembered as a great teacher, though he too produced little in the way of scholarship. More typical was Sidney Willard, Hancock Professor of Hebrew, who described himself as "a permanent instructor of youth" and took grim pride in having no time "to make it his business . . . to furnish himself with literary and scientific knowledge." In response to the charge that his colleagues were "leading a life of ease," he boasted that they "are generally employed with their classes to the exclusion of great literary undertakings, to which their choices might lead them." Not surprisingly, the botanist Thomas Nuttall, a Harvard instructor in the early 1820's, dismissed his years there as "vegetating" and "doing nothing for science." Whatever enthusiasm, scholarly or otherwise, men like Popkin, Professor of Greek (1815-1833), had was soon dried up by the monotony of their duties and being made the continual butt of undergraduate pranks. Rather than teach they became "verbal drillmasters," who, as Popkin did, obliged students "to wade through Homer as though the *Iliad* were a bog, and it was our duty to get along at such a rate *per diem.*"[19]

Only George Ticknor avoided the *vis inertiae* that Emerson thought pervaded the Harvard faculty, but he was the exception. His continuing interest in reforming Harvard's discipline and teaching was inversely related to his involvement in either. By the stipulations of his Smith professorship he was, unlike other faculty members, exempted from the residency requirement, parietal responsibilities, and daily recitations. Living in Boston and coming to Cambridge infrequently to deliver a formal lecture or supervise the instruction of modern languages, he remained to his colleagues during his seventeen years on the faculty an "outsider."[20]

In the summer of 1821 Ticknor began trying to persuade the Corporation to institute reforms along two fronts: curriculum and discipline. By recommending that limited electives be permitted in some subjects, particularly in modern languages, he hoped to break up the lock-step curriculum and to add variety to its heavily classical orientation. He also favored grouping students according to proficiency rather than alphabetically by class as was the prevailing practice. Similarly, other changes which he advocated—a longer, less frequently interrupted school year, teaching by subjects rather than books, written examinations, and formal lectures in place of daily recitations—were all designed to make Harvard "a school where the instruction shall be thorough."[21]

Of more immediate concern to Ticknor, however, was that "discipline be exact." Indeed, at times he seemed to argue that curricular reform was a means of achieving the more important end of disciplinary reform. This was most apparent in his plan to group students according to proficiency. Often described as Harvard's early

champion of the European university system, he was far more enamored of the regimentation of West Point than of the *Lernfreiheit* of
Göttingen. "If we can ever have a University at Cambridge, which shall
lead the intellectual character of the country," he advised Corporation
Fellow William Prescott in 1821, citing the Military Academy as his
model, "it can be I apprehend only when the present college shall
have settled into a thorough and well-disciplined high school."[22]

To this end Ticknor made several specific recommendations. The
first and most sweeping was that Harvard students be confined to
Cambridge even on weekends and to the Yard after dark. Nine
o'clock bed-checks were proposed as the mechanism by which
compliance with the prohibition against going over to Boston would
be assured. As a further check he suggested sumptuary regulations
which would oblige the students to wear easily recognizable uniforms
and would limit their spending money. Ticknor also called for the
establishment of a three-man tribunal, composed of faculty members, which would be empowered to dismiss "without trial or
assigned cause" any student it suspected of failing to fulfill "the
purposes for which he came to college." "In this perfectly arbitrary
power, and its constant and free exercise," argued the ex-lawyer
calmly, "are to be found the only means of supplying the place of
parental authority, and maintaining constant discipline in College
over a large body of boys and young men."[23]

While Ticknor's proposals slowly circulated among the Corporation, a veneer of complacency continued to hide Harvard's declining
fortunes from all but its closest observers. Then within a period of
eight months, in two closely related events, that veneer was peeled
off and the troubles in Cambridge laid bare. The first episode
occurred on May 2, 1823, when President Kirkland, six weeks before
Commencement, announced the dismissal of forty-three of the
seventy-member senior class. The incidents that forced this action,
initiated by a dispute between the class and one of its dissident
members, could have been avoided had Kirkland interceded earlier.
At least that was how one irate father of an expelled senior,
Secretary of State John Quincy Adams, viewed it.[24]

The second event, following hard on the adverse publicity attending the dismissals and the election for the first time in a decade of a
Democratic governor and lower house, was the General Court's

announcement in February 1824 that it would not renew the state grant about to expire. Harvard had already received $95,000 from the Commonwealth, $25,000 of which had been mandated and used for scholarships. Yet the capital expenditures of the college during the years of the grant far exceeded the $70,000 balance, University Hall alone costing $64,000. "University funds have been so reduced," pleaded the Corporation, "that the usual expenses for the support of the institution and its various officers cannot be sustained without a continuance of such aid." The legislators were unmoved, intimating that they would never again underwrite the riotous goings-on over in Cambridge. "It was formerly the pride and the care of the state," Andrews Norton wrote sadly but accurately of his *alma mater.* "It is now doubtful whether a majority of the inhabitants of the state do not view it with jealousy, hostility or indifference."[25]

The definitive rejection by the college's largest benefactor could not have come at a worse time. Enrollments had been dropping steadily since 1820; now Harvard suddenly found itself without the scholarship funds it had depended upon for a decade to attract and retain a sizable student body. In 1826, with a freshman class of thirty-six, for the first time since the 1790's the total number of students dropped below two hundred. This meant reduced receipts from fees in addition to an operating deficit of $4,000 which would have to be covered from the endowment. When a New England institution starts spending its capital, matters are indeed serious.[26]

Retrenchment and reform were clearly in order. The problem was how to implement them. While the Corporation and the Overseers quickly approved most of Ticknor's proposals, incorporating them in the 1825 *Statutes of Harvard University*, the resident faculty objected. Already overworked, underpaid, and generally put upon, the heretofore quiescent faculty, fearful that changes were about to be made at their expense, temporarily roused themselves in 1824. Eleven of the twelve resident faculty members, led by Edward Everett, seized upon a vacancy on the Corporation to assert their claim to representation. Theirs was an old argument, first raised during the Leverett administration a century before, based on the contention that all members ("Fellows") of the Corporation must reside in the college. But John Lowell, speaking for the Corporation, showed how little they thought of the faculty claim when he bluntly told the professors to confine themselves "to the pleasant duties of the classroom" and leave "the real and personal estate of the college" to those who "see it in the best and clearest light."[27]

Rebuffed in their attempt to gain a voice in the governance of the college, the faculty succeeded in displaying their negative power by thwarting nearly all of Ticknor's reforms. The fact that he had close social ties with the Corporation and had opposed their claims to representation was not lost on his colleagues in Cambridge. Nor was the fact that the parietal responsibilities as expanded in the new Statutes fell on them, not him. In addition, the proposed academic changes threatened to upset the personal accommodations they had long since made with the archaic but familiar curriculum. To Popkin, the encouragement of modern languages smacked of utilitarianism and challenged the supremacy of the classics. Finally, the faculty sided with the students in opposing grouping-by-proficiency as destructive of class loyalties and tending to stimulate unhealthy competition. Although they did not say so, it would also have put them on their mettle.[28]

On each of these issues Kirkland went along with the faculty. When individual instructors began sabotaging the curricular reforms authorized by the Statutes, they depended on him, if not to support their efforts, at least to ignore them. Of all those officially involved in Harvard affairs, he seems to have been least distressed by the events of 1823 and 1824. Forced to expel more than half the Class of 1823, he then proceeded to recommend several of them for law school in glowing terms! His attitude about college funds, which he dispensed without even bothering to ascertain their existence, remained casual as ever. In this he was abetted by his old friend, John C. Davis, who had managed Harvard's finances during the state-grant years without recourse to bookkeeping.[29]

That left only the Corporation to deal with the manifold crisis besetting Harvard. Fortunately for the college, four resignations in 1825-1826 permitted committed reformers Joseph Story and Nathaniel Bowditch, both long active on the Board of Overseers, Francis Calley Gray and Charles Jackson to move on to the Corporation and take charge of its tangled affairs. While Story concentrated on the curriculum, Bowditch tended to more immediate matters. His first action, after discovering that Davis' accounts consisted of little more than a notebook and some entries made on the backs of envelopes, was to force his resignation. It took a full-time clerk six months to reconstruct the financial history of the college since 1810 and to reconcile a cumulative error of $100,000.[30]

In Davis' place, Bowditch secured the election of a Salem businessman, Ebenezer Francis. Although neither Bowditch nor Francis was an alumnus—a fact that distressed Edward Everett and Ralph Waldo Emerson—they almost singlehandedly saved Harvard from financial collapse by imposing a rigid austerity program. Beginning in 1826 faculty salaries were cut twenty percent; professorships were consolidated, left vacant, and in four instances eliminated. Operating expenses were cut to the bone and for the first time since 1810 college provisioners found their bills being scrutinized.[31]

Bowditch, a gruff, humorless man, an autodidact and a successful businessman who did not suffer fools gladly, went about his economizing duties "with the zeal of an apostle." Eliza Susan Quincy, altering the metaphor slightly, remembered him "as the Martin Luther of Harvard College." It was only a matter of time before he and the genial Kirkland would clash. "The President," Bowditch wrote, in what for him was a grave indictment, "is no businessman."[32]

Kirkland in turn ignored Bowditch and carried on much as before, only, if possible, a bit more distractedly. A mild stroke in the summer of 1827, and his marriage that fall, at fifty-eight, into the Cabot family, cost him whatever interest he had in the college. During the winter of 1827-1828 he absented himself from several Corporation meetings, thereby infuriating Bowditch who valued punctuality more highly than conviviality. Finally, at a Corporation meeting on March 27, 1828, Bowditch told the president what he thought of him and his administration. The next day Kirkland resigned, thus bringing Harvard's Augustan Age to an ill-tempered close.[33]

There's a President for You

It took the Corporation eight months to find a new president. Story and Bowditch both proposed Ticknor but others, like Charles Jackson, were less than enthusiastic about him. As one of Ticknor's warmest supporters acknowledged, "the public would not swallow such a potion." His *Remarks on Changes Lately Proposed or Adopted in Harvard University* (1825), as well as his widely circulated critique of Kirkland's 1827 *Report*, had offended many of the president's well-placed friends. It was generally known that Ticknor was unacceptable to the resident faculty. Moreover, not even the most concerned alumnus enjoyed being told by a Dartmouth graduate that his college's "reputation compared with that of other institutions has been for many years suffering and is now seriously impaired." As for his habit of comparing Harvard unfavorably with the Military Academy, John Lowell once told him bluntly, "I would as soon send my son to a brothel, as I would send him to West Point."[34]

Ralph Waldo Emerson, still intoxicated by his undergraduate exposure to "our Cicero," thought Edward Everett the obvious choice. Nor was he alone in this preference. Among the leading Everett-boosters was the mayor of Boston. "Other names have been mentioned," Everett's father-in-law wrote only two weeks after Kirkland's resignation, "but Mr. Q. thinks none of them will do. . . . Mr. Ticknor, he said, was rather a particular friend and acquaintance of his—but he had still been frank and open in his opinion that you are the man."[35]

Though gratified by the vote of confidence, Everett knew Harvard well enough to know that he wanted no part of its presidency. "The academic life," he told Brooks, "presents fewer attractions to a man of letters than you probably think." Now in his second term in Congress and his future in politics hopeful, Everett refused to have "his spirits exhausted and his facilities scattered," as he believed Kirkland had, "by a succession of petty causes and business details." Moreover, he doubted that his constitution could survive another tour in Cambridge.

I assure you that my share of the gov't of College, as a professor, often gave me more anxiety, than I have ever encountered as a member of Congress. In the latter capacity I have never lost 1/4 of an hour's sleep. In the former, I had my digestion destroyed for a week altogether, by intense anxiety.

Everett's bearish estimate of the Harvard presidency did not prevent him from recommending that it be given to his older and as yet unemployed brother, Alexander Hill Everett.[36]

Several Harvard faculty members were cited in the press, along with Ticknor and the two Everetts, as worthy of the presidency. But the names of these "mere bookmen [who] understand but little about business" were quickly passed over by the Corporation. A number of Unitarian ministers were also mentioned, though here too the Corporation seemed more prepared to break with the tradition of electing an ordained minister than run the risk of another Kirkland. "I am ag't a clergyman," Joseph Story announced early in the canvass, and that was that.[37]

As the search continued the Corporation became more precise in what they wanted in Harvard's next president. "The place requires a man with powers of administration, and government, and knowledge of character, and competent to a vigorous supervision of all subordinate functionaries," Story persuaded his fellow members. Not a minister, not a scholar, and not necessarily someone with teaching experience; what was needed was a vigorous executive of demonstrated competence. "He is not to scan the shrouds, nor to go out in the boat," Story wrote, "but to stand at the helm and look at the needle." Unfortunately, such captains were in short supply and 1828 drew to a close with the billet unfilled.[38]

"There's a President for you," Mrs. Bowditch informed her husband after learning that Quincy had withdrawn from the mayoral race. Bowditch, who was a friend of Quincy and like him an unreconstructed Federalist, snapped up his wife's suggestion and immediately polled the rest of the Corporation. Exasperated by their fruitless search and worried about letting the college muddle along without a president, they seized upon the new candidate, whom they all knew personally, with enthusiasm and relief.[39]

Bowditch approached Quincy even before he vacated his municipal office, and found him hesitant but interested. Hale and hearty at fifty-seven, he had no immediate plans and clearly did not intend to retire from public life. Friends were already expressing concern that "our former mayor will want occupation for the moment—a condition of all others the most insupportable to him." The Harvard presidency impressed him as a less strenuous office than the one he was vacating, which after nearly six years had become "on many accounts irksome as well as attended with great responsibility." After convincing Mrs. Quincy that her sizable family could be accommodated in Cambridge, Bowditch received permission to present Quincy's name formally to the Corporation. On January 15, 1829, less than two weeks after relinquishing the Boston mayoralty, Josiah Quincy was unanimously elected the fifteenth president of Harvard University, contingent upon the Overseers' approval.[40]

The announcement caught many by surprise. Edward Everett, who as late as January 8 thought his brother would be chosen, complained bitterly of what he called the Corporation's precipitancy. "I think Mr. Quincy's nomination ought to be negatived," he wrote to a member of the Board of Overseers which had yet to approve the Corporation's selection. "It is a very hasty act . . . after nine months deliberation, in which I venture to say that he was thought of as a candidate by no living man." While Everett might have had a point in faulting the Corporation for a hurried decision, his charge that Quincy "did not possess the requisite qualifications" was equally true of Alexander Everett. As for his singular qualifications, Ann Gilman Storrow, who had originally favored Ticknor, stated them admirably:

I believe Mr. Quincy is a high-minded, honourable, independent man, and I do not believe he will follow anybody's lead. He lacks judgement they say, and the poor man is subject to fits of abstraction, and occasionally he is taken with a metaphor, whereupon he gets stuck. But what of all that? He is very handsome, and remarkably agreeable, and as honest as the day. Is he not fit for President, with these qualifications?[41]

Except for the rabidly Republican *Boston Recorder*, Quincy's election evoked surprisingly little opposition from the press. On January 29 the Board of Overseers approved the Corporation's choice by a vote of forty to twenty-six, the negatives coming from Republican or Calvinist state senators who served *ex officio* on the board. Despairing alumni like Dr. George Shattuck took heart, hoping that "under Mr. Quincy Harvard will attain her ancient rank." Even the *Boston Courier*, a violent critic of Quincy as mayor, gave him an endorsement of sorts. "We shall be disappointed indeed, if under the administration of the new president," it editorialized, "there does not grow up a system of industry, economy, and order, where for half a century there has been nothing but *improvidence, laziness, prejudice*, and *rottenness*."[42]

Prior to his election as president Quincy had given little thought to academic life. His interest in Harvard was that of loyal alumnus, occasional benefactor, and father of two undergraduates. His election to the Board of Overseers in 1810, when laymen were first eligible, was due to his political prominence. Even as an overseer he was not among those who actually set policy in Cambridge. So preoccupied had he been during the 1820's with municipal affairs that Bowditch's rendering of the state of the college in December 1828 came as a rueful revelation. "There has been a great deal wasted and lost at Cambridge," Bowditch told him, "but there is noble property left." The presidency of Harvard then, as his acceptance statement to the overseers indicated, was seen as another job that needed doing: "I recognize the right of society to command my services; and I accept the appointment, as a duty, which I have no authority to decline."[43]

Quincy began preparing for his presidential responsibilities by immediately undertaking a five-week tour of eastern colleges. Along the way he hoped to give himself a cram course in academic administration. New Haven was his first stop. Harvard's president-elect might be new to the problems of collegiate life, but Yale's President Jeremiah Day was decidedly not. Like most American colleges in the 1820's, Day's Yale had received its share of public scrutiny, some in the form of an investigation by the Connecticut legislature, which concluded that its curriculum "must be new-modelled . . . , adopted to the spirits and wants of the age," and better accommodated "to the business of the nation." Criticism had focused on the prominence of Greek and Latin in the prescribed curriculum which left little room for modern languages and none for vocational courses. But unlike other colleges, Yale had decided to answer its critics.[44]

The Yale Report of 1828, largely the work of President Day, was a ringing endorsement of the academic *status quo*. In a clearly argued statement, it presented an impressive defense of the centrality of classical studies by demonstrating how they successfully, and economically, provided what any college curriculum should: "the *discipline* and the *furniture* of the mind." The report insisted that the former, best acquired by heavy doses of Greek and Latin, ought to have priority over the latter. The fact that Greek and Latin were "dead languages," or that students disliked studying them, only enhanced their disciplinary value, whereas the study of modern languages was lacking in sufficient rigor. Also defended were daily recitations, study of particular books rather than subjects, and the prohibition of vocational courses. In summary, all was thought to be well in New Haven and, by implication, at any other American college where the traditional classical curriculum persisted.[45]

Quincy was impressed. Himself a serious student of the classics

and long persuaded that they provided "the sure and solid founda-
tion, on which you may, in after life, build whatsoever intellectual
frame you will," he departed New Haven with all his conservative
suspicions about curricular innovations confirmed. This was unfortunate as these suspicions would later prove difficult to exorcise. A
more positive outcome of his academic grand tour, however, was his
resultant conviction that an effective educational program, whether
traditional or innovative, must wait upon the establishment of a
sound system of discipline. Visits to Columbia and the University of
Pennsylvania, both of which had been having difficulties with unruly
students, convinced Quincy to ignore Day's misgivings and to handle
all of Harvard's disciplinary problems personally.[46]

Inaugural ceremonies began on the morning of June 2, 1829, with
an academic procession, followed by a felicitous Latin exchange
between Governor Levi Lincoln and the new president, and then by
the Inaugural Address. After praising his predecessor, Quincy assured
his audience that he would "adopt innovations with great caution."
The *Boston Courier* thought the speech manly in style and conservative in content, and worthy of Burke on both counts. Later that
evening, the students, on their best behavior, illuminated the windows of Holworthy and Hollis Halls, spelling out "KIRKLAND" and
"QUINCY." It was an auspicious if cautious beginning.[47]

After settling his family into Wadsworth House, Quincy began to
make his executive presence felt. His first project was to standardize
the chaotic grading system he had inherited. Under Kirkland,
instructors devised their own grading schemes and reported only the
final results to the president, a practice that was both confusing and
open to charges of partiality. After examining how his predecessor
had handled this ticklish matter, Quincy concluded that Kirkland's
"had been a government of favoritism but should be no longer." The
new president's solution was to institute "The Scale of Comparative
Merit," a complicated, multi-weighted system by which points in
multiples of eight were awarded or denied for virtually every move
made by an undergraduate during his four years in Cambridge. Total
possible point accumulation was 29,920! Each instructor submitted
daily reports to Quincy who insisted on keeping the ledgers himself,
in his effort to eliminate the possibility of faculty collusion and to
keep informed of each student's performance.[48]

The new grading system had other drawbacks in addition to its cumbrousness. Instructors were saddled with even more in-class bookkeeping than previously, scholastic performance was confounded with deportment, and, because the system assumed daily recitations and a uniform program, it proved an obstacle to opening up the curriculum and instituting lectures as part of the regular academic fare. Nonetheless, it put to rest charges of favoritism and reflected at least implicit support of the grouping-by-proficiency reform. For Quincy it constituted an important first step in bringing both the academic and disciplinary affairs of the college under his personal control. Anyone familiar with his centralizing proclivities as mayor should have expected as much.[49]

Predictably, the ranking system did not sit well with those being ranked. Students believed, not entirely without cause, that it was intended to generate "a spirit of ungenerous rivalry" within the classes. They were finding that they much preferred the old president's "charities which secured our hearts" to the business-like efficiency of his successor. But Quincy was less interested in securing his charges' love than their obedient respect. He did not, however, underestimate the obstacles he faced. "An age almost lawless from its love of liberty," he sadly noted in his Inaugural Address, "is calling for restraints to be taught and practiced here, which it neglects itself to teach and practice, and has no disposition to countenance elsewhere."[50]

While even Yale's kindly President Day acknowledged that "there may be perverse members of a college as well as a family," separating them out was no simple matter. Unless caught red-handed by a college officer, most campus criminals went undetected. "The esprit de corps was strongly against tale-bearing," one Harvard student of the 1830's recalled, "if anyone knew the offender, . . . he did not reveal it." Few undergraduates would risk even talking with an instructor outside of class for fear of being thought by his classmates an informer. Because of the lock-step curriculum and small classes, which enrolled never more than seventy during Quincy's era, loyalties quickly developed that were carried into later life. Lavish class dinners (the Class of 1835 ordered six gallons of whisky and rum for the forty members expected at their *freshman* banquet) further instilled a sense of common identity, to say nothing of communal inebriation. Class reputations were made not from academic ranking—an administrative matter dismissed as inconsequential—but by defiance of the faculty. Suspension was regarded not as a disgrace but rather as personal triumph, and assured a rousing reception upon the suspended student's return. Richard Henry Dana Jr., rusticated in 1832, revealed the prevailing student mores in a letter to a "dear ex-classmate": "I hear some of your relations in Cambridge say that you had nothing to do with our disturbances; If I were you, I would not let such a report, so much to my discredit, be circulated if I could help it."[5][1]

Some colleges, like the University of Pennsylvania, when confronted with collective assaults on its authority, simply gave up all responsibility for regulating the students' lives. Closing its dormitories and obliging students to secure their own room and board, the college authorities left all undergraduate violations of the law to the Philadelphia police. Yale was not willing to abandon its parietal responsibilities to that extent, but President Day readily admitted that there were some students "whom nothing but the arm of the law can reach." This same fatalism found expression in Cambridge, where on July 20, 1826, following a series of explosions in the dormitories, the Harvard Corporation directed President Kirkland to make use of "the proper civil tribunal" in future cases of student violations against "any person or property, which is cognizable by the Laws of the Land." Three weeks earlier, after Professor Popkin had been assaulted in the Yard, the faculty had asked the president to turn over uncooperative student witnesses to the Middlesex County grand jury where they would be obliged to testify under oath. But as long as "jolly old Kirkland" remained president, Harvard students knew that "being sent to Concord" was an idle threat.[5][2]

They could not be so sure with Kirkland's successor, whose reputation as a stern judge of the municipal court, vigorous enforcer of the licensing laws and scourge of Boston's prostitutes, had preceded him to Cambridge. If any doubt lingered on into the fall that Harvard was under new management, Quincy's first talk with the undergraduates erased it. After congratulating them generally on their good behavior, he went on to specify a number of recent lapses: the blowing up of a recitation room; the ransacking of the Cambridge armory for shells and powder which one student planned to use in blowing up the library; a short but destructive riot in commons; widespread pilferage and selling of library books. "Knowledge of the facts," he reminded his audience, "is not and can not be confined within the walls of the university. They are blazoned abroad."[5][3]

Quincy then proceeded to lay down the law as unanimously voted a week earlier by the Corporation:

In all cases of gross theft and depredations upon the property of the University or of others, or of gross trespasses or injuries done to persons or property within the precincts of the University, or charged upon any of its members, it shall be the duty of the President, first taking the advice of the faculty or Corporation, in that respect to cause prosecution to be instituted before the established tribunals of the state; and the usual forms of proceeding to be pursued which are applicable to like crimes and offenses when committed by other citizens or residents, according to the laws of the Commonwealth.

The Corporation had been brought to this decision, Quincy told the students, both because the faculty lacked the necessary coercive powers of the courts and because they were persuaded that the traditional exemption of undergraduates from criminal prosecution had the effect of licensing campus rowdiness. He described the new policy as "a Magna Charta for the young men of this seminary"; suspected students would now be able to prove their innocence before a judge, availing themselves fully of due process. The students, however, interpreted the Corporation's action as a unilateral change in the ancient rules of campus warfare.[54]

Whether momentarily intimidated or unusually phlegmatic, Harvard students declined to rise immediately to the challenge implicit in the new policy. Quincy's first year passed quietly. Not until the spring of 1831, when the faculty sent off a popular sophomore, George William Amory, for neglecting his studies, did a disturbance occur. Upon hearing of the dismissal, the sophomores expressed their disapproval by setting fire to Amory's vacated dormitory room and disrupting chapel services. The president first tried reasoning with them by reading a letter from Amory's father approving the faculty's decision, but this, "instead of silencing them as it *should have done*," a scandalized freshman reported, "made them more turbulent, and the confusion continued until the services were over."[55]

When a similar disturbance disrupted chapel services the next morning, Quincy announced that expulsions were in the offing. He further threatened to send the entire sophomore class to testify before the grand jury about the destruction of Amory's room. That terminated the disturbance, "the first serious difficulty President Quincy has met with."[56]

The following spring a more serious challenge to the president's authority occurred, this time from the freshman class. Augustus

Kendall Rugg, when summoned before the faculty to discuss his knowledge of events surrounding a recent dormitory explosion, refused to cooperate. Quincy then informed him that he would be sent to Concord where his testimony would be extracted under oath. Rugg's classmates, assuming he was covering for someone, rallied to his aid. "A meeting was called at which all the class but two or three very timid and mean spirited lads attended," Richard Henry Dana Jr. later recalled. "We passed resolutions that we would sustain our classmate and proceeded to act accordingly." Chapel services were disrupted for three days running and so complete was a boycott of classes that the faculty announced the cancellation of freshman classes for a week.[57]

What had begun to look like "an open Rebellion" suddenly fizzled when Rugg, thoroughly frightened by his imminent trip to Concord, confessed to Quincy that he was personally responsible for the dormitory explosion and that only the desire to save his own skin had prompted his earlier refusal to talk. He received a two-year suspension while Dana and seven other leaders of the freshman disturbances were rusticated for six weeks. "They went off," sophomore George Moore recorded, "amid the huzzas of the students," but Quincy had won round two. More importantly, it began to appear that, by invoking the threat of criminal prosecution, he had found the answer to student combinations.[58]

A Bone for Old Quin' to Pick

Except for a brief town-gown scuffle, which Quincy personally halted, Cambridge remained placid throughout the 1832-1833 academic year. The fall and winter terms that followed were uneventful. "College thus far this present year has been more calm and still than I ever knew it before," wrote Moore, now a somewhat restive senior, on March 8, 1834: "Everything goes on regularly—we scarce have a bonfire to vary the dull monotony of College life. I have some time thought that a rebellion, or some scrape would be a good thing for the sake of variety—but far be it from me to wish any such thing."[59]

Six weeks later, on Monday, May 19, a classroom disagreement arose between a freshman, John Bayard Maxwell, and his twenty-two year old Greek instructor, Christopher Dunkin. After declining Dunkin's invitation to recite and then refusing a directive to do so, Maxwell challenged the young instructor's authority to direct the class. He was promptly sent to the president who told the freshman that he must either apologize to Dunkin or give up his connections with the college. After weighing his options for two days, Maxwell decided Harvard was not worth an apology and quit.[60]

Such bravado evoked an immediate and sympathetic response from Maxwell's classmates. "Crackers were fired off in Chapel" following the announcement of his departure on Friday evening, "and a continuous noise by scraping and kicking kept up during the services." Later that night Dunkin's recitation room was set afire, the furniture shattered and thrown out into the Yard. On one of the room's walls was scrawled, "A Bone for Old Quin' to Pick." When two night watchmen tried to intervene, they were beaten. Chapel services all that weekend were disrupted by rampaging freshmen.[61]

On Monday, May 26, several sophomores joined the freshmen in causing another chapel disturbance. Their apparent reason for doing so, other than for the fun of it, also involved a classroom disagreement with Dunkin. The zealous instructor had decided earlier in the spring that Harvard sophomores ought to learn to write Greek as well as read it. His students immediately protested the assignment as onerous and unprecedented, and in a petition informed the president to that effect. Quincy rejected the petition with his opinion that writing Greek would not inflict permanent damage on either their health or college traditions. The sophomores had rejoined with their feet.[62]

Isolating the instigators of a disturbance in a room crowded with two hundred students and officers was not a simple matter, as the students well knew. But procedural difficulties notwithstanding, Quincy thought it imperative that he respond forcefully and promptly to Monday's outbreak. Less than two hours after the close of chapel he announced the rustication of four freshmen and the expulsion of a sophomore transfer student, Jonathan Barnwell. Why Barnwell was singled out was much disputed at the time. Quincy insisted that he had been the only sophomore positively identified by the tutors and, while certainly not the only offender, was, under the *University Statutes'* "selective punishment" provisions, liable to expulsion. Students dismissed this explanation as casuistical and continued to believe that Barnwell had been selected "as one who was but little acquainted, as a Southerner, and one concerning whom no disturbance would be made—but they were here mistaken."[63]

News of the Barnwell expulsion precipitated a series of unauthorized class caucuses in the Yard to "take some measure on the subject." Out of these came a petition signed by nearly all the undergraduates which called upon the president and faculty to reinstate Barnwell. Although described by one student as "couched in mild terms and without any abusive or menacing tone," the petition did demand a response—"by tomorrow morning." "We are on the eve of a Rebellion," wrote the no-longer-bored Moore, "and something serious will—must—soon be done."[64]

While the president conferred with the faculty about the student ultimatum, the sophomores seized control of the rebellion. They boycotted morning chapel and classes on Tuesday; on Wednesday they stormed into Chapel, completely disrupting services. When Quincy ordered them to take their seats, they turned in defiance and marched out. Furious, he suspended the entire class on the spot, and by three o'clock that afternoon forty-four sophomores had departed from Cambridge.[65]

On Thursday Quincy announced that he and the faculty, after reviewing the student petition, had no intention of reinstating Barnwell. "Groans and hisses" greeted the announcement as did calls for another round of class meetings. Far less restrained than those earlier in the week, these were highlighted by "speeches, flaming rebellious speeches, denouncing the Government and their proceedings." With the sophomores chased from the field, the freshmen again asserted their claims to the rebellion's leadership by hoisting above Holworthy Hall "the black flag of rebellion."[66]

Most upperclassmen, however, remained aloof. "We can look coolly on these matters," one senior wrote, perhaps recalling the Rugg incident two years earlier, as "we have experienced enough to know that the Government [is] generally right in [its] decisions and that they would not take rash measures without good cause." On Friday, a week after the disturbances had begun, Quincy appealed to this segment of student opinion by assuring the seniors that Barnwell had not been expelled, merely suspended for two years. This "concession" apparently satisfied not only the seniors but the juniors, who rescinded inflammatory statements they had issued earlier. Friday evening the Yard was quiet, leading some to believe the rebellion had run its course.[67]

Unfortunately, the freshmen were not so easily appeased. Saturday morning found them back in Chapel, stomping away. Two of them were suspended for creating a disturbance as was a junior who had joined in. However justified the junior's suspension, it had the effect of inciting still another class to rebellion. In memory of their departed comrade, and as a symbol of their opposition to Quincy, juniors took to wearing black armbands.[68]

By Sunday, having recovered from his lapse into conciliatory politics, Quincy decided to wheel out his major weapon. During the course of the day each member of the freshman class was notified that on June 12 he was to appear before the grand jury in Concord to testify as to his involvement in the destruction of Dunkin's room and the attack upon the night watchmen. That did it. Even seniors like George Moore, long straddling the barricades, now leaped over to the rebels' side. "This is a course that will never favorably operate," he declared upon hearing of the president's intention to resort to the courts. "The Community will not tolerate it—the members of the College will not suffer it."[69]

As Moore implied, the Harvard disturbances had already attracted considerable public notice. "No one can talk about anything else," he wrote after attending Artillery Election Day in Boston on June 2 where the principal topic of conversation was Quincy's difficulties in Cambridge. Critics of the college and its president revelled in the prospect of Harvard tearing itself apart. They were to have more cause to do so when reports of what was transpiring back in the Yard reached Boston. As Moore described it:

This evening, about 11 o'clock, a disgraceful scene took place in the College yard. An effigy of Pres. Quincy was hung with a rope about the neck from the Rebellion Tree,—a bonfire built near it—a loud shouting raised—and after being exhibited for some time in this way—it was set on fire, and burnt, while crackers were firing around, and explosions going on continually from powder in the body! This was done by the Junior Class, and by a vote of the Class!

What began as a simple classroom argument had escalated in the course of two weeks into a confrontation between the entire Harvard student body and its president, with the whole state looking on.[70]

If Quincy retained any illusions of support in the senior class, whose tenure at Harvard coincided with his, they were shattered on June 11 with the publication of *A Circular of the Senior Class of Harvard College on the Recent Disturbances.* Intended for wide circulation, the eight-page pamphlet offered a point-by-point refutation of the official explanation given a week earlier by the president in a letter to all parents of suspended students. Blame for the disturbances was placed squarely upon Quincy and his "want of discretion." The *Circular* concluded by questioning his personal qualifications to remain at the head of the college:

The manners of President Quincy toward many of the students have not been such as to conciliate their esteem and affection. His defective memory, and the natural impetuosity of his character, often give the appearance of acting in an arbitrary and capricious manner; and though his friends allow his sincerity and integrity, yet it can not be wondered at that many of the students, whom he has not made his friends, should entertain a different opinion.[71]

Those Boston and sectarian newspapers traditionally critical of Harvard joined the seniors in calling for Quincy's resignation. Editors vied with one another in resurrecting incidents out of the president's political past to corroborate the charge of impetuosity, hardly a difficult task. Even the *Boston Courier* and the *Columbian Centinel*, generally more sympathetic to the college, reprinted the *Senior Circular*, appending only a few words of support for its beleaguered president.[72]

"I am not a man to be frightened from a post of duty and usefulness," the sixty-three year old Quincy kept assuring his friends all through the spring; "the harder the tempest rages, the tighter I shall stick to the rudder." Deriving a certain amount of pleasure from the turmoil surrounding him, he likened it to his days in Congress and in the mayor's office. "I have known what it is to endure the calumnies and clamour of grown men," he stated after reading the *Senior Circular*, "there are no terrors in those of half fledged boys." But more than half-fledged boys were after him.[73]

Although the Corporation unanimously backed Quincy's summary handling of the student rebels, including his invoking the state courts, comparable support was lacking from the faculty and Board of Overseers. Students thought of the president and faculty as a single unit, "meeting like the Inquisition, ever ready to proceed against new offenders," when actually they were seldom in complete agreement. Quincy's hard line policy usually prevailed but never without generating opposition from individual faculty members. On the issue of whether to suspend all the seniors who signed the *Senior Circular*—virtually the entire class—or only those who instigated it, the president's preference for the more extreme action failed to receive the faculty's support, obliging him to settle for the suspension of seven instigators.[74]

The leader of the dissident faction within the faculty was Karl Follen, then in the fourth year of a five-year appointment as Professor of German Literature. Active in the student-led Burschenschaft movement of the 1820's, Follen left Germany after being implicated in the assassination of a ranking government official. Shortly after migrating to the United States and taking an instructorship at Harvard, he married Eliza Lee Cabot, whose father set him up in a temporary chair. The long-standing feud between the Quincy ladies and Eliza was only aggravated by her move out to Cambridge in 1830, accompanied not only by her new husband but by two unmarried sisters-in-law, all of whom "were given to hospitality." With four unattached females in her own household, Mrs. Quincy did not take such encroachment kindly.[75]

Eliza Susan, writing many years later, charged the Follens with fomenting the 1834 Rebellion. They were unquestionably popular with many students, their home serving as a sanctuary from the dormitories. Furthermore, Follen's frequently expressed wish "to see less outward government in college, and to induce the young men to govern themselves," suggests where his sympathies were. Although never able to gain the consistent support of the rest of the faculty for his conciliatory position towards the rebels, his efforts to undercut the president's authority prompted Quincy to label him a troublemaker. It was this, not his abolitionist sympathies, as his wife later charged, that led to his being sacked.[76]

More formidable was the opposition Quincy encountered from members of the Board of Overseers. Strained relations antedated the student disturbances, going back to 1833 when the Corporation conferred upon President Andrew Jackson Harvard's highest award, an honorary LL.D. Because the college had conferred the same degree upon President Monroe in 1817, Quincy and the Corporation, after being informed early in June that Jackson would pass through Cambridge later that month, felt they were obliged to follow the precedent. The honor was hardly intended as a political endorsement but rather as a prudent act of institutional self-defense. It was one thing for John Quincy Adams to write in his diary that Jackson was "a barbarian who could not write a sentence of grammar and hardly could spell his name," and was therefore "unworthy of literary honors," quite another, as Quincy unsuccessfully tried to persuade him, for the Corporation to deny him those honors and have the omission "imputed to party spirit—a charge they wished to avoid."[77]

Approval for the conferral of such a degree had to be obtained from the Board of Overseers. Accordingly the board, consisting of the governor, lieutenant governor, twelve members of the governor's council, all thirty-six state senators, and thirty permanent members elected by the board, was hastily called together two days before the President's scheduled arrival in Cambridge. A mix-up with some of the announcements for the meeting, the short notice, and the Saturday-morning meeting time combined to produce a meeting at which only thirty of the eighty overseers were present. Nevertheless, those who were in attendance approved the Corporation's recommendation and the conferral took place on June 23 without incident.[78]

At the next regularly scheduled meeting of the Board of Overseers several of those who had not been present to vote on Jackson's degree charged Quincy and the Corporation with duplicity. "You have probably heard . . . the proceedings of the Overseers," a correspondent of Joseph Story wrote following a January 1834 meeting, "and how the Pres't bears his *baiting*." James Trecothick Austin and George Blake, both old Republican foes of Mayor Quincy and now prominent Whigs, and Alexander Hill Everett, still with his eye on the Harvard presidency, were the principal baiters. The fact that a majority of the overseers were not Harvard graduates, and that many were far more interested in challenging the Corporation than protecting the college, lent virtually any criticism of Quincy and the Corporation an attractiveness, if not plausibility. It took two special meetings, a voluminous correspondence and the help of legal counsel before Quincy could convince a majority of the overseers that no "deep design" had existed.[79]

Messrs. Everett, Austin and Blake were ready and waiting when the rebellion provided further grounds for an attack on Quincy. At the overseers' meeting on July 17, 1834, Everett introduced the *Senior Circular* for discussion. During the ensuing debate he and Austin, who a month earlier as attorney general had offered Quincy his support in prosecuting the student rebels, espoused the seniors' position by contending that the disturbances would not have occurred but for a series of presidential "indiscretions." When Quincy's supporters on the board moved that he be given an immediate vote of confidence, they found most of their colleagues unwilling to comply. Instead they directed that a committee of overseers examine the allegations made in the *Senior Circular* and report its findings before any judgment be made on the president's handling of the rebellion. Everett was appointed to the committee, but fortunately for Quincy, so was John Quincy Adams.[80]

On August 21 the Harvard Board of Overseers held what must rank as one of its stormiest meetings. It was certainly one of its least productive. Everett moved at the outset that the meeting be opened to the public, and only after a heated debate was this unprecedented proposal narrowly rejected. There followed an even more heated debate over which of two committee reports to accept, that drafted by Adams and approved by a majority of the committee, or that "corrected" by Everett which promised to be far more critical of Quincy. Unable to decide between the two, the overseers adjourned for four days, directing the investigating committee to determine in the interim which report represented its collective view.[81]

Finally, on August 25, John Quincy Adams had his say. He wasted no time making clear where the responsibility for the rebellion lay. "There is within the recollection of your committee," he stated in his opening paragraph, "no previous example of disorders, in their origin or in their progress so unprovoked and unjustifiable, on the part of the students, as in the present case." Though he went on to condemn all the student rebels and those overseers who seemed prepared to condone their unlawful actions, Adams saved his most impassioned remarks for those responsible for the "untenable pretensions" of the *Senior Circular*. Here his argument went beyond a defense of his old friend and became an eloquent plea in behalf of, if not filial deference, at least generational comity:

In estimating the true character of this charge of want of discretion, preferred by the undergraduates, scarcely yet themselves of the ordinary age of discretion, against the President of the University, a man of more than three score winters, who, for nearly forty years, has successfully filled, by the confidence of his fellow citizens, offices of the highest trust, legislative, executive, judicial, civil and literary, and always with unsullied honor; always with untainted reputation; the first sentiment that forces itself upon the Committee is, that of the rule of proportion in the moral standing of the two parties, the accusers and the accused, before the committee.

The Circular of the Seniors *claims*, from the Government of the College toward them, the delicacy of and the tenderness of the parental relation, and descants upon the *duties*, which this relation imposes. . . .

Have the authors and avowed approvers of that Circular, fathers of their own? And if they have, and should, in the course of their lives, unhappily, have had occasion to observe in them 'a want of discretion,' do they feel, as if it was for them, in their *filial* relation, to proclaim that indiscretion to the world? . . . Have they yet to learn, that the primeval curse pronounced in Holy Writ was upon the son, who beheld and exposed his father's frailties? Have they yet to learn, may they never learn by the contamination of their own example,

> 'How sharper, than a serpent's tooth it is
> 'To have a thankless child?'

Everett denounced Adams' report as a "fulsome apology," but most of the overseers were sufficiently moved to give Quincy and his policies their endorsement* while denouncing the *Senior Circular* as "entirely inconsistent with the station and duties of the undergraduates of this University."[82]

But Quincy was still not out of the woods. Rumors had been circulating since the close of college on July 15 that the seniors intended to boycott Commencement Day, as a protest against the suspension of seven classmates responsible for the *Circular*. As graduation approached, however, some seniors began to reconsider their plans. Ironically, one of the contributing causes appears to have been the reaction that followed the burning of the Ursuline Convent in Charlestown on August 11. "Reports reached Cambridge that the Catholics in order to retaliate upon our citizens for the loss of what they deemed their most sacred property," George Moore wrote the next day, "were coming to attack and burn down the library: several Irishmen were seen during the day going around the college and examining the premises." In the accompanying hysteria, many seniors put their own arguments with Harvard aside and joined with faculty and alumni to form a company of armed volunteers to defend the college against this external threat. Though the Irishmen never appeared, the experience of students and faculty standing together ready to repulse them may well have served to vent some of the pressure that had been building since May.[83]

On August 20, seven days before graduation, the seniors still refused to agree to accept their degrees or participate in the ceremonies unless their suspended classmates were reinstated. Never-

---

*The attempt in the Board of Overseers to unseat Quincy may have been more coordinated than can be proved by the available documentation. There is circumstantial evidence to suggest that Austin, Blake, and Alexander Everett were all seeking Edward Everett's election to the presidency. Everett's announced resignation from Congress during August of 1834, when Quincy's position was problematic, and then his change of heart in October after Quincy managed to contain the rebellion, does not detract from this admittedly conspiratorial explanation.

theless, the margin by which this motion was carried at the class meeting was so slight as to suggest that the united front was beginning to crumble. Three days later the seniors voted to participate in the ceremonies but continued to insist that they would not take their degrees until such time as the suspended seven received theirs. Quincy, sensing he had them on the run, responded that they would take their degrees at the prescribed time, or never.[84]

On Commencement Day thirty-seven of the fifty-four-member Class of 1834 stepped smartly forward to receive their degrees. To the relief of all in attendance, the ceremonies "passed off without disorder." "Mr. Quincy and his family appeared in a state of considerable elation," one guest remarked at the end of the day, "and on the whole I do not wonder."[85]

Quincy had won; he had also been lucky. But for the intervention of John Quincy Adams, "half-fledged boys" and a few dissidents on the faculty and Board of Overseers nearly brought his tenure as president of Harvard to an ignominious and abrupt end. His heavy-handed tactics had at times aggravated the situation. The Barnwell incident was poorly if not disingenuously handled; the timing of the announcement to send freshmen to Concord was provocative; the lack of rapport between him and the more moderate students was continually evident. Too often he gave the appearance of acting unilaterally while regularly minimizing the resourcefulness of his antagonists. He did restore order, but only after two months of disruptions, a moratorium on all academic activity, the suspension of the entire sophomore class, the dismissal of seven freshmen, one junior and seven seniors, plus two indictments (subsequently dropped by Quincy) against three undergraduates in the Middlesex County Court of Common Pleas.[86]

Nor did victory come cheaply in personal terms. After conversing with Quincy in the fall, John Quincy Adams estimated its toll on his friend:

He spoke of the present condition of the University as satisfactory; but while the words were cheering, his tone was dejected. He can never again regain his popularity with the students, and the public treat him as they treat all old men, with cold neglect and insulting compassion. He is not made of the stuff to struggle long against this.

Although Adams underestimated the stuff of which his friend was made, he correctly saw that Quincy, and all the Harvard presidents who followed, would have to get along without the love Harvard students had given so freely to his predecessor.[8][7]

Yet the essential fact remains that Quincy won; he outlasted his challengers. For better or worse, the most important outcome of the Rebellion of 1834 was to confirm the fact that control of Harvard rested not with the Overseers, not with the Faculty, and not with the students, but with the President and the Corporation. What they intended to do with their "well disciplined high school" remained to be seen.

9 / Toward a University

There was another person who began much earlier (1829-1845) than I the conversion of
Harvard College into a university. He did not get far with it, because he encountered such
intense opposition to the measures he favored. That was Josiah Quincy.
— Charles William Eliot, 1923

After 1834 coordinated and sustained student rebelliousness
ceased to be a primary fact of life at Harvard. Isolated incidents
occurred but never again—until the late 1960's—would campus order
become a major concern, preoccupy the faculty, or put a president's
tenure in jeopardy. John Gorham Palfrey, a professor in Cambridge
during the 1830's, believed the establishment of order to be the
signal accomplishment of Quincy's presidency. "Proving to your
associates that it was possible to govern," Palfrey wrote to the
retiring president in 1845, "and to your pupils that it was necessary,
as well as honourable to obey, made the future task of control far
easier." More importantly, it enabled Quincy and his faculty to begin
altering the basic nature of their academic enterprise.[1]

A Chivalric Expedition

American colleges in the 1830's were on the defensive; never had
dissatisfaction been more general nor calls for immediate reform
more insistent. The essentially self-congratulatory Yale Report of
1828 promised that "improvements will continue to be made as
rapidly as they can." While a consensus existed that basic changes
were in order, there was none as to their nature and focus.
Nevertheless, it is possible to abstract from the plethora of reform
proposals a number of models of what constituted for most reformers the "ideal college." Four such models are sufficiently
distinctive to permit analysis: (1) the college as "a nursery of
orthodoxy"; (2) the college as transmitter of the utilitarian, democratic "spirit of the age"; (3) the college as refuge from that same
materialistic, levelling "spirit of the age"; (4) the college as the

embryo out of which a university might emerge. In one way or another, all four were superimposed on Quincy's Harvard.[2]

Not since the seventeenth century, if then, had Harvard approximated the first model: the college as an efficient promoter of sectarian dogma. But with the election of a Unitarian to the Hollis Professorship of Divinity in 1805, the doctrinally liberal Corporation publicly withdrew Harvard from the Calvinist wing of the Congregationalist Church. The break had been in the offing for nearly a century. Harvard's competitors—Yale, Williams, Amherst, Brown, and Middlebury—had retained doctrinal and financial ties with their original sectarian sponsors.[3]

If the Corporation eschewed the model of Harvard as "a nursery of orthodoxy," the same cannot be said of some of its alumni. As late as 1825 the Reverend John Brazer of Salem expressed the wish that his alma mater would again become "a proselytizer . . . a propagandist for what we believe to be the truth of the Gospel." Most of his colleagues in the clergy, however, had long since given up hope and transferred their affections—and their sons—elsewhere. When the Reverend Chandler Robbins, Class of 1782, ventured back to Cambridge in 1824 on Commencement Day, he found the students, as he had feared, "very intelligent but ungodly." If Harvard wanted nothing to do with the propagation of orthodoxy, the orthodox wanted nothing to do with Harvard. "We have (thanks to the Providence of God and the liberality of our people)," the *New England Puritan* assured its readers, "colleges of our own, which afford ample accommodations, and which without perverting the heart, give a better training to the intellect than does that at Cambridge."[4]

Some Calvinists contended that Harvard had never ceased to preach orthodoxy but had only exchanged dogmas. The ties between the college and the unabashedly Unitarian divinity school in Cambridge, as well as the preponderance of Unitarians on the Corporation, gave this charge a certain plausibility. But the college had not in 1805 simply switched over to producing Unitarian clergy in place of Congregationalist; it had begun getting out of the religious vocation business altogether. As late as 1790 more than a quarter of the graduating class entered the ministry; in the 1830's the ratio was one-in-ten and declining. More revealing, the laicization of Harvard's graduates occurred during a period when the percentage of graduates going into the ministry from many American colleges, including

Yale, remained fairly constant and from some, such as Dartmouth, actually increased. And finally, Boston Unitarianism was simply not the stuff out of which religious zealots were made.[5]

The imposition of religious qualifications was a standard practice at most American colleges prior to the Civil War and not unheard of later. The Harvard Corporation, however, prided itself on its faculty's heterodoxy. Francis Calley Gray, defending the college in 1831 against charges that it was dominated by Unitarians, pointed out that for fourteen academic positions filled since 1821, the Corporation had appointed three Catholics, one Lutheran, one Calvinist, one Quaker, one Episcopalian, and one Sandemanian, along with six Unitarians. "The complaint urged against Harvard with the greatest zeal," he noted sadly, "is that it is *not orthodox;* this is probably the real difficulty. The college is condemned, not because it is in the hands of a sect, but because it is not in the hands of the *right sect.*"[6]

Quincy, himself a Unitarian, was particularly sensitive to the charge of Unitarian domination of the college and sought during his presidency to counteract it. In 1834 he dissented from the Corporation's decision to appoint other than Congregationalist clergy to ministerial seats on the Board of Overseers as doing so denied what Quincy insisted was their special prerogative. Further, he opposed the appointment of his friend John Gorham Palfrey as an overseer in 1843 on the grounds that there were too many other Unitarians on the board. Upon his retirement he informed the Corporation of his continuing willingness to give of his time to Harvard—"especially to the greatest of all causes—her *Religious Freedom.*" By adhering to this ideal Harvard successfully resisted the model of "a nursery of orthodoxy" which outsiders wished to impose upon it, but at considerable cost in terms of student enrollments and popular as well as financial support.[7]

More compelling than the complaints of sectarian critics were those emanating from secular sources. The demand that American colleges should get in step with "the spirit of the age" was clearly audible in Cambridge as in New Haven where it had provoked Yale's classic rejoinder. But with its expanding enrollment, reasonably good press, and substantial financial backing from its sectarian sponsors, Yale could afford to be skeptical about what the 1828 Report patronizingly called "the bustle and the energy of the population"; Harvard could not.[8]

Another factor obliging Harvard to listen respectfully to the utilitarian argument was the reputation of its leading Cambridge exponent, Jacob Bigelow. Elected Harvard's first Rumford Professor on the Application of Science to the Useful Arts in 1816, and one of Boston's first great medical researchers, Bigelow spent his professorship trying to "incorporate a little more of what is practical with what is intellectual" in the college curriculum. Upon assuming his professorship he had defended the study of applied science precisely because it did not require "too much preparation." Citing the "infancy of our institutions," he counted it among America's blessings that "we have not often individuals among us, like the laborious Germans, spending their lives in endless acquisitions." So long as the country had "many useful ones," it could survive nicely without those "few learned men" whom colleges seemed determined to produce.[9]

Although himself a serious student of the classics, Bigelow believed the Harvard curriculum, in concentrating on them, failed to address itself to the "actual wants" and expectations of its undergraduates. Accordingly he asked the college's new president in 1830:

Is it not useful that education in our seminaries should have reference to the conditions and future pursuits of the young men who compose them? A great majority of graduates at our colleges are dispersed through the interior of the country, where their lives are spent in contact with the middling and operative classes of the community, to those pursuits they must in some measure assimilate to their own. . . . A professional man may pass his whole life without a single call for his knowledge of astronomy, of metaphysics, of Greek or of German. But it is not so with the practical and useful applications of science.[10]

Like others of the utilitarian persuasion, Bigelow buttressed his case with a kind of democratic determinism. "Whatever the majority of the people desire to know," he warned Quincy, "seminaries must sooner or later teach. If I mistake not, the spirit of the age is already showing itself in our schools." The question for Harvard's new president was not whether he would comply with the popular imperative, but whether he intended "to lead or follow in the path which is about to be beaten."[11]

Those anxious to have Harvard address itself "to the practical wants of the community" held out another inducement. If the college could convince the merchants and factory owners that their money and their sons' time would not be wasted at Harvard parsing Greek and memorizing Latin, its financial problems would be over.

And the way to do this, they argued, was to abandon all pretense of providing a classical education, to emphasize instead technical and commercial training, and to lower admission standards. Extension courses and abbreviated programs ("partial education") would also help attract a wider clientele. "I want the college to be brought nearer and dearer to the people," William Ellery Channing told Quincy in 1834, "to be made more an object of public attention and interest, to be talked about and thought of more, to be regarded and felt as a mighty object in society." His expressed hope was that Harvard could "be made popular, *popular* in the lowest sense of that word."[1][2]

Neither Bigelow nor Channing, nor for that matter Ticknor who aligned himself with both, demanded that Quincy succumb to the notion that the popular wisdom constituted the ultimate wisdom, only that no institution could ignore public sentiment with impunity. Nevertheless, few arguments could possibly have had less appeal to him than this one based on its consonance with the prevailing egalitarian and utilitarian thinking of Jacksonian America. Even if Bigelow was right when he argued that few Harvard graduates "find time for a life of literary leisure and intercourse of polished society," that struck Quincy as an insufficient justification for setting Harvard standards by the grubby needs of the factory and the frontier. To Channing's argument that Harvard's enrollment would grow if it instituted a more utilitarian curriculum, he peevishly responded: "Let there be at least one institution in the country, the criterion of whose worth and merit shall be measured by something other than the number of its polls."[1][3]

The model of the ideal college Quincy had brought to Cambridge was far closer to that espoused by the Yale Report. "The spirit of the age," he warned in his Inaugural Address, "requires to be watched on the subject of the claims . . . perpetually being made on the greater institutions of learning." Time and experience had not in the least modified his Federalist inclinations. "To follow public opinion is easy and popular," he reminded his audience, "but it is not always sound, and is liable to be corrupt; to resist it is hard and ungracious; yet often made necessary by conscience and duty."[1][4]

Quincy might have begun his presidency by restoring the reforms advocated by Ticknor and incorporated in the 1825 *University Statutes*, but this he chose not to do. On the contrary, his first alterations of the curriculum were in the opposite direction. Rather than reduce the classical emphasis and the required nature of the curriculum, his *Report . . . on a General Plan of Studies* (1830) made clear his intention to "effect a more thorough education in the Greek and Latin languages . . . than the present course of studies is calculated to attain." Under Ticknor's plan freshmen had been encouraged to study a modern language, but were now prohibited from doing so. The entire first year, with eighteen hours of recitation per week, was to be devoted exclusively to Greek, Latin, and mathematics. Symbolic of the direction in which Quincy wished to take the college was his first academic appointment—another Greek instructor.[15]

Although the new president disappointed those who had hoped he would institute basic changes in the curriculum, he was not without his supporters. "It is a comfort to me in these days of reform and wild speculation," Joseph Story wrote upon receipt of the *General Plan*, "that there are those among us who stick to the good old doctrines of other times, and to the studies, by which learning and taste and genius have been achieved in other days." Apparently having second thoughts about his earlier endorsement of Ticknor's reforms, Story voiced no complaint with Harvard's traditional curriculum in 1830 except that it had failed to accomplish all that it had promised. "I shall be very glad," he told Quincy, "if you can revive the desire of classical attainments less superficial and more thorough than we had." No more able to come to terms with the prevailing sentiments of Jacksonian America than was Harvard's new president, Story envisioned the college as a counterweight to the egalitarian and materialistic thrustings of that society. It was James Hillhouse, however, a Yale graduate and son of one of Connecticut's most doctrinaire Federalists, who provided the metaphorical description of their ideal Harvard: "a tower of light to preserve rational liberty, amidst the fogs and shallows of democratic fanaticism."[16]

In order to implement such a model, Quincy proposed, in addition to a demanding classical curriculum, stiffer entrance requirements and more exacting degree standards. But what if large numbers of students failed the entrance requirements, found the curriculum unsatisfying or the degree requirements too exacting, and simply went elsewhere? In the 1830's this was more than a hypothetical question. "The fear of reducing our numbers by acts of strictness and raising the standards of admission," Quincy kept insisting as late as the spring of 1835, "has no terror for me." He did acknowledge, however, that it had become "a bugbear for some." And with good reason, as the enrollment figures for the college during Quincy's first six years as president show a drop from 252 students in 1829-1830 to 210 in 1834-1835. Yale was graduating more students than Harvard, and so were Union, Princeton, and Dartmouth. That year's graduating class of thirty-nine was the smallest in twenty-seven years.[17]

What ultimately obliged Quincy to abandon his model of Harvard as a standing reproach to the rest of American society was his recognition that in adhering to it he would very likely destroy the college. Accommodation to the fact that "railroads and low motives are the present order of the day" had to be and were made. Although he continued to oppose lower admission standards, after 1835 he gave up trying to raise them. Beginning in 1835 "special students" were admitted and "probationary admissions" were made, with remedial sections established to deal with them. That same year a "partial education" scheme was discussed, designed for those students "peculiarly situated and peculiarly destined"—in other words, peculiarly resistant to the classics. While still honoring the ideal that a Harvard degree ought to be evidence of "qualities attained," Quincy came to recognize the practical necessity of granting it to those "who do their best to attain the minimum."[18]

These represented very tangible concessions to the quantitative standards of American society and testify to Quincy's acceptance of the severe constraints these standards imposed upon any college president. "Now in Republics," he sadly allowed, "numbers are ever made the criterion of success—and of power—and too often of virtue." He had come to Cambridge determined to make a Harvard degree "unobtainable, except by means of evidence of a thorough acquisition of all the branches of education of which a degree is a natural sign"; four years later he had come to fear that such "a chivalric expedition" was not only futile but possibly fatal. "In a state of things which exist in this country," he warned President James Marsh of the University of Vermont, who had expressed his own preference for pursuing quality:

such an attempt would make any University . . . obnoxious to the clamour of favoritism and aristocracy. It would find leagued against it, not only the children, but the fathers, and what is more the mothers. And what is more would find every time-serving rival growing fat and sassy on its spoils.

Acceptance of this state of affairs did not result in Quincy's succumbing to the utilitarians and transforming Harvard into an open-enrollment trade school. Rather, he turned to the model of the ideal college being espoused by certain members of his own faculty, that is, the college as the embryo from which a university might emerge.[19]

An End to Scholastic Uniformity

Aside from lack of funds and presidential indifference, the principal obstacle to reforming the Harvard curriculum in the 1820's had been an obstructionist faculty. Yet a decade later the faculty was the vanguard of the reform movement. By 1834 Emerson's three representatives of Cantabrigian *vis inertiae*, Professors Hedge, Willard, and Popkin, were gone. A year later Ticknor, convinced that there was little hope for Harvard or his reforms, turned his professorship over to a poet-professor from Maine, Henry Wadsworth Longfellow. By the time Longfellow reached Cambridge in the fall of 1836, the experimental Modern Language Department which he inherited was no longer isolated. Those traditional bastions of the *status quo*, the Latin and Greek Departments, and even more so, the Mathematics Department, had begun to stir with the infusion of new blood. Here were the educational views and political leverage that would soon convince Quincy and, in turn, the Corporation of the wisdom and necessity for "a radical change in the object and character of the college."[20]

"It will very much facilitate any system of improvement, to allow the very dull sons of rich parents to pursue a different course of Mathematics—under a private tutor." Such was the considered opinion of Benjamin Peirce, in 1832 a twenty-three year old tutor, son of the recently deceased Harvard librarian. A child prodigy, Peirce had been certified a genius by no less an authority than Nathaniel Bowditch who judged him to have, as a freshman, the finest mind for mathematics in Cambridge. During his sophomore year he spent his spare time correcting Bowditch's translation of Laplace's *Traité de Mécanique Céleste*. Peirce returned to Harvard in

1831, two years after his graduation, and remained a member of the faculty until his death in 1880. There, in addition to teaching, he pursued his own mathematical studies and achieved international recognition first in 1846 for his questioning of Leverrier's mathematical "discovery" of Neptune and subsequently as director and superintendent of the United States Coast Survey. Through his half-century on the faculty he was not only one of its luminaries but, as viewed by supporters and critics alike, also the leader of the university cause in Cambridge.[21]

Peirce, as a professional scientist, went beyond Ticknor's critique of the recitation system and the classical curriculum. In so doing he was much like Jacob Bigelow, though unlike him he had no use for the utilitarians' distinction between "applied" and "pure" science. Similarly, he opposed the recitation system because it failed to evaluate students "with a certainty that the exact sciences deserve."[22]

Much of the impetus behind Peirce's reforms was selfish. A rigid curriculum prescribed the duties of teachers no less than students, and if undergraduates found recitations uninspiring, instructors, who conducted several each day, found them far more so. For Peirce the enervating aspects of the daily routine were compounded by the fact that the students continued to be grouped together with no regard for relative proficiency. As one of his duller students later recalled, he had "little respect for pupils who had not a genius for mathematics and paid little respect to them." A supremely confident, physically imposing man, equally at ease with legislators and international scholars, Peirce was not without intellectual arrogance. Unlike Popkin or Willard, he cared little about providing all Harvard students with what the Yale Report called "the common foundations." Furthermore, he hoped that most students, if given the option, would avoid his classes. "May it not be forgotten," he observed with satisfaction, "that Mathematics is a far more difficult and therefore less attractive department than almost any other."[23]

As Hollis Professor of Mathematics, Peirce began in the fall of 1835 his frontal assault on the prescribed curriculum by requesting that all mathematics courses beyond the freshman year be made optional. Peirce believed that the required three full years of mathematics—a veritable forced march ending in what was for most the impenetrable thicket of differential calculus—was a waste of time, his as well as the students'. Convinced that even the most obtuse freshman could be exposed to enough arithmetic to satisfy his probable future needs, "to add up the bills of his tradesmen," he asked that all upperclassmen "with a disinclination to Mathematics, drop it."[24]

One of the novel aspects of his proposal was that it appeared to be departmentally self-denying, something that Ticknor's support of a more flexible curriculum had not been. Peirce did indicate, however, that he hoped all other departments would follow his lead and release unwilling students by making advanced courses optional. Superficially, his proposal had much in common with suggestions being made by the utilitarians. Like them he rejected the central premise of the Yale Report, that college ought to be primarily an experience in mental discipline. He believed, rather, that a student should be allowed to discontinue a subject "for which he has *no taste or capacity*." He also exposed himself to the charge of permissiveness.[25]

Beneath the surface similarities of his position and that of the utilitarians lay an essential difference: Peirce was not an academic egalitarian. On the contrary, remarks accompanying his 1835 proposal reveal a patently elitist philosophy:

However exalted mathematical truth may be, I am aware that much time is wasted in College in pretending to study it; and the key which explains this unpleasant fact is contained in a wise observation of Coleridge; 'there are very few who care for the good, for the good's sake; and still fewer who care for the truth for the truth's sake.' The very necessity of the stimulus of college rank and college honours confirms this remark.

Quincy clearly understood the radical thrust of Peirce's proposal. As he told James Walker, a newly elected Corporation member, Peirce was not so much trying to exempt lazy students from a difficult part of the traditional curriculum, though his plan had this effect, as insuring that "the study of mathematics would be in effect confined to the very few who have a taste and aptitude for it." It was, the President correctly inferred, the extension of the division-by-proficiency reform to its logical end. Although he had supported such divisions since becoming president, he had not, as of 1835, yet come to the point of regarding certain areas of the curriculum as proscribed to all but certain carefully selected students. Finding most of the faculty and the Corporation equally hesitant, Quincy tabled Peirce's proposal.[26]

Not an ideological disagreement, but the differing perspectives of the scholar and the administrator had prevented an accord. Peirce conceived of Harvard in vertical, individualistic terms; Quincy, horizontally and in aggregates. Whereas one naturally thought in terms of a few carefully selected students being impelled to the limits of their capabilities, the other thought of raising the common level of competence, a difference which was not irreconcilable. One thing is certain: Quincy's initial wariness about Peirce's model of the college as an embryonic university, stressing individual scholarship and research more than uniform instruction, was not because of its elitist implications. As he told Charles Francis Adams, after listening to him complain of how little he had learned at Harvard, "it is with students as with horses led to water. . . . "[27]

Though differing with Peirce in approach, Charles Beck, Professor of Latin, was another university-oriented member of the Harvard faculty. The stepson of Wilhelm de Wette, an eminent biblical scholar at the University of Berlin, and recipient of an 1822 Göttingen doctorate, Beck left Germany in 1825, coming to Harvard as an instructor in 1831. He proved a valuable addition to the faculty, not only as a teacher of the classics, but as a serious scholar in the Teutonic tradition. Much of the German scholarship that found its way to provincial Cambridge in the 1830's and 1840's did so through his efforts. His utility was further enhanced by the fact that he, unlike his fellow political refugee, Follen, got along splendidly with Quincy.[28]

Only months after arriving at Harvard, Beck began recommending additions to the academic program. On June 23, 1831, Quincy and the faculty received his plan for creating a philological seminary. Beck's ultimate objective was nothing less than the creation of an entire graduate program, distinct from the college and with its own faculty. As a modest first step in that direction, he proposed an intensive two-year program in classical philology, open only to seniors interested in becoming teachers of classical literature and prepared to spend a fifth year in Cambridge for the requisite training.[29]

Beck's "brainchild" impressed Quincy on at least two counts. If the seminary prospered, Harvard would have a highly qualified pool of classicists from which to draw its instructors. The effect of this on the general level of classical attainments in the college, he assumed, could only be positive. That such a seminary offered a domestic alternative to European study likewise made the proposal attractive to Quincy, since he was a firm believer in the notion that such study unsuited Americans for life in their own country. He forbade his sons to go abroad after graduation and, hearing of Charles Sumner's intentions to do so, told him that it would "spoil" him and be productive of nothing but "mustachios or a club cane."[30]

Formal instruction for the six seniors enrolled in the seminary began in the spring of 1832. The students, along with Beck and Cornelius Conway Felton, the new Greek instructor, set to their duties with an enthusiasm befitting pioneers. As the term went on, however, it became clear that more than enthusiasm was needed to keep the six seminarians in Cambridge beyond the time of their regular graduation. Beck asked the Corporation to provide them with stipends for a fifth year of study, but funds were not available. The seminary failed to reopen in the fall—a good idea born too soon. It would be another forty years before Henry Adams would pick up the graduate-studies idea where financial exigencies had obliged Beck to leave it off.[31]

Having watched his own reform plan come to grief in 1832, Beck might have been expected to offer his support in 1835 to Peirce's. He shared with the mathematician an abiding belief in the academic relevance of the parable of talents. Beck's annoyance at teaching dull students exceeded even Peirce's. "However kindly or delicately we treat the slowest sections," he reminded Quincy in 1835 when asking to be relieved of such obligations, "we ought not to carry this delicacy to such a point as to shut our eyes to the fact that they are inferior in knowledge and talent." Nonetheless, Beck's first reaction to Peirce's efforts to open up the curriculum was negative.[32]

At least three reasons can be suggested for this. Unlike Peirce's proposal, Beck's seminary had not attacked the integrity of the traditional curriculum but offered a supplement to it. His idea was rather to superimpose a university upon the college than to develop the one from the other. Furthermore, his negative reaction reflected a confounding, not peculiar to him, of Peirce's ends with those of the utilitarians and anti-classicists. "At a time when the best Friends of sound and thorough learning look to us for doing our part in raising the standard of classical attainments," he complained to the Corporation, "we are considering, and I fear, recommending the most effective means of limiting and lowering it forever." Finally, Beck feared, as did earlier classicists on the faculty, that any relaxation of the requirements would produce a mass exodus from Greek and Latin courses. Like the 1835 Corporation committee which decided against making third-year courses in the classics optional because "the junior . . . would probably be tempted to discontinue them by the variety of interesting courses then offered him for the first time," he was convinced that, whatever else, Harvard students must be spared the temptation of interesting courses.[33]

Peirce refused to be silenced by the initial resistance to his proposal. On January 21, 1838, after more than two years of intensive lobbying, he again moved that all mathematics courses beyond the freshman year be made optional. This time, however, he elaborated on the nature of his department's proposed optional offerings. They were to be divided into three categories: (1) a one-year course for those "who wish to become better conversant with Practical Mathematics" (e.g., surveying, navigation); (2) a more theoretical one-year course to prepare mathematics instructors; (3) a three-year course for "those who have the ability and inclination to become mathematicians, and to be qualified for mathematical professorships." Clearly, Peirce envisioned admission to this third category at the election fully as much of the professor as of the students. Nor did he deny that the numbers in the most advanced group "will be very small and sometimes be entirely wanting," but, he quickly added, "if successfully instructed, they will add more to the reputation of the college than either of the others."[34]

Peirce's new proposal neatly combined his earlier recommendation for an open curriculum with Beck's professionally oriented seminary scheme. Rather than wait until the fourth year, however, he wanted students to begin advance study much earlier, before "their minds hardened." The proposal also took into account the demands of the utilitarians. While advocating that a portion of the college be transformed into a university so as to provide advanced instruction for the few students "who have the inclination and the ability," his plan envisioned a wide range of practical instruction for the many students who had neither.[35]

Altogether it was a brilliant accommodation of his elitist conception of higher education with the demands of institutional finance and democracy. However belatedly, Quincy now recognized the genius of Peirce's proposal: it conceded to the demands of the utilitarians and the needs of the college treasury only what was necessary to enable Harvard to serve those professors and students in pursuit of "the truth for the truth's sake." As one professor later assessed the institutional ramifications of Peirce's proposal: "Harvard would still furnish, to say the least, the same means of improvement to the students but it would free itself from the responsibility of obliging the students to avail themselves of them. The public would lose nothing, but the college would gain much." Moved by a similar logic, Quincy, on June 2, 1838, persuaded the Corporation to adopt Peirce's plan to introduce the elective system in the mathematics department on a two-year trial basis.[36]

Once converted, Quincy became the most effective promoter of the elective system. In an attempt to allay Beck's fears that making Latin optional after the first year would deprive his department of students, the President suggested that a Latin certificate might be awarded to those who chose to continue in the subject. It "would be of the nature of honours which would . . . retain all ambitious of carrying into life evidence of having pursued the highest course of studies. . . . Would not this element," he asked Beck rhetorically, "constitute generally the *elite* of the class, and would not the spirit and the heights . . . carried by this class be probably ample indemnification to Latin Literature in this country for the loss of those who might be tempted to abandon it?" Peirce's position and Quincy's were now indistinguishable.[37]

Beck's response to Quincy's proposal for a Latin certificate indicated that he no longer looked upon the prospect of an open curriculum with as much trepidation as formerly. Of the students enrolled in Latin, he now estimated that less than half would drop the subject if given the option. And those, he believed, concurring with the president's view, would be "no loss to Latin Literature in the country."[38]

But then Beck hesitated, unwilling to endorse what he correctly saw as "a radical change in the object and character of the college" without a final weighing of its implication. "If the object of the college," he wrote to Quincy,

be to cultivate a branch of literature or a science, and to engage in its study those who are best calculated, from natural talent and predilection, to make rapid progress, and to advance in their turn that branch, the principle of election can not but operate beneficially.

"But," he went on,

> if the object be to impart a complete education to all who frequent the institution, that is to develop their various intellectual powers by a thorough instruction in those branches which reason and experience were proved to be the best means to this end, I am not certain whether the right of selection ought to be granted which, if exercised, necessarily tends to impair that harmonious culture of the mind which the collegiate institutions of this country profess to make their object.

Having thus paid his respects to the ideal that had informed the traditional curriculum, Beck then announced himself in favor of the elective system.[39]

Four days after Beck's announcement, Cornelius Conway Felton, now Eliot Professor of Greek Literature, told Quincy that, despite earlier reservations, he now favored "a full trial of the voluntary system" in his department. A competent scholar, though possessing neither Beck's learning nor Peirce's genius, he shared with his two colleagues a decided preference for those students "who are ready to learn." Like Beck, who thought the elective system would free him from the obligation of dealing with all but those students "pursuing a subject who considered it important," he also hoped it might generate "a spirit which would most advantageously react upon the instructors and stimulate them to constant exertions." Thus was completed the conversion of the three pillars of the traditional curriculum to support of the elective system.[40]

The experiment in the Mathematics Department quickly proved to be a success. Of the fifty-five sophomores given the choice of dropping the subject, only eight did so; thirty-five enrolled instead in one of the two terminal courses and twelve brave souls opted for Peirce's three-year course. Whatever doubts Beck had were put to rest. "It begins to appear," Felton enthused in August 1839, "that the age of scholastic uniformity and conformity has gone."[41]

Two weeks later Quincy recommended to the Corporation that the experimental program in the Mathematics Department be made permanent, and that it be extended to the Latin and Greek Departments as well. With the faculty now united behind Peirce's plan, and with the President its enthusiastic spokesman, the Corporation needed only four days to consider the plan before giving it their unanimous approval. Quincy made certain that there was no confusion as to what they were doing. "We regard this question as precisely the question," one Fellow later explained, "whether Harvard College shall or shall not become a University.... In no institution intended to answer the purposes of a University, and to be called by that name," he added, "is it attempted to carry all the scholars to the same degree of advancement in all departments of study.... We hope, therefore, that our College may become, in fact, a University."[42]

Approval from the Board of Overseers was slower in coming. John Pickering, long a defender of the classical curriculum, suspected that the faculty and the Corporation, in supporting the elective system, had succumbed to "the spirit of the age"; he also feared that if it were instituted the humanities would be slighted in favor of the sciences. His opposition stalled implementation for two years. Only Quincy's assurances to the board in 1841 that the elective system would undoubtedly raise "the standard of classical learning in the seminary," and that the college was not about to become a trade school, finally extracted the overseers' less than enthusiastic endorsement.[43]

By 1843 virtually all courses beyond the freshman year at Harvard were optional. They remained so, however, only as long as Quincy remained president. With Edward Everett's election in 1846, a reaction set in against the elective system despite the support it continued to have among the faculty. During Everett's three years as president, all sophomore options were eliminated. His successor, Jared Sparks, abolished junior options. "The voluntary system, as it has been called," Sparks wrote in 1853, "is still retained to a certain extent—rather from necessity than preference." Even academic revolutions can go backward.[44]

In James Walker, president from 1862 to 1868, the elective system again found an enthusiastic, if largely ineffective supporter. Only during the presidency of Charles William Eliot (1869-1909) did it enjoy the executive backing that was necessary to reverse the trend begun by Everett. Even then it took fourteen years to make the curriculum as flexible as it had been in 1843. It was Eliot who took the final steps necessary to transform the college into a university; but his way had been made easier by Josiah Quincy who, a generation earlier, had anticipated his vision of what Harvard might become.[45]

The President as Mendicant

Although "Harvard College aspires to the title of an University," Quincy told the overseers in 1841, it lacked some "of the efficient means an institution of that character should possess." What he was referring to was money. While that alone could not create a university, without it any attempt to create one was doomed. An open curriculum required the college to provide students with an intellectually demanding range of courses, properly staffed. Furthermore, if Peirce's proposal that professors be relieved of burdensome teaching loads and encouraged to carry on independent research were to be implemented, additional instructors would be needed. Only greatly expanded resources for scholarships would attract bright students and answer the charge that Harvard was a refuge for the lazy rich. Finally, money could guarantee the independence of the college from both sectarian and political pressures, which were likely to work against the creation of the university as envisioned by Peirce, Quincy, and the Corporation.[46]

The refusal of the Massachusetts General Court to extend the state grant in 1824 had marked a turning point in the history of Harvard College, however reluctant the Corporation was to acknowledge it. As late as 1831 Corporation Fellow Francis Calley Gray and Quincy were addressing appeals to the state for funds to build a new library in Cambridge. Both argued, recalling the 1764 fire, that the loss of the college's 40,000-volume collection would constitute a public calamity and that, therefore, the state ought to help provide for its safe storage. Not until 1834 did the Corporation resign themselves to the fact that no public money was forthcoming for this or any other Harvard undertaking. They then decided to go ahead and build the much needed library with college funds. Thus the bulk of the $100,000 Christopher Gore bequest, given to Harvard in 1829 and originally set aside for faculty salaries, went instead into brick and granite.[47]

The biggest patron of American private higher education prior to the Civil War was the American Educational Society, founded in 1815 by, among other prominent Congregationalist and Presbyterian laymen, Quincy's maternal relatives, the Phillipses. The Society's principal function was subsidizing the education "of young men of piety and promise for the ministry, who have not the means of educating themselves." Unfortunately for Harvard, its beneficence was theologically delimited. Of the 352 students subsidized by the Society in 1836 at twelve New England colleges, only one attended Harvard. For him the college received nineteen dollars. In contrast, more than half of Amherst's students that year were beneficiaries of the Society and the five thousand dollars which Amherst received constituted about one-quarter of that college's total income. Middlebury had sixty-one beneficiaries; Dartmouth, forty-four; Williams, twenty-eight; Bowdoin, twenty-six. Even Yale owed fifteen percent of its enrollment to its popularity among "young men of piety and promise." "No year passes," the Society's *American Quarterly Register* concluded in 1837, "without the descent of the Holy Ghost to a greater or lesser degree upon our colleges." Pentecostal visitations to Cambridge were obviously to a lesser degree.[48]

Traditionally, the college received little financial support from its alumni. Indeed, prior to the establishment of the Smith professorship in 1816 all its principal benefactions had been from outsiders. Harvard graduates apparently found too many other causes, either temporally more satisfying or giving promise of greater eternal reward, to consider Harvard as a recipient for their philanthropy. Many felt, especially during the state-grant years, that the college did not need their support. Whereas Kirkland never disabused them of this notion, both Bowditch and Quincy felt constrained from painting the financial situation in its truest colors for fear of revealing just how badly the college had been managed.[49]

The rigid economies effected by Bowditch after 1826 restored Harvard to reasonably good financial shape by the early 1830's; but when the college's substantial holdings in the Charles River Bridge Corporation were rendered worthless by the opening of the toll-free Warren Bridge in 1836, the situation again became desperate. Quincy estimated the loss at $35,000. No longer could Harvard wait upon the unsolicited benevolence of friends; it would have to go hat-in-hand among its sadly neglectful progeny.[50]

As Joseph Story's efforts two years earlier revealed, ideological as well as organizational obstacles had to be surmounted before the alumni could be successfully solicited. Calling together a select group of graduates in 1834 to get support for a beneficiary fund to reduce the cost of a Harvard education, Story encountered opposition from alumni no less loyal than John Lowell, Leverett Saltonstall, and John

Quincy Adams. Adams thought such a fund would be "a mere bonus to the merchants of Boston and to a few clergymen, throughout the state to send their sons to Cambridge rather than to Amherst, or Williamstown, or New Haven, or Providence for Education." Story's argument that such a fund was essential if Harvard was to compete for students left the group unpersuaded. "I likened it," Adams wrote in his diary, "to a stage or a steamboat competition in which the parties underbid each other, for customers, until one offers to convey passengers for nothing, and the other to pay them, instead of receiving pay for them for their passage."[51]

A second attempt to organize alumni financial support took place at the Harvard Bicentennial on September 8, 1836. A subscription banquet to which all Harvard alumni were invited, and which nearly eleven hundred attended, was held in the Yard beneath a massive tent. Dinner was served, toasts offered and drunk, speeches made, and vague promises of future support received. Then everybody went home. "They get up these things very well," acknowledged Charles Francis Adams who left early; nevertheless, he remained convinced that "the University has entirely lost her hold on the feelings of the State and is doing worse than nothing in the way to regain it." "I am sorry," he added, "not so much on my account for little is there of gratification to me in her reminiscences, but because my father and grandfather felt otherwise." From such stones was Harvard expected to squeeze her sustenance.[52]

Quincy held aloof from these early efforts at alumni fund-raising. Although he encouraged Story's efforts and certainly supported the idea of a beneficiary fund, he believed that, as "President of a Seminary like that of Harvard," his duties were already such as to exempt him from "the pain and drudgery of a common solicitor of charities." By 1838, however, his personal sense of responsibility for the welfare of the college obliged him to reconsider. "At every Commencement great things are talked of; glorious visions are hung in the clouds; 100,000 dollars are to be raised to give a lift to the University," he complained to Samuel A. Eliot, then Mayor of Boston, but then "Nothing is done. 'The bear is lost' while the hunters are disputing how they should divide the skin after he is taken."[53]

What particularly irritated Qunicy were the continued insinuations that Harvard's failure to increase its enrollment was due to mismanagement or because "its morals are worse than other colleges." As he insisted to the Corporation in 1834, when he tried unsuccessfully to lower the tuition, the problem in attracting students was essentially one of cost. Four years later he decided to prove his point. "I am about to adopt a course," he informed Eliot on August 30, 1838, "which I have hitherto, from delicacy or prudence, scrupulously avoided." Pledging five hundred dollars himself, and vouching for another thousand, Quincy launched a subscription campaign to provide Harvard with a fund sufficient to help the forty students he turned away each year because they could not pay the full tuition. "At least let us raise ten thousand dollars," he pleaded, "make the trail. Do not let us postpone, promise change and do nothing."[54]

Once into the fund-raising business, Quincy moved quickly to answer the objections raised earlier by Adams and other alumni about a beneficiary fund. " 'We do not wish to increase the numbers in the seminary,' " he paraphrased their argument. " 'We wish few to be educated and that thoroughly. Let the best scholars be those educated; and those come, who are able to pay for it!' . . . This language," he went on, "I know to be used." Yet no position could be more destructive of the college or more "false to the interests of men of property."

The class of men, who are thus excluded from the education they desire, are the very men which the wealthy ought to desire and *earnestly seek to be associated with their sons*. They are generally advanced in years—staid in their habits—fixed in their principles—right in their views. The good order and good spirit of the College is essentially modified by their influence. . . . It is a great misfortune to a College to have for its inmates, a very great proportion of the sons of men of wealth.

Nature has provided a compensation for their prosperity in the certain deterioration of their sons, unless some strong counteracting influences are provided by themselves to destroy the corrupting effect of the expectation of property.

Still a long way from sounding like a democrat, Quincy was not above turning a little Jacksonian rhetoric to the purposes of Harvard College.[55]

The beneficiary fund-drive proved to be an immediate and lasting success. The original goal of $10,000 was subscribed in less than two months and was surpassed several times over in the following years. By December 1840, twenty-one students were receiving tuition aid. As Quincy had predicted, the college's competitive situation improved accordingly. During the six years prior to the fund's establishment, enrollment had averaged 224 students; during the first six years of the fund's operation, 252 students. Harvard's years of declining and static enrollments were over; but gone too were the days when one of its presidents could imagine that his duties did not include that of "a common solicitor of charities."[56]

During Quincy's later years as president, he involved himself in a number of other successful subscription campaigns, including one for the library which netted more than $21,000. But the fund-raising project with which he was most closely identified was that for an astronomical observatory in Cambridge. Harvard had prided itself on its contributions to astronomy ever since the college treasurer Thomas Brattle recorded his observations of solar and lunar eclipses at the end of the seventeenth century. Still more illustrious was the work of John Winthrop whose observations of the transit of Venus in 1761 won him membership in Britain's Royal Society. As early as 1804 the Corporation seriously considered the possibility of building an observatory which would have been the first in the country.[57]

Although nothing came of the 1804 discussions, eleven years later William Cranch Bond, a young Dorchester clockmaker and amateur astronomer, was commissioned by the Corporation to examine the operations of England's Greenwich Observatory and report on the feasibility of equipping an observatory in Cambridge. Again interest waned and Bond, who had been promised the directorship of the contemplated observatory, returned to Dorchester where he spent the next twenty-three years making astronomical and meteorological observations through a hole in his parlor roof.[58]

In 1823 as Secretary of State, and again in 1825 as President, John Quincy Adams urged the Corporation to seize the opportunity to build the country's first observatory. He subscribed $1,000 in the hope that others would follow, but few did and the subscription failed. Affecting the utilitarian attitude, if not that of frontiersmen, wealthy Bostonians were too preoccupied with China clippers, factories, and railroads to underwrite any of Adams' frivolous ideas about "lighthouses in the sky."[59]

With Quincy's personal intervention in 1839 the idea of building an observatory in Cambridge was revived. Several reasons can be suggested for his interest in such an expensive project. His interest in science, as attested by his faithful attendance at meetings of the

Society for the Study of Natural Philosophy thirty-five years earlier, was genuine, however dormant in the intervening years. Moreover, his life-long affection for John Quincy Adams may well have prompted him to take up a project dear to the old President's heart. The most important reason for his involvement, however, was his realization that an observatory in Cambridge would further substantiate Harvard's claims to the title of university.[60]

Like the Quincy Market project fifteen years earlier, the Harvard Astronomical Observatory drive bears Quincy's distinctive signature. It was he who asked Bond in 1839 to transfer his astronomical activities from Dorchester to Cambridge. The next year he launched a subscription campaign to acquire the $3,000 necessary to outfit Dana House for Bond's observational purposes. When the fund was fully subscribed he asked the Corporation to appoint Bond to the unsalaried post of "Observer of Harvard University."[61]

Dana House, located on the site of the present Lamont Library, served as the college observatory until 1844. Long before that, Bond, Peirce, now Perkins Professor of Mathematics and Astronomy, and Joseph Lovering, Hollis Professor of Mathematics, had found its facilities inadequate for their needs. The limitations were clearly revealed when Peirce and Bond were able to get only the most rudimentary data on "a comet of surpassing size and splendour" that blazed across the Boston sky on the night of March 6, 1843.[62]

Several of Boston's wealthiest gentlemen, suddenly fascinated with astronomy, conferred with Quincy after this incident to learn how they might help improve the observatory's facilities. The president promptly announced another drive, this one for $20,000 to buy a fifteen-inch refracting telescope, the largest then made, and to provide a building in which to house it. Although David Sears launched the drive with a $5,000 contribution, other potential subscribers seemed hesitant. Harvard's reputation among Boston students of science was not what it might have been.* Members of the old Linnaean Society, for example, had never forgiven President Kirkland for allowing a natural history collection, on loan from the society to the college, to rot away in the basement of Harvard Hall. Others thought the proposed observatory ought to be built in Boston, safely removed from student disruptions. Ultimately these

---

*The decision of the Lowells in 1840 to establish their lecture institute in Boston rather than in Cambridge under the auspices of Harvard is indicative of the dubious reputation of the college among Boston promoters of science.

fears were put to rest when Quincy assured potential subscribers that the observatory would not be used "as an instrument of instruction of undergraduates," but would be devoted to "the advancement of astronomical science in the world."[6 3]

Without waiting for the funds, Quincy proceeded to purchase land for the new observatory. The location he selected, two miles northwest of the college and commanding an impressive view of the entire Charles River Basin, confirmed his reputation as a shrewd investor and showed him to be well aware of the scientific needs of an observatory. On September 12, 1844, Bond transferred his equipment to the new site and immediately resumed his observations. During the summer of 1847 the "Giant Refractor" arrived, permitting Bond and Peirce to begin a series of stellar observations that would win them and the Harvard Astronomical Observatory international acclaim.[6 4]

Quincy's interest in the observatory extended beyond his retirement in 1845. He continued to serve as an overseer of the observatory, and maintained a close friendship with Bond along with an active curiosity about his work. It was on Quincy's advice that his grandnephew, Edward Bromfield Phillips, decided shortly before he died in 1848 to make the observatory his principal beneficiary. This $100,000 windfall not only assured the institution's survival but finally enabled the overseers to begin paying a salary to Bond and his assistants. In 1855 Quincy himself gave the observatory $10,000 to underwrite the *Annals of the Astronomical Observatory of Harvard College*, the first regularly published contribution of the Harvard community to the larger world of scholarship.[6 5]

It took far more money than Quincy could command to implement fully his aspirations for Harvard. That money became available only after the Civil War and enabled President Eliot during the 1870's and 1880's to complete the transformation from provincial college to one of the world's great centers of learning. Yet the desire, the energy, and the executive ability to have done so had existed in Cambridge forty years earlier.

Into the Politico-Theologico Sea

On December 26, 1840, the Cambridge printer Charles Folsom announced the long-awaited publication of *The History of Harvard University*, by Josiah Quincy. Published in two octavo volumes and elegantly bound in cloth, it contained more than nine hundred pages of text, four hundred pages of appendices, and twenty-one steel engravings. "As far as we know," surmised the *North American Review*, "nothing in style of such completeness and luxury has before proceeded from the American press," while the *Christian Examiner* was equally impressed with the *History*'s "beauty of execution, both in type and pictorial illustration." In conception as well as execution, Quincy intended this historical labor for the ages.[66]

Six years in the making, the *History* owed its origins to a Corporation request in 1834 that Quincy prepare an historical discourse for the Bicentennial festivities scheduled for the fall of 1836. Though he promptly set to work on it, and devoted the two intervening summers to his task, he managed to get Harvard's story only as far as 1708 by delivery time. Nevertheless, his efforts were well received and he decided to take up the long-standing appeal of the Corporation for a full-dress history of the college. At the age of sixty-four, and with all his other responsibilities, this was no small undertaking. But once committed, he gave to the pursuit of Harvard's past the same enthusiastic energy he gave its present administration. Neither time nor expense was spared as he and his daughter Eliza Susan combed the college and state archives, those of the Massachusetts Historical and American Antiquarian Societies, and collected materials relating to Harvard from several English sources. In its documentation, Quincy's *History of Harvard University* deserves to be ranked alongside the work of Bancroft, Prescott, and Parkman.[67]

The *History* is, however, more than a collection of documents strung together by a date-filled narrative. Quincy wrote with vigor and purpose; his central theme, the gradual divestment by Harvard of its original sectarian purposes and the adoption of the ideal of disinterested scholarship, is continually in evidence. The narrative is both dramatic and highly personalized, crowded with confrontations between villains like "the restless, violent, selfish and passionate" Cotton Mather and heroes on the order of the "calm, chastened, disinterested" John Leverett. In contrast with most academic histories, Quincy's does not pass over the seamier aspects; full coverage is given to Headmaster Nathaniel Eaton and his financial improprieties, to Hollis Professor of Mathematics Isaac Greenwood and his drinking problem, and to John Hancock, College Treasurer during the 1770's, and his "extraordinary and wayward conduct" in that office. Asked why he bothered to detail the revolutionary hero's malfeasance, Quincy explained: "I had no choice between giving them in their fullness, or proving myself recreant and without nerve to execute a task I had undertaken."[68]

Quincy served his larger purposes well by subdividing Harvard's two centuries into four periods. The first, from the founding of the college in 1636 to the granting of the 1692 Charter by King William and Queen Mary, is described as "the theological phase." During this period and despite the 1642 Constitution's "independence of a sectarian spirit," Harvard existed "as an instrument destined to promote and perpetuate the religious opinions predominating at the time." Particularly in their dealings with President Henry Dunster, whose views on infant baptism brought him into conflict with the prevailing orthodoxy and forced his resignation, the early directors of the college were "neither kind nor just."[69]

The second period, from 1692 to the installation of President Edward Holyoke in 1737, is depicted in the context of intense religious controversy, controversy which split the Congregationalist Church into two irreconcilable camps and made control of Harvard a major objective of both. The defeat of Cotton Mather for the presidency in 1708 by John Leverett represented a decisive victory for the religious liberals who had aligned with Corporation Fellow William Brattle; it also marked the point when "High Calvinists began to look elsewhere for instruments to propogate their sentiments and extend their power." During this period Quincy's narrative approaches epic dimensions, wherein "Christo et Ecclesiae," the sectarian motto the Mathers had imposed upon Harvard, is overcome by the sentiments implicit in the earlier, but, until Quincy's researches rescued it, all but forgotten motto, "Veritas."[70]

The third period of Harvard's history, extending through Holyoke's long presidency and the Revolution, is viewed as one of "relative tranquillity." Although the college continued to be an object of sectarian wrangling, political issues after 1760 obliged the churches of Massachusetts to put aside their local differences in the face of what they conceived to be a common external threat to their liberties. Quincy also argued that the Great Awakening, and particularly George Whitefield's attack on "corrupt Harvard," had a quieting effect. "The controversy with Whitefield," he wrote, "was the last of a theological character in which the governors of the college directly engaged. As doctrinal disputes grew more intense and critical, they stood aloof, realizing the wisdom of conducting the seminary exclusively as a literary, rather than as a theological institution."[7 1]

The last period, from the 1780's to 1840, is rendered in more muted tones than those used in the earlier three. Discussion of the struggle over the Hollis Professorship of Divinity in 1804-1805 is circumspect. The impression is conveyed, however, that its outcome was a victory not for Unitarianism over Calvinism but for those who conceived of Harvard "as a tree, destined to support and develop all the objects of human knowledge and pursuit, in proportion to their respective value and importance; of which Theology should always be a branch, but no longer the stem."[7 2]

About Harvard's continuing financial troubles Quincy showed a similar reticence. Nothing is said of the General Court's decision not to renew the state subsidy in 1824 except that it came "under circumstances rendering vain expectation of relief from the legislature in the future." In part this can be attributed to the author's personal affection for Kirkland and his reluctance to condemn his contemporaries on the Corporation for bringing the college to the brink of bankruptcy. A more compelling reason seems to have been Quincy's fear that detailing the financial sins of his predecessor would not serve his secondary purpose in writing the *History*: to impress upon its readers the fact that Harvard, having divested itself of sectarian backing and state support, was now wholly dependent for survival upon the generosity of private benefactors. Accordingly, the sixty-four appendices which accompany the text are largely given over to proving that the college's principal support had always been from private rather than sectarian or public sources. "Because of the views it presented of the foundations and finances of the institution," Quincy told the Corporation when he explained why he set the price of the *History* at a modest five dollars, "I think it both desirable, and for the advantage of the university, that it should have as wide a circulation as possible, particularly among Alumni and friends of the College."[7 3]

Fully as much an ecclesiastical history of New England as a history of Harvard, Quincy's account was assured a wide and not always uncritical audience. From some quarters, especially where theologically liberal opinions prevailed, came warm approval. The *Christian Examiner* praised its "fidelity, accuracy, fulness, and, as we think, signal impartiality of detail." No less a critic than Francis Parkman concluded that "it needs no prophetic sagacity or boldness to assert, that it will endure." Others, however, hoped it would not. The Reverend Enoch Pond, writing in the Calvinist *American Biblical Repository*, flatly rejected Quincy's thesis that Harvard owed its success to the support it had received from Massachusetts liberals. He responded to Quincy's slashing attack upon the Mathers with a labored defense of Harvard's only absentee president and his Yale-boosting son. Unquestionably the most succinctly damning criticism of the book came from the Reverend William M. Rogers, a leading Congregationalist spokesman and pastor of Boston's Central Church: "President Quincy's History of Harvard College is a partisan work, by a partisan man, and written for partisan purposes."[74]

Quincy had not calculatedly given offense to Harvard's traditional enemies. He was not himself a particularly disputatious Unitarian and as president of Harvard had tried to keep the college out of sectarian and political controversies. His endorsement of Jackson's honorary degree in 1833 was but one instance of his defensive non-partisanship. Six years later, when Abolitionism was splitting the Boston Whig community into two distinct camps, he dissuaded John Gorham Palfrey from using the divinity school as a forum for his anti-slavery views. "Whatever may be your, or my private opinion, on the main question," Quincy advised, Harvard should not add to "the state of excessive excitability of the public mind on the topic."[75]

But when this sense of moderation failed to impress certain critical readers of his *History*, Quincy refused to soften those passages which Edward Everett and others construed as evidence of his "religious partizanship." "The work was well considered and diligently labored," he answered those who thought him unduly harsh on the Calvinists. "The hopeless design, or the vain desire, of pleasing everybody was not mine. Those who think history and eulogy are terms identical, and whose maxim is 'de mortues nil nise bonum,' will be dissatisfied in advance."[76]

If his forthrightness offended some, it served to awaken others to the pressing needs of the college. Six months after the publication of Quincy's *History* the first formal meeting of the Harvard Alumni

Association was held. And, like the *History*, the meeting was a response to what Charles Greeley Loring described in 1839 as "the extraordinary state of apathy towards the College of those who were its members." Quincy's daughter later contended that it was her father's *History* that provided the catalyst which transformed Harvard's apathetic alumni into an organized, functioning reality. Whatever the impetus, it has been a reality that has impressed itself upon the life and fortunes of the university ever since.[77]

In January 1843 the voters of Massachusetts, in a political turnabout, awarded twenty-six of the state senate's thirty-six seats to Democrats. Having already elected a Democrat governor the previous November, they merely confirmed the Jacksonian sweep of the state and the routing of the Whigs. The implications of this for Harvard were obvious and frightening. Since the Board of Overseers was composed principally of elected state officials, the college now found one of its two governing boards in the hands of politicians who were numbered among its harshest critics. While the Whigs had controlled the General Court during the previous decade, acknowledged friends of Harvard like James Savage, Lemuel Shaw, and Leverett Saltonstall kept the overseers from questioning the Corporation. The Visiting Committee had made only cursory inspections and subscribed to Saltonstall's view that "nothing could be more ridiculous or pernicious than for the Overseers to enter into the details and minute arrangements of the *great family* at Cambridge."[78]

But this was precisely what the new Democratic overseers were intent on doing when they gathered on February 3, 1843. The way in which they handled the first order of business, the election of a permanent member to fill the vacancy created by John Pickering's retirement, was an indication of things to come. Rejecting the Corporation's endorsement of John Chipman Gray, the board proceeded to elect George Bancroft by a vote of thirty-nine to twenty-three. Bancroft, the state's best known Democrat, had a well-earned reputation as a Harvard-baiter, virtually a prerequisite for advancement within the Jacksonian ranks. Like Alexander Hill Everett, another Harvard-man-turned-Democrat, Bancroft had shifted his academic allegiances to Brown where it was thought "the common man" was more highly esteemed than at "old Tory Harvard."[79]

Overseers predisposed to be critical of Harvard had their task made simpler by the fact that of all American colleges it alone published an annual *President*'s and *Treasurer's Report*. These yearly unbuttonings, instituted in 1826, were a ready source of "incriminating" evidence with which to embarrass Quincy and the Corporation. John A. Park, for example, a Democratic state senator and prominent Calvinist layman, seized upon an entry in Quincy's 1842 *Report*, which he interpreted as meaning that there were more unexcused absences from chapel recorded against the seniors than against the other classes, and demanded an immediate explanation. Clearly irritated by such petty harassment, Quincy took up most of the next meeting to inform Park that he had misread the figures and that "no such excess of unexcused absences from public worship exists as requires remedy."[80]

A more substantive challenge to the Corporation's control of the college was raised at the February 22, 1844, meeting of the overseers. The Reverend Rodney A. Miller, one of the board's permanent clerical members and an outspoken Calvinist, moved that the Visiting Committee be directed to look into student expenses at Cambridge and recommend steps to reduce them. Although the overseers had in the past always left such matters to the Corporation, Bancroft, who was a member of the Visiting Committee, enthusiastically endorsed the motion and promised to take an active part in the investigation. After approving the motion, the Democrats proceeded to stack the committee with dependable Harvard-baiters. "It was enough," a Whig overseer concluded, "to make one perfectly disgusted with mankind."[81]

Fortunately for Harvard, Democratic control of the General Court proved to be short-lived. The 1844 elections restored the Whigs to power in Massachusetts and assured a Whig majority on the Harvard Board of Overseers. Thus, while the findings of the Visiting Committee, when presented in January 1845, were not a clear endorsement of the Corporation's management of the college's finances, they were hardly incriminating. The expected report from Bancroft on student expenses was not presented because, according to the committee chairman, it had not been submitted. Bancroft, who had spent the fall unsuccessfully running for governor, promised to deliver it at the next meeting.[82]

When finally presented on February 7, Bancroft's *Report on Diminishing the Cost of Instruction in Harvard College* proved long on accusations and short on documentation. Striking a properly Jacksonian note at the outset, Bancroft charged Harvard, "an institution which belongs to the public," with being willfully derelict in its responsibility to make access to it "as free as possible." Among his specific complaints were: tuition and living expenses were prohibitive; admission standards were exclusionary; professors were underworked; students were overworked; the construction of Gore Library had been an unjustifiáble extravagance. Nor did he stick at personal accusations. "The capital defect in the system at Harvard is this," he informed the overseers, "the President of the College teaches nothing." The *Minority Report* closed by recommending that Quincy's salary be cut by sixty percent and faculty salaries by twenty, that the elective system be abolished as it was too taxing on the students, that admission requirements be abandoned, and that no future capital expenditure be undertaken by the Corporation without first securing the approval of the overseers.[83]

Three committees, all chaired by Whigs critical of Bancroft, promptly set about to bury his *Report*. With the Democrats again in the minority on the board, some Whigs thought it best simply to ignore his charges. "The public sentiment is sufficiently strong against him," Charles Greeley Loring advised Quincy, "it is thought that your dignity and that of the College will be best served by keeping as far from him as possible and avoiding all allusions to him." However sound the advice, there was little chance that the president would heed it.[84]

Quincy's *Speech on the Minority Report by George Bancroft*, delivered to the overseers on February 25, 1845, is one of his best polemics. He demolished Bancroft's case by showing his statistics to be inaccurate, personal accusations unfounded, and proposed remedies either impractical or ill-considered. In answering the charge that expenses at Harvard had increased greatly during his presidency, Quincy had dug out Bancroft's bills as an undergraduate and showed them to be greater than those of a typical student in the 1840's. The good order of the college, Bancroft's "non-committal insinuation" notwithstanding, was documented by figures attesting to the steadily declining cost of special repairs required because of student vandalism. As to the charge that Quincy had not been pulling his weight in the classroom, he dared Bancroft to cite a Harvard president since Samuel Langdon, an acknowledged disaster, who had. "Is it not a little remarkable," the Reverend John Pierce, who, as Secretary of the Overseers, had closely followed the debate, "that Mr. Bancroft did not seek access to the only authentic source of correct information to substantiate his severe charges?"[8 5]

Disposing of this clumsy effort to discredit himself and the Corporation was only part of Quincy's purpose in addressing the overseers. What bothered him most about Bancroft's accusations was that, though essentially irresponsible, they were guaranteed a respectful hearing by virtue of the fact that they were made by a member of an official body of the state and college. The next effort might not be so clumsy. "It is the fate of Harvard College," the president argued, "to be cast by the constitution of its Board of Overseers, into the very troughs of a politico-theologico sea, which has tossed that seminary in successive periods of its history, always to its injury, sometimes nearly to its destruction." What Quincy was calling for was nothing less than the removal of the Board of Overseers, and Harvard, from that sea. He wanted a board no longer dominated by state officials but comprised of alumni of the college. While this reform was not to be accomplished for another seven years, Quincy's earlier advocacy of Harvard self-rule helped make it possible. Like his efforts on behalf of the college's intellectual and financial independence, those to secure Harvard's political autonomy served to clear the way for the university-builders who followed him.[8 6]

Four weeks after his speech to the overseers, Quincy informed the Corporation that "unless internal difficulties in the seminary should render a temporary postponement of that purpose necessary," he would resign at the end of the academic year. "In point of actual labor, expenditure of time, mental application, wear and tear of feelings, and consequent exhaustion," he complained in 1842 when he had first informed the Corporation of his desire to retire in 1845, "the office of the mayor is in every particular less onerous, is less attended with the oppressive sense of responsibility than is the Presidency of Harvard College." For sixteen years he had awakened at four o'clock to meet the demands of his office—"the universal superintendency of all its concerns, moral, literary, economical and fiscal." And now, at seventy-three, he was tired. "In spite of his hale look and vigorous habits," an undergraduate during Quincy's last years in Cambridge later recalled, "he passed there for a man who was growing old. His forgetfulness and uncertain manners gave a slight impression of senility; he was loved and ever respected but it was the respect due to an old man."[8][7]

On August 28, 1845, Harvard's sixteenth president officially resigned. The most frequently cited evaluation of his tenure is Emerson's: "Old Quincy, with all his worth and a sort of violent service he did the College, was a lubber and a grenadier among our clerks." But Emerson's judgment in these matters was far from faultless, as indicated by his belief that Everett would make an excellent successor. Whatever else one may say of "Old Quincy," he found Harvard in 1829 on the brink of despair and left it sixteen years later on the threshold of greatness.[8][8]

10 / A Final Eminence

> Rightly it is said
> That man descends into a Vale of years;
> Yet have I thought that we might also speak,
> And not presumptuously, I trust, of Age,
> As of a final EMINENCE; though bare
> In aspect and forbidding, yet a point
> On which 'tis not impossible to sit
> In awful sovereignty.
>
> —William Wordsworth

"Instead of rolling in the dirt as other animals do under a state of like regained liberty, I intend to repose on the green sward." So Quincy assured friends upon resigning. Preparations for doing so had been in progress since 1842 when a large house was purchased in Boston's Bowdoin Place, a quiet cul de sac just off Beacon Street. It was there, he told those who asked of his plans, "I hope to pass softly and quietly and thankfully the last days. . . ."[1]

Nestor

For a while it looked as if he might take retirement seriously. "I have at length the felicity of being my own master," he wrote on the eve of his seventy-fourth birthday, "relieved from the servitude of place and office, and have entire liberty to devote my time according to my duty to myself and Heaven." Once away from Cambridge, his household resumed the seasonal pattern of thirty years earlier. Summers were spent on the farm in Braintree. On Sundays the family attended services at the First Congregationalist Church where Quincy sat stiffly in his main-aisle pew, directly behind the congregation's other distinguished senior member, John Quincy Adams. Both were the object of Adams' nine-year old grandson's rapt attention. As young Henry observed the backs of their ancient heads, one graying and the other bald, he surmised that they must have "sat there, or in some equivalent dignity, since the time of St. Augustine, if not since the glacial epoch."[2]

During the winters spent in Boston, visitors were received, historical society meetings attended, and, on clear nights, trips were made
to Cambridge to observe the stars with Mr. Bond. In addition to
renewing his classical studies, Quincy began to keep a diary; both
were conscious efforts to elude what Cicero warned were the vices of
age—"indolence and indifference to labor."[3]

Such precautions were hardly necessary. During the first thirteen
years of his retirement, Quincy wrote and published more than ever
before. Along with *The History of the Boston Athenaeum* (1851)
and *A Municipal History of Boston* (1852), he wrote memoirs of
James Grahame, the English historian of the American Colonies, and
of Samuel Shaw and John Bromfield, two early China merchants, as
well as a masterly tribute to John Quincy Adams. Beginning in 1846,
and for the next decade, he personally managed his farm and busied
himself with various agricultural experiments, this time with more
favorable results. "My corn is flourishing, my barley excellent, rye
abundant, and my general products so great," he boasted in 1856,
"that for aught I must pull down my barns and build larger." Two
years earlier, Richard Henry Dana Jr. acknowledged that "the old
gentleman, at 83 . . . had an excellent farm, and is a thoroughly
practical farmer."[4]

These literary and agricultural occupations notwithstanding, Quincy found it impossible to avoid being drawn into polemical combat.
By asserting his proprietary interest in the local institutions which he
had served during his public career, he succeeded in embroiling
himself in several enjoyable skirmishes.

Of the many "reforms" instituted at Harvard during Edward
Everett's brief and unhappy presidency, only one drew Quincy into
print: the alteration of the institution's title from "Harvard University" to "the University of Cambridge in New England." While most
alumni regarded this change with indifference, or were mildly
amused by Everett's anglophilia, the author of *The History of
Harvard University* viewed the matter more darkly. Quincy warned
Jared Sparks, who succeeded to the presidency after Everett's escape
to the State Department in 1849, that the change was intended "to
rid the institution of 'the tang of Puritanism.' This," he insisted,
"could not fail to be pleasing to Episcopalians, and to men Episco-
palianly inclined; a party which was growing into great influence in
consequence of the recent infusion into our religious system of

Roman Catholicism." Sparks, while not fully persuaded of Quincy's theory of a Popish plot to undermine Harvard, did agree that "the University of Cambridge" was historically indefensible and abandoned it.[5]

Proposals to alter Boston's municipal arrangements also received Quincy's closest scrutiny. In 1849 he argued unsuccessfully against the transfer of the jurisdiction of the Boston municipal court—*his* court—to the state superior court. Two years later he helped delay the expansion of the Board of Aldermen and a plan for its selection by ward voting. These were proposals he had opposed twenty-five years earlier as mayor; his belief that the board should be small and elected-at-large so as to attract "men of energy, of appropriate talent, and approved fidelity," had not changed. Despite his continued opposition, both changes were adopted in 1854.[6]

A decision by Mayor Benjamin Seaver in 1852 to sell city-owned property around Quincy Market also drew the ex-mayor's ire. The land, which Quincy had acquired during the early stages of the market project, provided the city with considerable revenue and remained, or so he tried to convince Seaver, a sound civic investment. Accordingly when Seaver, pleading poverty, went ahead and offered the property for sale, Quincy himself bought it for $411,000. After the city declined his offer to buy it back, he decided to develop the area commercially. At the age of eighty-two he found himself the city's largest landowner. During the next few years he showed himself to be one of its shrewdest. Boston's loss was the Quincys' gain as income from this property remained the family's principal support long after the death of their crafty father.[7]

The most heated civic controversy in which Quincy engaged was over the annexation of Charlestown by Boston in 1854. As he viewed it, this would be the first step in Boston's absorption of all its neighboring towns and would ultimately end in the creation of "a gigantic metropolis, vying in numbers and extent with New York and Philadelphia." In arguing against such a plan, he revealed all his old Federalist distrust of economic complexity and cultural heterogeneity, as well as his fear of what he now called "new social organizations." Bostonians, he wrote in his *Considerations . . . on the Proposed Annexation of Boston and Charlestown*, "ought never to let the example of any means of population and extent be the criterion of their character and dignity." Again he found it useful to call upon his political nemesis for moral support: "Great cities Mr. Jefferson long ago denominated 'great sores,' and, undoubtedly their tendency is not conductive to the morals or health of the body politic."[8]

Quincy's pamphlet elicited several responses. W. W. Wheildon, a leading annexationist, tried to discredit his argument by labelling him, not without cause, "in opposition to the enterprise of the age." "The ideas are almost antideluvian," Wheildon went on, "and would not only have prevented any enlargement of the Garden of Eden, but any increase of its inhabitants!" Despite the sarcasm it evoked, and the characterization of his views as "conservative as a cramp," Quincy's pamphlet succeeded in arousing enough opposition to oblige the annexationists to shelve their plans for fifteen years.[9]

During the 1850's both the Boston Athenaeum and the Massachusetts Historical Society had occasion to call upon their oldest living member to defend them against the encroachments of newer organizations of cultural betterment. When, in 1853, George Ticknor proposed that the Athenaeum turn over its collection and building to the newly established, but as yet unhoused, Boston Public Library, not many of the seven hundred members seemed disposed to protest. To the author of *The History of the Boston Athenaeum*, however, the idea of "surrendering one of the oldest monuments which patriotism and public spirit, and love of learning, in this country, ever raised," to "a political body, annually shifting its members, and changing principles and policy with every turn of party or passion," was preposterous. Due largely to Quincy's *Appeal in Behalf of the Boston Athenaeum*, Ticknor's proposal was rejected by the membership and a commitment to sustain the institution was made that continues to be honored.[10]

"Was ever a legislature," Quincy asked a committee of the General Court on February 18, 1858, "called upon to legislate on a matter so small and trivial?" The matter in question was a petition presented to the legislature by the New England Historic-Genealogical Society to change its title to the New England Historical-Genealogical Society. "Nothing is wanted by the petitioners to make them happy and great," Quincy acknowledged, "but the additional *al* to their already sesquipedalian name." Nevertheless, speaking for the Massachusetts Historical Society, he argued against the granting of the petition as an encroachment upon the older organization's use of the appellation, "*the* Historical Society." When the legislative committee denied the petition, Quincy's friends had yet another opportunity to honor him as "the Nestor of our fellowship," while the disappointed members of the Historic-Genealogical Society, who later reconstituted themselves as the Prince Society, preferred to think of him as a meddling old fool.[11]

Father and Sons

Aside from these gratifying diversions, Quincy enjoyed two other consolations in his old age: good health and the companionship of a large and attentive family. Conscious of his father's early death from consumption, he had always taken fastidious care of himself. He did not drink, watched his diet, and exercised. Work on the farm, long walks, and early morning gallops had allowed him while mayor to retain a trim figure into his fifties. When confronted with the essentially sedentary duties of the Harvard presidency, he devised an elaborate series of exercises for keeping "the vital juices surging," which he continued after leaving Cambridge. "He rises at 5 o'clock every morning," an acquaintance reported in 1857,

bathes his head and feet and sits down in water, then exercises himself violently for fifteen minutes without any clothing whatever, in winter when there is a fire, endeavoring to move every muscle instead of one set of muscles as would be the case if the exercises were limited to walking. Thus he excites a glow and then uses a cloth and flesh brush. All the pores are thus opened and this being done without any obstructions from garments the exhalations all pass off without being confined by his clothes. He needs no more exercise.

At eighty-five, one would hope not.[12]

In 1848 the Quincys celebrated their fiftieth wedding anniversary. During all those years, except for five winters Quincy spent alone in Washington, they had virtually never been apart. Shortly after the family moved out to Braintree in the spring of 1850, Eliza's health began to fail. On September 1 she died. "Few have on the whole," Charles Francis Adams said of her, "enjoyed more uninterruptedly moderate prosperity." As for her bereaved husband, Adams wrote: "Mr. Quincy seemed affected, but not overcome." Beneath his composed appearance, however, he was devastated. "It is the will of heaven," Quincy wrote two months after his wife's death. "I submit, but nature cannot be stayed in vindicating its affections. Life is not, it cannot be to me hereafter, what it once was."[13]

Eliza Susan became mistress of her father's household, while retaining her responsibilities as his amanuensis. Abigail and Maria, now resigned to spinsterhood, remained an integral part of the family. When Quincy purchased Francis Calley Gray's mansion on Park Street in 1857, Eliza Susan, Abigail, and Maria made the move from Bowdoin Place with him. His two other daughters, Margaret and Anna, lived nearby with their gentlemen-of-leisure-and-learning husbands, the non-ministering Reverend Robert Cassie Waterston and the non-practicing Dr. Benjamin Greene. And then there were his two sons, Josiah Jr. and Edmund.[14]

Both sons had attended Andover before going on to Harvard. Despite competition from his classmate Ralph Waldo Emerson, Josiah Jr., Class of 1821, won the Boylston Prize in English Composition. Edmund, Class of 1827, though less successful as a student than his brother, like him was elected to Phi Beta Kappa. Both held commissions in the Washington Corps and were members of Hasty Pudding and Edmund was president of Porcellian.[15]

Allowed all the options of young men with "too much expectation of property," each in his turn decided to study law. Fortunately, neither was dependent upon the profession for subsistence. After marrying daughters of wealthy Boston merchants, both were able to abandon their practices almost immediately upon being admitted to the bar. It was at this point that their paths separated: Josiah Jr. became a railroad entrepreneur and a Whig politician; Edmund turned to newspaper work and abolitionism.[16]

Josiah Jr.'s political aspirations were acknowledged in 1832 when he was selected to deliver Boston's Fourth of July Oration. The following year he won election to the Common Council and from 1834 to 1837 served as its president. During this period he became interested in the possibility of linking Boston by rail to Albany and the Erie Canal. Without such a connection, he warned his fellow Bostonians, the city's days as a commercial center were numbered. In January 1836, following a reorganization of the recently chartered Boston and Albany Railroad, Quincy was elected its treasurer. While the company's engineers cut their way through the Berkshires, he managed to keep the railroad solvent through stock subscriptions, loans, and state aid. Once the Albany hookup was made in 1841, the stockholders began realizing a handsome return. When Quincy resigned as treasurer in 1846, he left with a reputation for financial shrewdness and a lot of money.[17]

Meanwhile, his political star continued to rise. On December 8, 1845, he was elected Mayor of Boston. During his three terms, he presided over the most efficient and innovative administration since that of his father. The police department was reorganized and greatly expanded while heroic, if inadequate, efforts were made to meet the needs of the thousands of Irish immigrants beginning to pour into Boston. The most notable accomplishment of the second Mayor Quincy, however, was the completion of the $2,500,000 Cochituate waterworks project to meet the city's needs for fresh water—needs recognized but not acted upon by the first Mayor Quincy.[18]

After his voluntary resignation in 1849, Quincy accepted the treasurership of another railroad, the Vermont Central. Regarding the plan to link Boston and Montreal as both practical and potentially lucrative, he invested $100,000 of his own money in the railroad. Two years later, however, with the tracks still not laid and over $1,500,000 of the debt of the overextended railroad backed by Quincy's personal notes, his fellow directors panicked. Although never formally filing criminal charges against him, they placed the blame for the railroad's problems upon what they charged was his mismanagement and demanded his resignation. Quincy thereupon declared personal bankruptcy, severed his Boston connections, and departed with his family for Europe. His reputation ruined, his wealth greatly reduced, he never recovered from this debacle. Upon his return to Massachusetts in 1854, he moved out to Braintree where, he assured friends, "as an occupation I find the cultivation of the fields . . . the most agreeable employment I ever engaged in."[19]

Before being obliged to abandon politics, Josiah Jr. had aligned himself with the Whig party. His last political statement was a eulogy of Zachary Taylor in which he commended this slave-holding Whig for his presidential defense of the Union and the Constitution. Whatever reform impulse he had was apparently sated by his exertions on behalf of municipal efficiency and prohibitionism. His views on slavery were those of his fellow "Cotton" Whigs: that it was an unfortunate institution but protected by the Constitution and best left to the South to handle. Accordingly, "Conscience" Whigs and later Free Soilers like Charles Francis Adams and Richard Henry Dana abhorred his politics, as did his own brother. "Edmund spoke in the worst manner possible of young Josiah's anti-slavery," it was reported in 1851, "he said he [Josiah] was not the least of an abolitionist and you would have thought he was talking of a person in Georgia."[20]

Reminiscing after the Civil War, Edmund Quincy recalled the personal circumstances that had propelled him into the antislavery movement. "It seemed to me that there was nothing in professional life or politics worth trying for or troubling one's self about until I stumbled on the Anti-Slavery cause. There was a thing that took hold of history and futurity and was worth working for." And work he did. No less than William Lloyd Garrison, his mentor, or Wendell Phillips, his cousin and close friend, Edmund made abolitionism his life.[21]

After witnessing the manhandling of Garrison by an anti-abolitionist Boston mob in 1835, Edmund became a lifetime subscriber to his newspaper, *The Liberator*. Two years later, following the murder of Elijah Lovejoy in Alton, Illinois, he joined the Massachusetts Anti-Slavery Society and soon became one of its most active members. He wrote regularly for *The Liberator* and filled in as editor during Garrison's frequent absences. His literary skills were featured in addition by *The Liberty Bell* and the *National Anti-Slavery Standard*. Prior to 1853, when he began writing a regular column in Horace Greeley's *New York Daily Tribune*, he had sole responsibility for compiling the Massachusetts Anti-Slavery Society's voluminous *Annual Reports*. No less an authority than James Russell Lowell thought Edmund Quincy the most prolific writer for the abolitionist cause, and the only one with a sense of humor.[22]

During his first years with Garrison, Edmund identified with all manner of radical activities. In 1839 he declared himself to be a Non-Resistant and pledged never to raise a hand against another man. More revealing, it was he who agreed to chair the Chardon Street Convention of Friends for Universal Reform in 1840, which Emerson characterized as that "assembly of disorderly and picturesque madmen, mad women, men with beards, Dunkers, Muggletonians, Come Outers, Groaners. . . ."[23]

Perhaps chastened by exposure to such fellow-reformers, Edmund's activities narrowed later in the 1840's and came to focus almost exclusively on the abolition of slavery. Here he gave no quarter. He subscribed to Garrison's demands for immediate freedom for the slaves and his non-political stance until Lincoln's Emancipation Proclamation in the middle of the Civil War. While remaining on reasonably good terms with Free Soilers like Charles Francis Adams and Richard Henry Dana, he found their policy of delimiting slavery without calling for its abolition morally unacceptable. "If the bond of this boasted Union be indeed but links of iron, binding our free limbs to the triumphal car of Slavery, as it crushes beneath its wheel all that we hold dear," he declared in 1843, "MAY THE UNION BE SHIVERED, AND THAT SPEEDILY, INTO A THOUSAND FRAG-MENTS."[24]

Edmund's father had no sympathy for most of the "ultratheories" his son espoused early in the 1840's; he later disparaged them as being part of "that fanaticism or pseudophilanthropy which has exercised such a baneful influence in our land." As a faithful church member, he found Edmund's "Come-Outer" phase particularly distressing. Neither did he approve of Non-Resistance. When Charles Sumner tentatively declared himself a pacifist in 1845, Quincy Sr. promptly told him that such a position was "as anchors cast to the windward, against the innate propensities of mankind." For corroboration of his belief that man's warlike tendencies were irrepressible, he recommended to Sumner a political philosopher seldom mentioned in Jacksonian America, Thomas Hobbes.[25]

It would appear that Josiah Sr. had far more in common with his namesake than with Edmund. Josiah Jr.'s academic success at Harvard, his ability as an orator, his early interest in politics, and his career as a municipal reformer identify him as his father's first son. Yet Josiah Jr. was a Whig while his father and brother were assuredly not. As a Whig he fully subscribed, at least until his bankruptcy, to that party's insistent meliorism, what Glyndon Van Deusen has called its faith in "a natural harmony of interests between all groups that made up the American social order." As mayor of Boston, for example, he tried to eliminate vice altogether, whereas his father had hoped only to contain it. As a railroad entrepreneur, he entered enthusiastically into the industrializing of America while his father and brother looked upon the process with foreboding.[26]

Above all else, Josiah Jr. was a conciliator, a party man in the narrowest sense. Such a political disposition was in large part a function of his personality, characterized by a contemporary as "his usual, fluent, little to the point way." It was temperament—so Henry Adams later argued when he attempted to describe the political options available in the 1840's and 1850's—that was *the* crucial variable. "Had Mr. Adams' nature been cold," Henry wrote of his father, "he would have followed Mr. Webster, Mr. Everett, Mr. Seward and Mr. Winthrop in the line of party discipline and self-interest." But had his father's nature "been less balanced than it was, he would have gone with Mr. Garrison, Mr. Wendell Phillips, Mr. Edmund Quincy and Theodore Parker into secession."[27]

Josiah Quincy Jr. deserved to be placed among the first group as much as Edmund among the second. Their father fell somewhere between. Like Charles Francis Adams, he chose "an intermediate path, distinctive and characteristic." Nevertheless, for reasons of temperament perhaps as much as principle, on the questions of slavery and secession Quincy Sr. tended to side not with his namesake but with his abolitionist son. "The Garrisonians," Edmund declared in 1849, "are the legitimate successors of the old Federalists, who dared to make the last stand against the encroachments of Slavery." His father's subsequent decision to reenter the political arena, and to do so as an uncompromising antislavery man, would lend credence to this claim.[28]

The Only True Conservative Doctrine

Josiah Quincy spent ten years preparing his *Memoir of John Quincy Adams*. Undertaken as a brief tribute to be read to the Massachusetts Historical Society, it emerged from the press in 1858 as a full-dress biography over four hundred pages long. During this period, he had access to all of Adams' papers, including his personal diary. As he worked through this mass of materials, Quincy came to realize just how valuable a friend he had lost. From the diary, for example, he first learned that Adams, out of respect for Quincy's political integrity, rejected Republican overtures in 1808 to contest his congressional seat. He also discovered how, during the 1834 Harvard Rebellion, Adams almost single-handedly saved him his job.[29]

Gratifying as these revelations were, the principal satisfaction Quincy derived from retracing Adams' career was the conclusion this allowed him to make about his own. That half-century trek from lukewarm Federalism, to the unbounded nationalism of his years as a Republican diplomat, to his unhappy term in the White House, and finally to his last years in Congress where, on January 24, 1842, he presented a petition calling for the dissolution of the Union, had been, by Adams' own admission, an exercise in futility. As such, it provided his first biographer with a final vindication of his own intransigent, stay-at-home Federalism.[30]

Although neither one had participated in the Missouri Debates of 1820, Quincy devoted twenty pages to recording Adams' private reflections thereon. Here, his biographer argued, Adams confronted for the first time the possibility that his continentalism served the interests of Southern slaveholders rather than the nation. The manner by which "the slave states have clung together in one unbroken phalanx" throughout the debates forced him to reexamine his belief that an essential harmony of intersectional interests existed. " 'It is a contemplation not very creditable to human nature.' " Quincy recorded Adams' conclusion upon hearing Calhoun's defense of slavery, " 'that the cement of common interest, produced by slavery, is stronger and more solid than that of unmingled freedom.' "[31]

Having gone this far in rethinking his political views, Adams doggedly went on to draw several conclusions: a politically irreconcilable sectional conflict did exist and was not amenable to compromise; the Constitution could not be looked to as a check on future Southern plans to extend "the peculiar institution," its very formulation having "sanctioned a dishonorable compromise with slavery"; only "a fundamental reorganization of the Union" could rid the country of slavery; and such a reorganization could not occur until after a violent disruption of the Union. It was Quincy's persuasive argument that these beliefs became the basis for Adams' subsequent politics.[32]

Adams had conceived of the sectional conflict as being between "freedom and slavery." Quincy, as a Federalist congressman, had occasionally invoked an equally moralistic vocabulary, but usually his antagonism with Southern Republicans had reflected his concern with their use of slavery as the means to gain a disproportionate voice in the national government. Adams came to hate the South because he hated slavery; he ultimately repudiated his expansionist beliefs because they furthered the cause of slavery. Quincy, on the other hand, from the outset of his political career hated the South and opposed expansionism; his objections to slavery, while sincere, were always part of a larger antipathy.[33]

If the plight of the individual slave was less central to Quincy's antislavery views than it was to Adams', both were equally convinced that the institution was morally corrupting of the men who practiced it, of the politicians who defended it, and of the nation that condoned it. Neither allowed himself the comfort of being anesthetized by the natural-limits-of-slavery argument or the emigration "solution" proposed by the American Colonization Society. Moreover, both were of a generation and a family which could not so easily dismiss the tenets of the Declaration of Independence as did Whigs like Rufus Choate. Though one was an obstinate Federalist and the other a chastened nationalist, both were firm in their opposition to slavery long before the first issue of *The Liberator* reached the streets of Boston.[34]

This is not to deny their lapses. While Adams privately recorded the fateful implications of the Missouri Compromise, he publicly endorsed it and thereby retained his standing as a presidential candidate. During his four years in the White House he managed to get along knowing that three million people were in bondage in the country over which he presided. Quincy, during the 1820's, had demonstrated a similar tolerance. In 1825 he published his *Memoir of Josiah Quincy Jun.*, only after quietly deleting from his father's "Southern Journal" passages wherein slavery was condemned. "While slaveholders were a component part of the nation," he later explained, "it was deemed wise and kind to abstain from publication."[35]

Yet as early as 1836 Quincy violated his self-imposed moratorium on political statements to applaud Adams for his "noble stand" in Congress against the extension of slavery. "As to Slavery in the new states," he advised Adams,

I think that Northern men owe it to their character as well as to that of their country, to meet every attempt to extend the evil to new states with the most decided opposition. It is the only way in which they can manifest that the acquiescence they have shown in the continuance of slavery in the Union has been compelled by their respect to the relations and obligations of the Constitution. Let their acquiescence be limited by those obligations. Let every attempt to extend the iniquitous traffic in human beings, and to plant the evil in other states, be manfully and perseveringly resisted.[36]

On February 23, 1848, Adams died, believing that his beloved Union was destined for a violent disruption. "For myself," Quincy wrote four weeks later, "I hear the hollow voice of the rushing waters, foretelling the coming storm,—for come it will. . . . Even now," he went on, "I feel the upheaving of the advancing tempest, I see the broken columns of our Union, and realize the grinding of their massive materials as they dash against each other—*not without blood.*"[37]

With Adams no longer there to speak for him, and because official responsibilities no longer restrained him, Quincy permitted himself to be drawn back onto the political stage. In the summer of 1850 he volunteered his support to several Free Soilers, including Charles Francis Adams, who were organizing a meeting to protest passage of the Fugitive Slave Act. Although his wife's death prevented his attending the Faneuil Hall gathering, his public letter was thought by the sponsors to have been "very good indeed." Among the names attached to the meeting's declaration repudiating the Compromise of 1850, his was reported to be "the only name of the gentility."[38]

This fact was not overlooked by Boston's "gentlemen of property and standing," among them Ticknor "and other Webster men." It was reputedly at their instigation that George Stillman Hillard, writing in the *Daily Advertiser* the following spring, attacked Quincy as one of those Free Soilers who persisted in believing that Daniel Webster's support of the Compromise of 1850 had been something less than a disinterested act of statesmanship.[39]

In the spring of 1852 Quincy's political sympathies were again revealed when he publicly protested the manner in which Rufus Choate, Robert C. Winthrop, and other Massachusetts Whigs were using the Joseph Story Association as a platform from which to defend the Compromise of 1850 and to condemn the Free Soilers for attacking it. On May 1, despite a boycott by what Charles Francis Adams classified as the local representatives of "the slave power," Quincy appeared at a Faneuil Hall banquet in honor of Louis Kossuth, the Hungarian revolutionary and critic of slavery. "Though long separated from such scenes," he wrote in his diary, "my presence was not disregarded." There would be no holding him back now.[40]

The introduction in Congress of the Kansas-Nebraska bill in early 1854 intensified Quincy's political activities. A meeting of Boston Whigs called for February 23 to reaffirm the party's support of the Compromise of 1850 drew his uninvited attendance. Because the crowd jamming into Faneuil Hall that night proved to be far less interested in honoring Daniel Webster's handiwork than in condemning this latest proposal to extend the boundaries of slavery, the organizers of the meeting decided to adjourn early. Before they could do so, however, the audience called upon Quincy to speak. He was more than willing to do so and proceeded to deliver the only unequivocal indictment of the Kansas-Nebraska bill heard that night. "He spoke in his best manner," Dana reported, "the thorough, independent, manly character shining out through every word."[4] [1]

By now he had discovered his special role in the antislavery movement: to demonstrate the fatuousness, if not the calculated ineffectiveness, of the Whig response to Southern attempts to extend slavery. Few were as free to protest as he. Removed from national politics for more than thirty years and never more than "a looker on" with respect to the Whig party, he was in no way implicated in its compromising tradition. Nor did he owe any personal allegiance to its leaders. His antipathy toward Clay was deep and was a matter of record. Although a casual acquaintance of Webster's in the 1820's, and an infrequent correspondent thereafter, Quincy had never been on politically intimate terms with him. As for Massachusetts' other leading Whigs—Everett, Winthrop, and Choate—he thought them, as did Charles Francis Adams, "fine 'chevaux de bataille' for a parade field day."[4] [2]

In taking on the Whigs, Quincy sided with the insurgents of the Free Soil party, men, for the most part, two generations removed from his own. He had known many of them, including Charles Sumner, John Gorham Palfrey, and Richard Henry Dana, since their undergraduate days in Cambridge. As was true of their slightly older colleague, Charles Francis Adams, they were political idealists, firm in their opposition to slavery, and contemptuous of the temporizing ways of their immediate elders. As such they were favorably disposed toward Quincy's old-fashioned Federalism and found it far more palatable than what they dismissed as the optimistic and egalitarian pap being dispensed by the Whig and Democratic parties. The fact that he had been removed from national politics during the previous thirty years—years Adams later disparaged as "the heyday of our prosperity, when banks and tariffs and internal improvements were argued as if vital points"—only enhanced his standing among the Free Soilers. Finally, his anti-manufacturing sentiments complemented their own distaste for those factory magnates they feared had come to dominate Massachusetts public life and who, in alliance with Southern planters, seemed to determine national policy.[43]

Quincy in turn responded enthusiastically to their moral fervor and gave ungrudgingly of himself on behalf of their cause. His mere presence among them gave the Free Soilers a measure of respectability they otherwise lacked; it also helped undercut charges that they were all radicals or, as Rufus Choate argued, that their views were the product of nothing more than "youthful enthusiasm and inexperience." Thus the Free Soilers welcomed his support and sought his counsel, although Dana, ever the innocent, occasionally thought "Mr. Quincy reasoned too much like a politician."[44]

An Adams or a Dana might argue that a "slave power" conspiracy existed among the planters of the South and the manufacturers of the North, but Quincy did so "as one who began stemming [it] more than fifty years ago." Although even more powerful with the inclusion of New England textile interests, the conspiracy was merely a continuation of the same arrangements that had permitted Jefferson to secure Louisiana's statehood. Although they knew that the free states would have agreed to its admission into the Union, Quincy wrote of the "conspirators" nearly a half-century later,

They foresaw such an appeal would foreclose forever the admission of other states unless under a like appeal and that the precedent then set would be conclusive and the opportunity forever lost of extending the field of slave power, and of the slave market. They chose therefore to *assume* the power as though it were given by the Constitution. Jefferson swallowed his objections, and with the acquiescence, or indifference, of the people of the free states, vested in themselves the power of admitting new states from the North Pole to Cape Horn, without any consultation or asking of the people of the states. We are at this day experiencing the evil consequences of that policy. From that day to the present, history will show, that not a step favorable to the slaveholders' power and progress *has failed to* be taken and be successful.

To a generation that had never known the United States without Louisiana, this argument helped legitimize the antislavery position by giving it a pedigree nearly as old as the Union itself—and far older than the Whig party. When Quincy argued, as he did in 1854, that further compromise with the South was futile, many were inclined to defer to his judgment if only because they could not gainsay his experience.[45]

With the passage of the Kansas-Nebraska Act in May of 1854,

Quincy's break with the Whigs became absolute. Uninvited, he appeared at their state convention in August, determined to deliver a speech "for which," Adams correctly prophesied, "they will not thank him." After condemning the Kansas-Nebraska "fraud" and the recent removal from Boston of the fugitive slave Anthony Burns, he charged the Whigs with complicity in both. Responding to earlier speakers who had warned against repudiating this latest extension of slavery because it might provoke the South into leaving the Union, Quincy insisted that the South had no reason to secede. On the contrary, he argued, the South realized the unique advantages of remaining in the Union where its plan to extend slavery throughout the continent enjoyed the protection of the Constitution. As for Quincy's feelings about that document, he infuriated his Whig audience by declaring the Constitution "at this moment abrogated."[46]

Unlike many Massachusetts Free Soilers, Quincy took no part in the Know-Nothing crusade which succeeded in capturing the state government in 1854 by replacing the divisive issue of antislavery with the more popular one of nativism. "Four fifths of the organization," Charles Francis Adams complained after the elections, "has left the standard of freedom to enlist itself against a shadow." But, as Quincy advised Dana and others who were discouraged by the public's willingness to chase shadows, there was little that could be done except wait for the anti-immigrant, anti-Catholic hysteria to subside. When that happened in early 1856, in part because of the political ineptitude of the Know-Nothing leadership, those Free Soilers who had not participated were able to point to their aloofness as proof of their commitment to the antislavery cause.[47]

The attack upon Sumner in the Senate in May, coming hard on the news from "bleeding" Kansas, brought Quincy again to the political fore. "My mind is in no state to receive pleasure from social scenes and friendly intercourse," he wrote in a widely reprinted letter to E. Rockwood Hoar,

I can think or speak of nothing but of the outrages of slaveholders in Kansas, and the outrages of slaveholders at Washington,—outrages which if not met in the spirit of our fathers of the Revolution (and I see no sign that they will be), our liberties are but a name, and our Union will prove a curse. . . . It is time to speak on the house-top what every man who is worthy of the name of freeman utters in his chamber and feels in his heart.[48]

Just a week later Quincy was given an opportunity to speak what every "freeman utters in his chamber" at a citizens' gathering on the South Shore. The speech was, according to Charles Francis Adams, "not much nor very well calculated for the feelings of the present age, yet it had its effect." Abolitionists thought it an "admirable Address" and well they might have. They could hardly improve on Quincy's characterization of the history of the Union as "little else than a record of triumphs of slavery, through the instrumentality of the ambition, cupidity, and baseness of men from the Free States." Not even Edmund could fault his father's concluding statement: "If this Union is destined to break to pieces, it cannot fall in a more glorious struggle than in the endeavor to limit the farther extension of Slavery—that disgrace of our nation and curse of our race."[49]

An Address Illustrative of the Nature and Power of the Slave States and the Duties of the Free States, first published in July and several times reprinted, was prefaced with an endorsement of the presidential candidacy of John C. Frémont. Still calling himself a Federalist, Quincy became one of the Republican nominee's most vocal supporters and regularly compared this Southern-born critic of slavery to Washington. In addition, he took it upon himself to answer the Whigs' charge that a vote for Frémont, whom they condemned as a sectional candidate, was a vote against the Union. In two other widely circulated campaign pamphlets, *The Duty of Conservative Whigs in the Present Crisis* and *Remarks . . . to the Whig State Committee of Maine*, he returned the charge by arguing that Choate and other Whig spokesmen for "the cotton spinners of the North" were supporting Millard Fillmore's candidacy in the knowledge that by so doing they guaranteed the election of the Democrat James Buchanan, the choice of "the cotton growers of the South."[50]

When not attacking the Whig leadership, Quincy spent the campaign coaxing the Whig rank-and-file into the Republican camp. Many Whigs, however disillusioned by their party's position on slavery, were reluctant to support a new party, fearing that it would be interpreted as an endorsement of radicalism in general. "Men dare not believe, much less act in contrariency with old creeds," Quincy admitted to Daniel A. White, an old friend who had sought his advice, "particularly when they force them into a partnership or with political bedfellows, with whom they do not like to lay, spoon fashion. But," he went on, "it has long ago been said that politics like misery often brings men into strange company." As for his own decision to support the Republicans, Quincy assured White that it reflected anything but a belated conversion to radicalism:

I see that one party are endeavoring to present my doctrines as tending, if not designed to break up the Union; and that the other are in a flutter, and are afraid to take up the thing lest it should burn their fingers and give their opponents the edge. But I can tell these gentlemen that mine is the only true conservative doctrine.[51]

During the last week of the 1856 campaign Quincy produced his fourth pamphlet, *Whig Policy Analyzed and Illustrated*, in which he detailed Daniel Webster's fall from grace and his final "unqualified acquiescence" to "the Northern Wing of the Slave Power." It was a forceful polemic and a fitting climax to the old gentleman's campaign labors. All that remained was for him to lead the contingent welcoming Senator Sumner back to Boston on election eve. "I am sometimes ashamed of myself at finding embers flaming," the eighty-four year old Quincy had written to the convalescing Sumner earlier in the campaign, "at a period when they ought naturally to be expiring under ashes as cold as the grave to which I am hastening. Heaven knows I have not willfully brought together either kindlings or wind. . . ."[52]

Willfully or not, Quincy's efforts had generated more than a little heat. His *Remarks to the Whig State Committee of Maine* was credited by at least one Republican there with securing the state for Frémont, while his *Address on the Slave Power* was one of the most widely circulated Republican pamphlets of the campaign. Never one to underestimate his own worth, Quincy was convinced that his endorsement in *Whig Policy Analyzed and Illustrated* provided Anson Burlingame with his margin of victory over the Whig William Appleton in a close Boston congressional race. Party officials thought enough of his views to devote six pages of their nationally circulated *Republican Scrapbook* to them. Conversely, the editors of the *Democratic Handbook* felt compelled to attack him as a disunionist and to remind their readers that this was the same Quincy who forty-seven years earlier had tried to impeach Thomas Jefferson![53]

The election went much as Quincy had hoped. Although Buchanan won the presidency, Frémont carried most of the North and all of New England. In Massachusetts he had a two-to-one margin

over the combined Buchanan-Fillmore vote. Not only was Burlingame returned to the House but Sumner's seat in the Senate was
assured by the election of a Republican General Court. The most
important result of the election, however, was the collapse of the
Whig party and with it the possibility of further sectional compromise. In 1860 the South would have to reckon with a North
politically united as never before. Satisfied with his own efforts in
bringing about this impasse, Quincy withdrew to await the inevitable
result.[54]

Land after a Long Navigation

According to an English journalist who visited Boston, Quincy had
become by the late 1850's "one of the lions of the place, and
strangers were taken to see him, as they were taken to Wesley's Oak
or to Washington's house." A lion perhaps, but one finally obliged to
acknowledge his mortality. While visiting Andover Academy in 1857,
he had a seizure; after that his eyesight began to fail. His hand-
writing, steady as late as 1856, by the end of the decade gave
evidence of palsy. An 1861 photograph shows his carriage erect and
his chin still firm, but the signs of old age are in his face. "When
death happens to the young, they seem to yield to an external
force," he had written a year earlier, "but the old pass voluntarily
away, as if by their own will. To me the approach of death is rather
pleasant than otherwise. I seem to see land after a long navigation."[55]

A fall in the winter of 1861 resulted in a broken hip and rendered
him bedridden for most of the following year and lame for the
remainder of his life. By this time, however, a new interest had seized
his mind and was to enliven his last days—the Civil War. Asked during
that cheerless summer of 1862, when the Union Army had yet to
prove itself and Northern morale was at its lowest ebb, what his
feelings were, Quincy replied: "I glory in the present state of
affairs!" He told Samuel H. Walley the following February, "I do not
share in your gloomy apprehensions, from the darkness, which now
surrounds our public affairs. You say that some years ago I intimated
to you that such times were coming. I have anticipated such an event
for more than sixty years. I am only disappointed and regret that it
has not come before."[56]

The Civil War was a family project for the Quincys. Edmund made several visits to Washington to press the cause of abolition on the President. Eliza Susan joined the United States Sanitary Commission. Even Josiah Jr. came in from the farm to praise the President before a Harvard audience in the summer of 1862, a time when praise was not often heard.[57]

More spectacular were the war efforts of Josiah Jr.'s son, Samuel Miller Quincy. Responding to Lincoln's first call to arms, Sam took a commission in the Second Massachusetts Infantry. In August 1862, after sustaining serious wounds at Cedar Mountain, he was captured and sent to Libby Prison. There he remained for eight weeks before being exchanged. Rather than return to civilian life, he rejoined his old regiment just in time to be almost mortally wounded at Chancellorsville. Forced now to resign his line commission, he took a staff commission in the newly organized 73rd United States Colored Infantry and served with it through the rest of the war. "Sam," his proud grandfather told all who inquired, and some who did not, "is just where he ought to be."[58]

Quincy, for his part, applauded Lincoln's every move. "What is to be the end of all this," he asked a Harvard Commencement audience in 1862, to which he answered: "I do not know; that is in the hands of a higher power than ours. We have only to do our duty, and that is, to support the President of the United States." On February 27, 1863, he delivered a short speech to the Boston Union League in which he both commended Lincoln's recent Emancipation Proclamation and urged him to go further. He had welcomed the war in 1861 quite apart from what it could mean for the slaves, and had earlier acknowledged "that my heart has been always much more affected by the slavery to which the Free States have been subjected, than with that of the Negro." But as the war went on, he came to see emancipation as the only goal that could possibly justify its human cost. The ultimate objective of the North, he told the Union League, must not be merely to defeat the Confederacy on the battlefield but to refute its "assumption that the African race have been constituted by God and nature unequal to the Caucasian."[59]

Such humanitarian concerns dominated his last public utterances. In a widely reprinted letter, dated September 7, 1863, Quincy pleaded with Lincoln to seize the opportunity, spoken of more than forty years earlier by John Quincy Adams and now given to him by the South's secession, to abolish slavery once and for all:

Your instrumentality in the work is to you a subject of special glory, favor, and felicity. The madness of Secession and its inevitable consequence, civil war, will, in their result, give the right and the power of universal emancipation sooner or later. If the United States do not understand and fully appreciate the boon thus bestowed on them, and fail to improve it to the utmost extent of the power granted, they will prove recreant to themselves and to posterity.[60]

That fall he completed a final round of public visits; these included a meeting of the Massachusetts Historical Society in honor of his sixty-seventh year of membership, and a farewell trip to Harvard and his beloved Observatory. On December 31, 1863, he made a closing entry in his diary. "The sun is withdrawing," he wrote, "but blessed be heaven, the light of the evening star reveals the hope of a coming immortality." In May he was brought out to the Quincy farm. There, during the afternoon of July 1, 1864, in his ninety-third year, he died.[61]

Never had he been held in such universally high esteem as at the last. Boston newspapers all mourned his passing and praised his loyalty to the Union, but so did the *New York Daily Tribune* which carried his obituary on the front page of its July 4 edition. At his funeral he was eulogized as "the patriarch of all public men in America," while at services at the Massachusetts Historical Society Richard Henry Dana said simply of him: "Mr. Quincy was a nobleman." Death had come after the North's eventual victory was assured but before anyone foresaw the agonies of the Reconstruction era and the cynical materialism of the Gilded Age that were to follow. Josiah Quincy's ultimate blessing was to die at one of those rare moments in his country's history when even a Federalist dared to believe that America might yet fulfill its liberal promise.[62]

Bibliographical Note on the
Manuscript Collections

Although Quincy thought enough of his incoming correspondence, diaries, drafts of speeches, and other manuscript materials to retain them, his first biographers did not. After completing the *Life of Josiah Quincy* in 1867, Edmund Quincy turned over "a trunkful of papers" to James Walker, President Emeritus of Harvard, who was then writing a "Memoir" of Quincy for the Massachusetts Historical Society. According to the college librarian, John Langdon Sibley ("Private Journal," II, 791: May 28, 1868, Sibley Papers), Walker later disposed of many of these papers. Included in the materials apparently put to the flames were Quincy's "retirement journals" (1846-1863) and the bulk of his incoming correspondence during that same period. Sibley wrote off Walker's action as carelessness, but one can hypothesize that Walker, very much a Cotton Whig in the 1850's, had his own reasons for destroying materials that could not have dealt kindly with men of his political persuasion.

Much, however, did escape the torch. Walker retained the Quincy materials that related to Harvard; they are now deposited in the Harvard University Archives and constitute not only the major source for chapters 8 and 9 of this study, but a valuable source of information on American higher education in the Jacksonian era. The Harvard College Papers and the Records of the Corporation, the Overseers, and the Faculty were also examined.

Materials relating to Quincy's mayoralty are to be found in greatest abundance in the Boston Public Library and the Massachusetts State Library in Boston. The City Clerk's Office in the Boston City Hall retains the original records of the Mayor, Aldermen, and City Council as well as a large collection of printed documents, unavailable elsewhere, relating to the 1820's. The Rare Book Room of the Boston Public Library has, in addition to the Boston School Committee Records, several political broadsides that convey some of the feeling generated by Quincy's mayoralty.

Eliza Susan Quincy kept some of her father's incoming correspondence as part of an autograph collection. These letters and several of his efforts to maintain a regular diary constitute a comparatively small part of the Massachusetts Historical Society's vast collection of Quinciana. The Quincy Family Papers, including those of Quincy's grandfather, father, and children, especially Eliza Susan and Edmund, all proved useful. The Norfolk and Suffolk County Probate Records provided considerable economic data on the family.

Small collections of Josiah Quincy Papers are also to be found at the Boston Athenaeum, Brown University, Columbia University, Connecticut Historical Society, Essex Institute (Salem, Massachusetts), Houghton Library (Harvard University), Library of Congress, New York Historical Society, New York Public Library, Phillips Academy (Andover, Massachusetts), and Theodore Crane Library (Quincy, Massachusetts).

A special comment should be made about another major source for this study, the Adams Papers, quotations from which are made from the microfilm edition by permission of the Massachusetts Historical Society. Because the Adamses and the Quincys came into contact at so many points over such a long period of time, the papers of John, John Quincy, and Charles Francis Adams are all rich in materials that bear on the life and careers of Josiah Quincy. Certainly one of the pleasures derived from writing a biography of Quincy has been the opportunity to become better acquainted with his often critical, but by no means unappreciative, neighbors.

ADDITIONAL MANUSCRIPTS cited

Cabot Family Papers, Massachusetts Historical Society
Cranch, William, Massachusetts Historical Society
Dana, Richard Henry, Jr., Massachusetts Historical Society
Everett, Edward, Massachusetts Historical Society
Gallatin, Albert, New York Historical Society
Griscom, John C., Special Collections, New York Public Library
Jenks, William, Massachusetts Historical Society
Loring, Ellis Gray, Schlesinger Library, Radcliffe College
Norcross Collection, Massachusetts Historical Society
Otis, Harrison Gray, Massachusetts Historical Society
Palfrey, John Gorham, Houghton Library, Harvard University
Peirce, Benjamin, Houghton Library, Harvard University
Pickering, Timothy, Massachusetts Historical Society
Pierce, John, Massachusetts Historical Society
Randolph, John, Library of Congress

Saltonstall, Leverett, Massachusetts Historical Society
Sedgwick, Theodore, Massachusetts Historical Society
Shaw, William S., Boston Athenaeum
Sibley, John Langdon, Harvard University Archives
Sparks, Jared, Houghton Library, Harvard University
Story, Joseph, Library of Congress
Sumner, Charles, Houghton Library, Harvard University
Ticknor, George, Harvard University Archives
Washburn Autograph Collection, Massachusetts Historical Society
Webster, Noah, Special Collections, New York Public Library
Winthrop, Robert C., Massachusetts Historical Society
Wolcott, Oliver, Connecticut Historical Society

Abbreviations

AAS *Procs.*	American Antiquarian Society, *Proceedings*
AC	*Annals of Congress*, Ninth—Twelfth Congresses. Washington, 1853
AHR	*American Historical Review*
BPL	Boston Public Library
CFA	Charles Francis Adams
DAB	*Dictionary of American Biography*. Ed. Allen Johnson and Dumas Malone. 20 vols. plus index and supplements. New York, Scribner's, 1928-1936
EQ, *Quincy*	Edmund Quincy, *Life of Josiah Quincy of Massachusetts*. Boston, 1867
HUA	Harvard University Archives
Coll. Papers	—Harvard College Papers
Corp. Minutes	—Minutes of the Corporation
Corp. Papers	—Corporation Papers
Faculty Recs.	—Records of the College Faculty
Overseers Recs.	—Records of the Overseers
JA	John Adams
JQ	Josiah Quincy
JQ, *Memoir*	Josiah Quincy, *Memoir of the Life of Josiah Quincy Jun. of Massachusetts. By His Son, Josiah Quincy*. Boston, 1825
JQ, *Speeches*	Edmund Quincy, ed., *Speeches Delivered in the Congress of the United States. By Josiah Quincy, Member of the House of Representatives for the Suffolk District of Massachusetts, 1805-1813*. Boston, 1874
JQ I	Josiah Quincy, grandfather of JQ
JQ Jr.	Josiah Quincy Jr., father of JQ
JQA	John Quincy Adams
LC	Library of Congress
MHS, *Colls., Procs.*	Massachusetts Historical Society, *Collections*, and *Proceedings*
MVHR	*The Mississippi Valley Historical Review*
NEQ	*The New England Quarterly*
NYHS	New York Historical Society
NYPL	New York Public Library
RCB	Records of the City of Boston: Mayor and Aldermen, 1822-1828, MS., City Clerk's Office, Boston City Hall
RCCB *Rpts.*	*Reports* of the Record Commissioners of the City of Boston. 39 vols. Boston, 1876-1909
SCR	Records of the School Committee of the City of Boston, MS., Rare Book Room, BPL
WMQ	*William and Mary Quarterly*

Notes

Notes to Chapter 1: A Dubious Legacy

1. Henry Adams, "Review of *Speeches of Josiah Quincy*," *North American Review*, 70 (January 1875), 235-236.

2. John Adams, *Diary and Autobiography of John Adams*, ed. L. H. Butterfield (4 vols., Cambridge, Mass., Harvard University Press, 1961), III, 203-204.

3. Eliza Susan Quincy, "Edmund Quincy (1681-1738)," *New England Historic-Genealogical Register*, 38 (April 1884), 145-146.

4. John Winthrop, *History of New England from 1630 to 1649*, ed. James Savage (2 vols., Boston, 1826), I, 109, 129n; Robert Francis Scybolt, *The Town Officials of Colonial Boston* (Cambridge, Mass., Harvard University Press, 1939), 2, 3, 5n.

5. William S. Pattee, *A History of Old Braintree and Quincy* (Quincy, 1878), 9-10; Charles Francis Adams Jr., "Quincy," *History of Norfolk County*, ed. D. Hamilton Hurd (Philadelphia, 1884), 307.

6. Ola Elizabeth Winslow, *Samuel Sewall of Boston* (New York, Macmillan, 1964), 48-54; Samuel A. Bates, ed., *Records of the Town of Braintree, 1640-1793* (Randolph, Mass., 1886), 25, 26. For a selective genealogy of the Quincy family, see L. H. Butterfield, *A Pride of Quincys* (Boston, MHS, 1969).

7. John Langdon Sibley and Clifford K. Shipton, *Biographical Sketches of Graduates of Harvard University, in Cambridge, Massachusetts* (Cambridge and Boston, 1873-   ), IV, 491-495; E. S. Quincy, "Edmund Quincy," 146-156.

8. E. S. Quincy, Quincy, to Robert C. Winthrop, July 7, 1879, Winthrop Papers.

9. Captain Isaac Freeman, St. John's, Newfoundland, to Messrs. Quincy, Quincy, and Jackson, August 1, 1748, Quincy Family Papers; Sibley-Shipton, *Harvard Graduates*, VIII, 467.

10. JQ, *Memoir*, 5; Bates, *Braintree Records*, 324, *passim*; JA, *Diary*, I, 100-101, 81-84.

11. *Ibid.*, 93-94, 140-141; John Adams, *The Earliest Diary*, ed. L. H. Butterfield (Cambridge, Mass., Harvard University Press, 1966), 82.

12. Sibley-Shipton, *Harvard Graduates*, XIII, 285-289; JA, *Diary*, I, 95, 207.

13. Sibley-Shipton, *Harvard Graduates*, XIII, 484-489; JA, *Diary*, I, 51-52, 57-58, 109, III, 261; JA, Quincy, to Jefferson, September 15, 1813, in Lester Cappon, ed., *The Adams-Jefferson Letters* (2 vols., Chapel Hill, University of North Carolina Press, 1959), II, 402.

14. JA, *Diary*, I, 176-177; Sibley-Shipton, *Harvard Graduates*, XIII, 455-457; JA, Quincy, to Richard Rush, December 10, 1810, in John A. Schutz and Douglas Adair, eds., *The Spur of Fame* (San Marino, Huntington Library, 1966), 174; JA to Jefferson, November 15, 1813, *Adams-Jefferson Letters*, II, 397-402.

15. Sibley-Shipton, *Harvard Graduates*, XII, 208-214, 288-289.

16. *Ibid.*, XIII, 484-489.

17. Abigail Adams, Braintree, to JA, September 14, 1774, in *Adams Family Correspondence*, ed. L. H. Butterfield (Cambridge, Mass., Harvard University Press, 1963-   ), I, 152.

18. Samuel Quincy, Boston, to JQ Jr., June 1, 1774, JQ Jr. Papers, MHS; JQ, *Memoir*, 7.

19. Faculty Recs., I, 342, 344-345, II, 112; JQ, *Memoir*, 8; *Legal Papers of John Adams*, ed. L. Kinvin Wroth and Hiller B. Zobel (3 vols., Cambridge, Mass., Harvard University Press, 1965), I, cvii.

20. JQ Jr., Boston, to JQ I, December 1768, in JQ, *Memoir*, 26.

21. *Ibid.*, 12-14, 18-25; *Boston Gazette*, October 3, 1768.

22. Philip Davidson, *Propaganda and the American Revolution* (Chapel Hill, University of North Carolina Press, 1941), 7, 8, 57; Arthur M. Schlesinger, *Prelude to Independence* (New York, Knopf, 1958), 12, 131, 161-162, 180; Thomas Hutchinson, Boston, to Francis Bernard, May 22, 1770, Hutchinson Letter Book, MHS; JQ Jr., *Observations on the Act of Parliament Commonly Called the Boston Port Bill* (Boston, 1774), in JQ, *Memoir*, 355-469, 451; JA, Arundel, to Abigail Adams, July 4, 1774, *Adams Family Correspondence*, II, 122; Mark A. De Wolfe Howe, ed., "Journal of Josiah Quincy, Junior, 1773," MHS *Procs.*, 49 (1915-1916), 426-481, and "Journal of Josiah Quincy, Jun., during His Voyage and Residence in England from September 28th, 1774, to March 3d, 1775," MHS *Procs.*, 50 (1916-1917), 433-470; Pauline Maier, *From Resistance to Revolution; Colonial Radicals and the Development of American Opposition to Britain, 1765-1776* (New York, Knopf, 1972), 23, 47.

23. Caroline Robbins, *The Eighteenth-Century Commonwealthman* (Cambridge, Mass., Harvard University Press, 1961), 3-21; Bernard Bailyn, "Political Experience and Enlightenment Ideas in Eighteenth-Century America," *AHR*, 67 (January 1962), 339-351.

24. JQ, *Memoir*, 366-367, 396-400, 467, 27, 149; JQ Jr., "London Journal," 433; JQ Jr., Boston, to JQ I, December 1768, in JQ, *Memoir*, 149.

25. JQ Jr., London, to JQ I, November 27, 1774, JQ Jr. Papers; JQ Jr., "Southern Journal," 458, 467.

26. Jack Richon Pole, *Political Representation in England and the Origins of the American Revolution* (London, Macmillan, 1966), 3-32; JQ Jr., "Southern Journal," 455-457.

27. MHS *Procs.*, 4 (1858-1860), 47-51; JQ, *Memoir*, 31-66; JA, *Legal Papers*, II, 402-404, III, 5-8; Peter Oliver, *Origin and Progress of the American Revolution*, ed. Douglas Adair and John Schutz (San Marino, Huntington Library, 1963), 87-93; JQ, *Memoir*, 365-369. For a similar view, see James Lovell, Boston, to JQ Jr., November 25, 1774, JQ Jr. Papers.

28. Abigail Adams, Braintree, to JA, October 16, 1774, *Adams Family Correspondence*, I, 173; [Gloucester] *Essex Gazette*, May 2, 1775.

29. John Lowell, Boston, to JQ, December 17, 1825, Autograph Letter Book, JQ Papers, MHS.

30. Josiah Quincy I, Braintree, to JQ, March 16, 1780, Josiah Phillips Quincy Papers, MHS; EQ, *Quincy*, 18-19.

31. Copy of JQ Jr.'s will in JQ Jr. Papers; in slightly altered form in EQ, *Quincy*, 29.

32. Josiah Quincy I, Braintree, to JQ Jr., January 3, 1775, JQ Jr. Papers; Josiah Quincy I, Braintree, to————, December 20, 1780; December 1781; January 8, 1782, JQ Jr. Papers; Bernard Bailyn, *The Ideological Origins of the*

American Revolution (Cambridge, Mass., Harvard University Press, 1967), 312; Sibley-Shipton, *Harvard Graduates*, VIII, 474-475; Bates, *Braintree Records*, 374.

33. ———, "A Tory View of the Boston Whigs," London, April 18, 1775, Boston MSS., MHS; Sibley-Shipton, *Harvard Graduates*, IX, 431-436, 560-570; JQ, Quincy, to Sprague, October 22, 1855, in William B. Sprague, *Annals of the American Pulpit* (9 vols., New York, 1857-1869), II, 44-47.

34. Claude M. Fuess, *An Old New England School: A History of Phillips Academy, Andover* (Boston, Houghton Mifflin, 1917), 51; Sibley-Shipton, *Harvard Graduates*, IX, 435; EQ, *Quincy*, 23.

35. Fuess, *Andover*, 58-60; Robert Middlekauff, "A Persistent Tradition: The Classical Curriculum in Eighteenth-Century New England," *WMQ*, 18 (January 1961), 54-67.

36. Sibley-Shipton, *Harvard Graduates*, XII, 286; Chauncy, Boston, to Dr. Amory, September 12, 1774, JQ Jr. Papers; Conrad Wright, *The Beginnings of Unitarianism in America* (Boston, Beacon Press, 1955), 36-38, 63-67, 264-265.

37. Fuess, *Andover*, 57-92; JQ, Boston, to J. L. Taylor, December 13, 1855; JQ, Boston, to W. Barnard, December 1, 1860, Phillips Academy Archives, Andover, Mass.

38. James Walker, "Memoir of Josiah Quincy," MHS *Procs.*, 9 (1866-1867), 86; EQ, *Quincy*, 532-533.

39. Walker, "Quincy," 88; JQ, Boston, to Oliver Wolcott Jr., December 3, 1804, Wolcott Papers.

40. Claude M. Fuess, *Men of Andover, Biographical Sketches in Commemoration of the 150th Anniversary of Phillips Academy* (New Haven, Yale University Press, 1928), 65-92.

41. *Quinquennial Catalogue of the Officers and Graduates of Harvard University, [1636-1890]* (Cambridge, 1890), 417, 419.

42. JQ, *The History of Harvard University* (2 vols., Cambridge, 1840), II, 174-175, 238-248; Samuel Eliot Morison, *Three Centuries of Harvard* (Cambridge, Mass., Harvard University Press, 1936), 133-163.

43. Brook Hindle, *The Pursuit of Science in Revolutionary America, 1735-1789* (Chapel Hill, University of North Carolina Press, 1956), 86-89, 380-387; Wilson Smith, "The Teacher in Puritan Culture," *Harvard Educational Review*, 36 (Fall 1966), 394-411; Sidney Willard, *Memories of Youth and Manhood* (2 vols., Cambridge, 1855), I, 97-99; Henry Adams, "Harvard College, 1786-1787," *Historical Essays* (New York, 1891), 88.

44. JQ, *Harvard*, II, 134; *The Laws of Harvard College* (Boston, 1790), 21-32; Eliphalet Pearson, "College Journal [of Disorders], 1788-1793," MS., *passim*, HUA; Faculty Recs., V, 240, 284, 297; Harold M. Ellis, *Joseph Dennie and His Circle* (Austin, University of Texas Press, 1915), 10; EQ, *Quincy*, 29.

45. Adams, "Harvard College," 94-96; Story, Cambridge, to Channing, September 23 and October 12, 1843, in William W. Story, *Life and Letters of Joseph Story* (2 vols., Boston, 1851), I, 47-55; folder on student costs, JQ Papers (1844-1845), HUA.

46. *Laws of Harvard College*, 41-53; "Commencement at Cambridge," *The Massachusetts Magazine*, 2 (July 1790), 431-432; Sumner, Boston, to Charlemagne Tower, September 27, 1830, in Edward L. Pierce, *Memoir and Letters of Charles Sumner* (4 vols., Boston, 1877-1893), I, 81; James Spear Loring, *The Hundred Boston Orators* (Boston, 1852), 258-278; EQ, *Quincy*, 448.

47. Daniel H. Calhoun, *Professional Lives in America: Structure and Aspiration, 1750-1850* (Cambridge, Mass., Harvard University Press, 1965), 1-19; Willard, *Memories*, II, 61-64; Robert A. East, *John Quincy Adams, the Critical Years* (New York, Bookman, 1962), 70; George Dexter, ed., *The Suffolk County Bar Book, 1770-1805* (Boston, 1882), 26.

48. JQ, *An Address Delivered at the Dedication of Dane Law College in Harvard University, October 23, 1832* (Cambridge, 1832), 17; James Jackson Putnam, *A Memoir of Dr. James Jackson* (Boston, Houghton Mifflin, 1905), 125; Ames, Dedham, to Christopher Gore, October 5, 1802, in Seth Ames, ed., *Works of Fisher Ames* (2 vols., Boston, 1854), II, 298-300; Docket Books for Court of Common Pleas (1794-1804), Suffolk County Court House, Boston; EQ, *Quincy*, 35-36.

49. *Centennial Celebration of the Wednesday Evening Club, 1777-1877* (Boston, 1878), 143; MHS *Procs.*, 1 (1791-1835), 112; Records of the Society for the Study of Natural Philosophy (1801-1807), MS., Boston Athenaeum; MHS *Procs.*, 49 (1915-1916), 418-424; Linda K. Kerber, "Science in the Early Republic: The Society for the Study of Natural Philosophy," *WMQ*, 29 (April 1972), 263-280.

50. Will of JQ I, Probate #18158 (1784), Suffolk Probate Court, Suffolk County Court House, Boston; Eliza Susan Quincy, unpublished "Memoirs," I, 86, Quincy Family Papers; EQ, *Quincy*, 58; Samuel Eliot Morison, *The Life and Letters of Harrison Gray Otis* (2 vols., Boston, Houghton Mifflin, 1913), I, 42-43; Harold Kirker and James Kirker, *Bulfinch's Boston, 1787-1817* (New York, Oxford University Press, 1964), *passim*; Records of the Neponset Bridge Corporation, Theodore Crane Library; Records of the Middlesex Canal Corporation, MS., Baker Library, Harvard Business School; Suffolk Registry of Deeds, Suffolk County Court House, Boston; Norfolk County Probate Records, Norfolk County Court House, Dedham; Walter Firey, *Land Use in Central Boston* (Cambridge, Mass., Harvard University Press, 1947), 1-45; Alexander S. Porter, "Changes of Values in Real Estate in Boston—The Past Hundred Years," Bostonian Society *Publications*, 1 (1886-1888), 57-74; *United States' Direct Tax of 1798* (RCCB *Rpts.*, 22), 60, 79, 89, 341.

51. JA, Philadelphia, to Abby (daughter), January 1, 1796, in Katherine M. Roof, *Colonel William Smith and Lady; The Romance of Washington's Aide and Young Abigail Adams* (Boston, Houghton Mifflin, 1929), 229; Eliza Quincy, "Memoirs," I, 16-17, 60-66, 72-73, Quincy Family Papers; EQ, *Quincy*, 35; *Christian Examiner*, 49 (November 1850), 521-522.

Notes to Chapter 2: A Federalist from Principle

1. EQ, *Quincy*, 261; Otis, Washington, to John Phillips, February 3, 1818, Otis Papers.

2. *Boston Town Records, (1796-1813)* (RCCB *Rpts.*, 35), 41, 45, 50, 80; JQ, *An Oration Pronounced July 4, 1798, at the Request of the Town of Boston, in Commemoration of the Anniversary of American Independence* (Boston, 1798); *Columbian Centinel*, May 21, 1800; EQ, *Quincy*, 59, 60.

3. *Catalogue of the Officers and Graduates of Yale University, 1701-1924* (New Haven, Yale University Press, 1924), 577; EQ, *Quincy*, 53; [Boston] *New*

England Palladium, November 6, 1804; *A View of the State of Parties in the United States of America* (Edinburgh, 1812), 50-51, quoted in David Hackett Fischer, *The Revolution of American Conservatism* (New York, Knopf, 1965), 30-31.

4. Morison, *Otis*, I, 210; Otis, Washington, to his wife, February 4, 1800, Otis Papers; *Columbian Centinel*, October 11, 18, 22, 25, 1800.

5. Morison, *Otis*, I, 190-191; JQ, Washington, to Wolcott, July 14, 1808, Wolcott Papers; Martin Duberman, *Charles Francis Adams, 1807-1886* (Boston, Houghton Mifflin, 1961), 39. That this preference lingered on, see David J. Rothman, *Politics and Power: The United States Senate, 1869-1901* (Cambridge, Mass., Harvard University Press, 1966), 119-120.

6. Richard Hildreth, *The History of the United States of America* (6 vols., New York, 1855), III, 429; JQ, Boston, to Wolcott, December 3, 1804, Wolcott Papers; JQ, Washington [to a Boston Federalist], January 18, 1806, JQ Papers, Houghton Library; JQ, "Diary," January 1, 1805, JQ Papers, MHS.

7. *Columbian Centinel*, November 1, 1800; [Boston] *Independent Chronicle*, October 27 and 30, 1800.

8. Voting returns recorded at Massachusetts Archives, State House, Boston; *DAB*: "William Eustis"; Frederick S. Allis, Jr., ed., *William Bingham's Maine Lands, 1798-1820* (2 vols., Colonial Society of Massachusetts *Publications*, 36, 37, Boston, 1954), II, 1085; *Columbian Centinel*, November 5, 1800.

9. JQ, Boston, to Wolcott, August 30, 1802, Wolcott Papers; Samuel Flagg Bemis, *John Quincy Adams and the Foundations of American Foreign Policy* (New York, Knopf, 1949), 113, 114; EQ, *Quincy*, 62.

10. Bemis, *Adams*, 114; *Columbian Centinel*, March 14, 1804; EQ, *Quincy*, 63.

11. *Columbian Centinel*, November 7 and 14, 1804; JQ, Boston, to Wolcott, December 3, 1804, Wolcott Papers.

12. JQ, "Diary," January 1, 1805, JQ Papers, MHS.

13. JQ, Boston, to Wolcott, December 3, 1804, Wolcott Papers; James Russell Lowell, "A Great Public Character," *Atlantic Monthly*, 20 (November 1867), 618.

14. EQ, *Quincy*, 38-39; Eliza S[usan] M[orton] Quincy, *Memoir [of the Life of Eliza S. M. Quincy]* (privately printed, Boston, 1861), 55-56; JQ, Boston, to Henry B. Dawson, December 27, 1863, Miscellaneous Manuscripts, NYHS.

15. Paul Goodman, *The Democratic-Republicans of Massachusetts* (Cambridge, Mass., Harvard University Press, 1964), 70; JQ, *Fourth of July Oration* (1798), 6. For Quincy's satirical rendering of the origins of the Jeffersonian party, see his remarks published under the pseudonym "Climenole" in *The Port Folio*, 4 (January-November 1804), esp. 81-83. See also [JQ], *An Answer to the Questions, Why Are You a Federalist? And Why Shall You Vote for Gov. Strong?* (Boston, 1805).

16. Charles A. Beard and Mary R. Beard, *The Rise of American Civilization* (4 vols., New York, Macmillan, 1927-1942), I, 400. This generalization does not apply to three recent studies: Fischer's already cited; James F. Banner Jr., *To the Hartford Convention: The Federalists and the Origins of Party Politics in Massachusetts, 1789-1815* (New York, Knopf, 1969); Linda K. Kerber, *Federalists in Dissent: Imagery and Ideology in Jeffersonian America* (Ithaca, Cornell

University Press, 1970). Nor does it apply to the genre of filiopietistic biographies of the late nineteenth century; see, for example, Henry Cabot Lodge, *Life and Letters of George Cabot* (Boston, 1877).

17. Louis Hartz, *The Liberal Tradition in America; An Interpretation of American Political Thought since the Revolution* (New York, Harcourt, Brace, 1955), 78-86.

18. EQ, *Quincy*, 357-358; Morison, *Otis*, II, 130-133. For Quincy's dealings with the Whigs, see Chapter 10 below.

19. Hartz, *Liberal Tradition*, 86; Bailyn, *Ideological Origins*, 312-319; James D. Richardson, ed., *A Compilation of the Messages and Papers of the Presidents* (10 vols., Washington, 1896-1907), I, 323.

20. JQ, *Fourth of July Oration* (1798), 10; [John Lowell], *The Road to Peace, Commerce, Wealth, and Happiness, by an old Farmer* (Boston, 1812), 2. This interpretation sharply distinguishes Quincy from those Bostonians described by Paul Goodman in his "Ethics and Enterprise: The Values of a Boston Elite, 1800-1860," *American Quarterly*, 18 (Fall 1968), 437-451.

21. See generally Marvin Meyers, *The Jacksonian Persuasion: Politics and Belief* (New York, Vintage Books, 1960); John William Ward, *Andrew Jackson: Symbol for an Age* (New York, Oxford University Press, 1962); Rowland Berthoff, *An Unsettled People: Social Order and Disorder in American History* (New York, Harper and Row, 1970), Part Two.

22. JQ, *An Address to the Citizens of Boston, on the XVIIth of September, MDCCCXXX, the Close of the Second Century from the First Settlement of the City* (Boston, 1830); JQ, *Harvard*, I, 1-67; JQ, *A Municipal History of the Town and City of Boston, during Two Centuries, from September 17, 1630, to September 17, 1830* (Boston, 1852), 1-19, 318-352. For Quincy's relations with Bancroft, see Chapter 9 below and JQ, *The Memory of the Late James Grahame, the Historian of the United States, Vindicated from the Charges of "Detraction" and "Calumny" Preferred against Him by Mr. George Bancroft, and the Conduct of Mr. Bancroft towards That Historian Stated and Exposed* (Boston, 1846).

23. JA, Quincy, to JQ, February 9, 1811, *The Works of John Adams*, ed. Charles Francis Adams (10 vols., Boston, 1851-1856), IX, 629-630.

24. JQ, *Fourth of July Oration* (1798), 8, 19; Edmund S. Morgan, "The Puritan Ethic and the American Revolution," *WMQ*, 24 (January 1967), 3-43.

25. JQ, *Fourth of July Oration* (1798), 12-13.

26. *Ibid.*, 15-16.

27. On this point, see JQ, *Considerations Respectfully Submitted to the Citizens of Boston—on the Proposed Annexation of Boston and Charlestown* (Boston, 1854) and *Address Illustrative of the Nature and Power of the Slave States, and the Duties of the Free States; Delivered at the Request of the Inhabitants of the Town of Quincy . . . June 5, 1856* (Boston, 1856), both of which are discussed in Chapter 10 below.

28. Manning J. Dauer, *The Adams Federalists* (Baltimore, Johns Hopkins University Press, 1953), 140-151; William A. Robinson, *Jeffersonian Democracy in New England* (New Haven, Yale University Press, 1913), 23; JQ, *Fourth of July Oration* (1798), 20.

29. Robinson, *Jeffersonian Democracy*, 36-42; Noble E. Cunningham, *The Jeffersonian Republicans in Power* (Chapel Hill, University of North Carolina Press, 1963), 3-11; Richard Hofstadter, *The Idea of a Party System* (Berkeley, University of California Press, 1969), 128-131.

30. JQ, Boston, to Wolcott, September 30, 1801, Wolcott Papers.

31. JQ to Wolcott, March 26, 1802, and September 30, 1803, *ibid.*

32. JQ to Wolcott, September 5, 1803, and Wolcott, New York, to JQ, September 12, 1803, *ibid.*

33. Henry Adams, *History of the United States during the Administrations of Thomas Jefferson and James Madison* (8 vols., New York, 1889), IV, 94-113; John Bach McMaster, *A History of the People of the United States from the Revolution to the Civil War* (8 vols., New York, 1883-1913), III, 7; Morison, *Otis*, I, 261-269.

34. William Plumer Jr., *Life of William Plumer* (Boston, 1856), 261-262, 285; Banner, *To the Hartford Convention*, 84; Ames, Dedham, to Thomas Dwight, October 31, 1803, in *Works of Fisher Ames*, I, 329-330; JQ to Wolcott, September 5, 1803, Wolcott Papers.

35. Ames, Dedham, to Christopher Gore, October 3, 1803, *Works of Fisher Ames*, I, 322-324; JQ to Wolcott, September 5, 1803, Wolcott Papers.

36. [James Madison], "Number Ten; The Size and Variety of the Union as a Check on Faction," *The Federalist*, ed. B. F. Wright (Cambridge, Mass., Harvard University Press, 1961), 129-135; JQ to Wolcott, September 5, 1803, Wolcott Papers.

37. JQ to Wolcott, September 5, 1803, *ibid.*

38. See also Quincy's "Speech on the Fortifying of Ports and Harbors of the United States, April 15, 1806," in JQ, *Speeches*, 22-23.

39. Justin Winsor, ed., *Memorial History of Boston* (4 vols., Boston, 1881), IV, 1-24; Dixon Ryan Fox, *The Decline of Aristocracy in New York* (New York, Columbia University Press, 1919), 162-165; Morison, *Three Centuries*, 164-191; Thomas Wertenbaker, *Princeton, 1746-1946* (Princeton, Princeton University Press, 1946), 120-121; JQ to Wolcott, September 5, 1803, Wolcott Papers.

40. On this point, see Rowland Berthoff, "The American Social Order: A Conservative Hypothesis," *AHR*, 65 (April 1960), 495-514.

41. Ames, Dedham, to Dwight, November 29, 1803, *Works of Fisher Ames*, I, 334; H. Adams, *History of the United States*, II, 160-171; Meredith Mason Brown, "The Northern Confederacy: High-Federalist Political Attitudes and the Separatist Movement of 1803-1804," 35, unpub. honors thesis, Radcliffe College, 1961, HUA.

42. H. Adams, *History of the United States*, II, 163-168; Brown, "Northern Confederacy," 35; Ames, Dedham, to Pickering, April 28, 1804, *Works of Fisher Ames*, I, 340.

43. Fischer, *American Conservatism*, 1-28.

44. Brown, "Northern Confederacy," Appendix II; JQ, "Speech on the Bill for Authorizing the President to Suspend the Embargo, April 1808," in JQ, *Speeches*, 49. See Henry Adams, ed., *Documents Relating to New England Federalism* (Boston, 1877), 56, 78, 300, and JQ's "Travel Diary," February 18, 1829, JQ Papers, MHS.

45. JQ, *Fourth of July Oration* (1798), 10; JQ, Boston, to JQA, November 23, 1804, reel no. 403, Adams Papers.

46. Fischer, *American Conservatism*, 29-49; JQ, Boston, to JQA, November 23, 1804, reel no. 403, Adams Papers; JQ to Wolcott, September 5, 1803, Wolcott Papers.

47. Bemis, *Adams*, 115; JQA, Boston, to Rufus King, October 8, 1802, in Worthington Chauncey Ford, ed., *Writings of John Quincy Adams* (7 vols., New York, Macmillan, 1913-1917), III, 9.

48. Bemis, *Adams*, 111-134; EQ, *Quincy*, 123-124.

49. JQ to JQA, November 23 and December 15, 1804, reel no. 403, Adams Papers; JQ, "Diary," September 10 and 25, 1805, MHS.

50. JQ to JQA, December 15, 1804, reel no. 403, Adams Papers. In chapters 3 and 4 I set forth my objections to Professor Fischer's characterization of Quincy as one who "generally subordinated himself to party discipline" (*American Conservatism*, 273).

Notes to Chapter 3: The Politics of Exasperation

1. JQ, Washington, to William S. Shaw, November 30, 1805, Shaw Papers.

2. Cunningham, *Jeffersonian Republicans*, 71-72.

3. H. Adams, *History of the United States*, III, 119; Cunningham, *Jeffersonian Republicans*, 30-70. For an analysis of the problems inherent in "outsized" majorities, see William F. Riker, *A Theory of Political Coalitions* (New Haven, Yale University Press, 1965), 1-10.

4. Norman K. Risjord, *The Old Republicans: Southern Conservatism in the Age of Jefferson* (New York, Columbia University Press, 1965), 18-71; Taggart, Washington, to John Taylor, January 4, 1805, in "Letters of Samuel Taggart, Representative in Congress, 1803-1814," introd. by George Henry Haynes, AAS *Procs.*, n.s. 33 (April 1923), 146; H. Adams, *History of the United States*, II, 210.

5. *Ibid.*, III, 128; JQ, Washington, to Wolcott, January 5, 1806, Wolcott Papers.

6. Cunningham, *Jeffersonian Republicans*, 74-82; Henry Adams, *John Randolph* (Boston, 1882), 122-152.

7. AAS *Procs.*, n.s. 33 (April 1923), 174-175: February 2, 1806; JQ, Washington, to Wolcott, February 3, 1806, Wolcott Papers; H. Adams, *History of the United States*, III, 147-171; Cunningham, *Jeffersonian Republicans*, 86-87.

8. Ames, Dedham, to JQ, December 16, 1805, in *Works of Fisher Ames*, I, 346; JQ, Washington, [to a Boston Federalist], January 18, 1806, JQ Papers, Houghton Library; JQ, Washington, to Shaw, January 1, 1806, Shaw Papers.

9. JQ, Washington, to Wolcott, December 11 and 18, 1805, January 6, 1806, Wolcott Papers; AAS *Procs.*, n.s., 33 (April 1923), 130,177: February 4, 1804, and February 24, 1806.

10. JQ, Washington, to Wolcott, February 3 and March 8, 1806, Wolcott Papers.

11. [JQ], "Climenole," *The Port Folio*, IV, 65-67: March 3, 1804; Adams, *Randolph*, 22, *et passim*.

12. Josiah Quincy, Jr., *Figures of the Past* (Boston, 1883), 175; Adams, *Randolph*, 6, 39.

13. William Cabell Bruce, *John Randolph of Roanoke* (2 vols., New York, Putnam's, 1923), I, 95; Adams, *Randolph*, 17; *AC*, 9th, 1st, 1040: April 15, 1806.

14. JQ, Washington, to Wolcott, March 8, 1806, Wolcott Papers.

15. *The Port Folio*, IV, 27-28: January 28, 1804; JQ, Washington, to JA, December 5, 1808, in EQ, *Quincy*, 146; Adams, *Randolph*, 48-53.

16. AAS *Procs.*, n.s. 33 (April 1923), 152, 198: February 3, 1805, and April

2, 1806; EQ, *Quincy*, 95; Randolph, Bizarre, Virginia, to Monroe, September 16, 1806, in Adams, *Randolph*, 200-202; JQ, *Speeches*, 376.

17. JQ, Washington, to Wolcott, December 11, 1805, Wolcott Papers; JQ, Washington, to Upham, January 6, 1806, JQ Papers, Houghton Library; Randolph, Georgetown, to JQ, July 12, 1812, in EQ, *Quincy*, 268.

18. *Ibid.*, 266-267, 301; Adams, *Randolph*, 268-269.

19. Russell Kirk, *Randolph of Roanoke, A Study in Conservative Thought* (Chicago, Chicago University Press, 1951), 9-12.

20. Bruce, *Randolph*, I, 222-286; H. Adams, *History of the United States*, III, 147-164; AAS *Procs.*, n.s. 33 (April 1923), 194: March 24, 1806; E. S. M. Quincy, Washington, to Abigail Adams, April 6, 1806, reel no. 404, Adams Papers.

21. Risjord, *Old Republicans*, 62-80; Jefferson, Washington, to Monroe, May 4, 1806, in Paul Leicester Ford, ed., *Writings of Thomas Jefferson* (12 vols., New York, 1892-1899), II, 106; Everett Somerville Brown, ed., *William Plumer's Memorandum of Proceedings in the United States Senate, 1803-1807* (New York, Macmillan, 1932), 446; AAS *Procs.*, n.s. 33 (April 1923), 194: March 24, 1806.

22. Risjord, *Old Republicans*, 86; Cunningham, *Jeffersonian Republicans*, 87-88.

23. JQ, Boston, to Noah Webster, June 30, 1806, Webster Papers; JQ, Washington, to Fisher Ames, n.d. [spring 1806], Washburn Autograph Collection.

24. JQ, Washington, to Shaw, February 10, 1807, Shaw Papers.

25. JQ, Washington, to Richard Cranch, March 9, 1806, Cranch Papers; JQ, Washington, to Upham, September 10, 1810, JQ Papers, Houghton Library; JQ, Washington, to his wife, 1808, in EQ, *Quincy*, 131; *ibid.*, 186.

26. Gaillard Hunt, ed., *Forty Years of Washington Society Portrayed by the Family Letters of Mrs. Samuel Harrison Smith* (New York, Ungar, 1906), 1; Constance McLaughlin Green, *Washington: Village and Capital, 1800-1877* (Princeton, Princeton University Press, 1962), 21, 41; James Sterling Young, *The Washington Community: 1800-1828* (New York, Columbia University Press, 1966), 28, 57. This section owes much to Professor Young's analysis of the dysfunctional aspects of early Washington as the seat of government. See also Sidney H. Aronson, *Status and Kinship in the Higher Civil Service* (Cambridge, Mass., Harvard University Press, 1969).

27. Joseph Story, Washington, to Samuel P. Fay, May 29, 1807, in Story, *Joseph Story*, I, 148-149; JQ, Washington, to his wife, March, 1808, in EQ, *Quincy*, 137; AAS *Procs.*, n.s. 33 (April 1923), 303: January 27, 1808; *AC*, 10th, 1st, 1531-1593: February 2-8, 1808; William Cranch, Washington, to Richard Cranch, February 28, 1808, Cranch Papers.

28. Story, Washington, to Fay, May 29, 1807, in Story, *Joseph Story*, I, 150; Green, *Washington*, 39; *Plumer's Memorandum*, 642.

29. E. S. M. Quincy, Washington, to Abigail Adams, April 6, 1806, reel no. 404, Adams Papers; JQ, Washington, to William Sullivan, December 21, 1810, Washburn Autograph Collection.

30. Young, *Washington Community*, 98-106; E. S. M. Quincy, *Memoir*, 130-131; JQ, Washington, to Sullivan, December 21, 1810, Washburn Autograph Collection.

31. E. S. M. Quincy, Washington, to Miss Storer, December 4 and 20, 1809, in E. S. M. Quincy, *Memoir*, 127, 129; EQ, *Quincy*, 131; Richard Beale Davis, ed., *Jeffersonian America: Notes on the United States of America Collected in the Years 1805-6-7 and 11-12 by Sir Augustus John Foster, Bart.* (San Marino, Huntington Library, 1954), 9.

32. JQ, Cambridge, to Sullivan, March 17, 1834, Essex Institute, Salem; Paul Goodman, "Social Status of Political Leadership: The House of Representatives, 1797-1804," *WMQ*, 25 (July 1968), 465-474; AAS *Procs.*, n.s. 33 (April 1923), 172: January 12, 1806; H. Adams, *History of the United States*, III, 126-128.

33. EQ, *Quincy*, 458-462; Davis, *Jeffersonian America*, 8. See also Eliza Quincy, Boston, to Charles Sumner, January 15, 1867, Sumner Papers.

34. Davis, *Jeffersonian America*, 5-10.

35. Young, *Washington Community*, 33; JQ, *Speeches*, 38-39.

36. Young, *Washington Community*, 91-98; see also Hofstadter, *Idea of a Party System*, *passim*, and Bailyn, *Ideological Origins*, 144-159.

37. AAS *Procs.*, n.s. 33 (April 1923), 223: December 22, 1807. On stereotyping, see Irving, Washington, to Henry Brevoort, February 7, 1811, in Pierre Irving, ed., *Life and Letters of Washington Irving* (4 vols., New York, 1864), I, 268, and Roger H. Brown, *The Republic in Peril: 1812* (New York, Columbia University Press, 1964), 7-15.

38. Davis, *Jeffersonian America*, 9.

39. JQ, *Speeches*, 38-39.

40. John Cotton Smith, Sharon, Mass., to JQ, August 25, 1806, in E. S. M. Quincy, *Memoir*, 104-105.

41. *Ibid.*, 115; AAS *Procs.*, n.s. 33 (April 1923), 307-308: February 28, 1808.

42. JQ, Washington, [to a Boston Federalist], January 18, 1806, JQ Papers, Houghton Library; *Columbian Centinel*, November 10, 1810; JQ, Boston, to Upham, September 17, 1810, JQ Papers, Houghton Library. Election returns, as recorded in Massachusetts Archives, State House, Boston:

1806	Josiah Quincy	1,968	James Prince	1,439
1808	Josiah Quincy	3,004	William Jarvis	2,074
1810	Josiah Quincy	2,273	David Tilden	1,024

43. JQ, Washington, to Shaw, February 10, 1807, Shaw Papers.

44. Ames, Dedham, to JQ, January 27, February 3, and November 19, 1807, JQ Papers, LC.

45. Ames to JQ, December 6, 1807, *ibid.*; JQ, Washington, to the Rev. Joseph McLean, February 13, 1811, JQ Papers, HUA.

46. JQ, "Diary," September 21, 1805, JQ Papers, MHS.

47. *AC*, 9th, 1st, April 15, 1806, in JQ, *Speeches*, 5-27; H. Adams, *History of the United States*, III, 180.

48. *AC*, 10th, 2nd, 1120: January 20, 1809. This paragraph owes much to the discussion of "a dramatistic theory of status politics" in Joseph Gusfield, *Symbolic Crusade* (Urbana, University of Illinois Press, 1963), 166-188.

49. *AC*, 10th, 2nd, 962: December 30, 1808, in JQ, *Speeches*, 117. For another example of Quincy's enflamed oratory, see his "Second Speech on the Report of the Committee on Foreign Relations," December 7, 1808, in *ibid.*, 83-107.

50. EQ, *Quincy*, 168.

51. JQ, Washington, to Shaw, January 19, 1811, Shaw Papers; EQ, *Quincy*, 303.

52. JQ, "Diary," September 10-21, 1805, JQ Papers, MHS; JQ, Washington, to JA, January 29, 1811, reel no. 411, Adams Papers.

53. EQ, *Quincy*, 115; Bradford Perkins, *Prologue to War: England and the United States, 1805-1812* (Berkeley, University of California Press, 1961), 34-35; AAS *Procs*., n.s. 33 (April 1923), 396: May 9, 1812.

54. Young, *Washington Community*, 143-153; AAS *Procs*., n.s. 33 (April 1923), 347: April 27, 1810.

55. JQ, Washington, to JA, January 29, 1811, reel no. 411, Adams Papers.

56. *AC*, 10th, 2nd, 1173-1182: January 25, 1809.

57. Ames, Dedham, to JQ, February 3, 1807, JQ Papers, LC; Gusfield, *Symbolic Crusade*, 1-12, *passim*; JQ, Boston, to Upham, April 6, 1809, JQ Papers, Houghton Library.

58. David Hackett Fischer, "The Myth of the Essex Junto," *WMQ*, 21 (April 1964), 191-235; Samuel Eliot Morison, *Harrison Gray Otis—The Urbane Federalist* (Boston, Houghton Mifflin, 1969), 530-531; Samuel Eliot Morison, *The Maritime History of Massachusetts, 1783-1860* (Boston, Houghton Mifflin, 1921), 167. For Quincy's view of the Junto, essentially that taken by Fischer, see JQ, Boston, to Waldo Higginson, March 4, 1858, JQ Papers, Houghton Library.

59. Morison, *Otis*, I, 275-277, 324-326; JQ, Boston, to Pickering, June 20, 1811, Pickering Papers; JQ, "Review of the *Works of Fisher Ames*," *The Monthly Anthology and Boston Review*, 8 (February 1810), 119.

60. JQ, Washington, to his wife, March 26, 1812, in EQ, *Quincy*, 254; Henry Dearborn, Boston, to Gallatin, April 2, 1809, Gallatin Papers; Merrill D. Peterson, *The Jeffersonian Image in the American Mind* (New York, Oxford University Press, 1962), 180.

61. JA, Quincy, to JQ, February 9, 1811, in *Works of JA*, IX, 629-632; JA, Quincy, to JQA, February 14, 1811, reel no. 411, Adams Papers; Eliza Quincy, Boston, to Winthrop, June 30, 1879, Winthrop Papers.

62. JQ, Washington, to his wife, February 10, 1811, in E. S. M. Quincy, *Memoir*, 145; JQ, Washington, to McLean, February 13, 1811, JQ Papers, HUA.

63. JQ, "Diary," September 1805, 51, JQ Papers, MHS; JQ, Washington, to Wolcott, December 20, 1806, Wolcott Papers.

64. JQ, Washington, to McLean, February 13, 1811, JQ Papers, HUA; EQ, *Quincy*, 306.

Notes to Chapter 4: Escape into War

1. [JQ], *An Address of Members of the House of Representatives of the Congress of the United States to Their Constituents on the Subject of War with Great Britain* [June 25, 1812] (Boston, 1812), 11; *AC*, 12th, 2nd, 571: January 5, 1813; JQ, Cambridge, to Sullivan, March 17, 1834, Essex Institute; William Sullivan, *Familiar Letters on Public Characters and Public Events from the Peace of 1783 to the Peace of 1815* (Boston, 1834), 320-321; EQ, *Quincy*, 235, 249.

2. JQ, Washington, to his wife, June 3, 1812, in E. S. M. Quincy, *Memoir*,

152; [JQ], *Address on War*, 36; AAS *Procs.*, n.s. 33 (April 1923), 352: January 6, 1813; Mathew Carey, *The Olive Branch, or Faults on Both Sides* (Philadelphia, 1814), 231-235.

3. JQ, Cambridge, to Sullivan, March 17, 1834, Essex Institute; [JQ], *Address on War*, 27; JQ, Washington, to Otis, November 8, 1811, Otis Papers. This was essentially the view held by Randolph and Foster.

4. EQ, *Quincy*, 255-257.

5. JQ, *Speeches*, 367.

6. *Ibid.*, 361-362.

7. Irving Brant, *James Madison: The President, 1809-1812* (Indianapolis, Bobbs-Merrill, 1956), 421-483; JQ, *Speeches*, 361-362, 367.

8. Warren H. Goodman, "The Origins of the War of 1812: A Survey of Changing Interpretations," *MVHR*, 28 (1941-1942), 171-186; Theodore Clarke Smith, "War Guilt in 1812," MHS *Procs.*, 64 (1931), 319-345; H. Adams, *History of the United States*, VI, 116-118, 123, 140.

9. Louis M. Hacker, "Western Land Hunger and the War of 1812: A Conjecture," *MVHR*, 10 (1923-1924), 365-395; Julius W. Pratt, "Western Aims in the War of 1812," *ibid.*, 12 (1925-1926), 36-50; George Rogers Taylor, "Agrarian Discontent in the Mississippi Valley preceding the War of 1812," *Journal of Political Economy*, 39 (1931), 471-505. Taylor's thesis has since been extended to explain Southern militancy; see Margaret Latimer, "South Carolina—A Protagonist of the War of 1812," *AHR*, 61 (1955-1956), 914-929.

10. Norman K. Risjord, "1812: Conservatives, War Hawks, and the Nation's Honor," *WMQ*, 18 (April 1961), 196-210; Brown, *Republic in Peril*; Perkins, *Prologue to War*, vii, 289. Support for the Perkins-Brown view about party loyalty as an important factor is to be found in Ronald L. Hatzenbuehler, "Party Unity and the Decision for War in the House of Representatives, 1812," *WMQ*, 29 (July 1972), 367-390.

11. *Niles' Weekly Register*, January 1, and April 4, 1812; AAS *Procs.*, n.s. 33 (April 1923), 382: February 6, 1812; Perkins, *Prologue to War*, 392, 418-434; Samuel Eliot Morison *et al.*, *Dissent in Three American Wars* (Cambridge, Mass., Harvard University Press, 1970), 31.

12. Jefferson, Monticello, to Monroe, May 5, 1811, in Perkins, *Prologue to War*, 262.

13. *AC*, 12th, 1st, 329-1606: November 4, 1811, to April 1, 1812; H. Adams, *History of the United States*, VI, 170-171; Perkins, *Prologue to War*, 262.

14. *Ibid.*, 350; Risjord, *Old Republicans*, 130-133.

15. JA, Quincy, to JQ, November 25, 1808, reel no. 118, Adams Papers.

16. Perkins, *Prologue to War*, 67-68.

17. H. Adams, *History of the United States*, IV, 1-20.

18. *Ibid.*, 27-31. For a recent critical assessment of Jefferson's policy, see Eric L. McKitrick, "The View from Jefferson's Camp," *New York Review of Books*, 15 (December 17, 1970), 35-38.

19. H. Adams, *History of the United States*, IV, 146-147; Ames, Dedham, to JQ, November 11, 1807, JQ Papers, LC; "Pacificus," *Columbian Centinel*, July 24 and August 12, 1807.

20. Otis, Boston, to JQ, November 19, 1807, in EQ, *Quincy*, 115.

21. JQ, Boston, to Timothy Bigelow, July 13, 1807, Washburn Autograph Collection; *AC*, 10th, 1st, 795-796, 1137-1141, 1167, 1195-1204.

22. *Ibid.*, 796, 1830-1838, 2199-2212; JQ, Washington, to JA, January 29, 1811, reel no. 411, Adams Papers.

23. JQ, *Speeches*, 31-49; *Columbian Centinel*, January 23, 1808; H. Adams, *History of the United States*, IV, 401; Story, *Joseph Story*, I, 171, 185; JA, Quincy, to JQ, December 23, 1808, reel no. 118, Adams Papers.

24. JQ, *Speeches*, 55-79.

25. *Ibid.*, 111-126.

26. *Ibid.*, 143-144.

27. *AC*, 10th, 2nd, 860-861: December 15, 1808; AAS *Procs.*, n.s. 33 (April 1923), 320: December 2, 1808; JQ, Washington, to his wife, December 17, 1808, in EQ, *Quincy*, 160.

28. Kirkland, Boston, to JQ, February 10, 1809, in MHS *Procs.*, 17 (June 1879), 113; JA, Quincy, to JQ, December 23, 1806, reel no. 113, and JQ, Washington, to JA, January 24, 1811, reel no. 411, Adams Papers; Cabot, Boston, to Pickering, January 19, 1809, in Lodge, *George Cabot*, 407; JQ, *Speeches*, 77.

29. J. D. Forbes, "Boston Smuggling, 1807-1815," *American Neptune*, 10 (1950), 144-149; Eliza Quincy, Boston, to Winthrop, May 15, 1879, Winthrop Papers.

30. EQ, *Quincy*, 185-186.

31. H. Adams, *History of the United States*, V, 183.

32. EQ, *Quincy*, 198-199; E. S. M. Quincy, *Memoir*, 130-131; JQ, Washington, to Sullivan, December 21, 1810, Washburn Autograph Collection.

33. JQ, *Speeches*, 196.

34. Irving, Washington, to Brevoort, January 13, 1811, in Irving, *Washington Irving*, I, 263.

35. JQ, Washington, to Sullivan, December 21, 1810, Washburn Autograph Collection.

36. Richardson, *Compilation*, I, 491-496.

37. Abijah Bigelow, Washington, to his wife, December 11, 1811, in AAS *Procs.*, n.s. 40 (October 1930), 319; *ibid.*, n.s. 33 (April 1923), 369: December 14, 1811.

38. The number of Federalists is that cited by *Niles' Weekly Register*, November 30, 1811. On the Federalist situation in Massachusetts, see Morison, *Otis*, II, 26-28.

39. JQ, Washington, to Otis, November 8, 1811, Otis Papers. Quincy was not the only Federalist with this view; see AAS *Procs.*, n.s. 33 (April 1923), 368: December 2, 1811.

40. H. Adams, *History of the United States*, V, 16-20; Charles Warren, ed., *Jacobin and Junto, or Early American Politics as Viewed in the Diary of Dr. Nathaniel Ames, 1758-1822* (Cambridge, Mass., Harvard University Press, 1931), 238; Richard Hofstadter, *The Paranoid Style in American Politics* (New York, Knopf, 1965), 11.

41. JQ, Washington, to Otis, November 8, 1811, Otis Papers. For evidence that Massachusetts Federalists took these elections seriously, see Banner, *To the Hartford Convention*, 257, 275-276.

42. JQ, Washington, to Otis, November 25, 1811, Otis Papers.

43. Gore, Waltham, to King, October 5, 1812, in Charles R. King, ed., *The Life and Correspondence of Rufus King* (5 vols., New York, Putnam's, 1894-1900), V, 282; Samuel W. Dana, Washington, to Pickering, January 30, 1812, Pickering Papers; H. D. Sedgwick, Boston, to Harmanus Bleecker, Decem-

ber 16, 1811, Sedgwick Papers; Eliza Quincy, Boston, to Winthrop, May 15 and June 30, 1879, Winthrop Papers; Robert A. East, "Economic Development and New England Federalism, 1803-1814," *NEQ*, 10 (September 1937), 430-446.

44. Abijah Bigelow, Washington, to his wife, December 4 and 11, 1811, AAS *Procs.*, 40 (October 1930), 317, 319. The fullest account of the plan, based on an 1861 interview with Quincy, is in Benson J. Lossing, *The Pictorial Field Book of the War of 1812* (New York, 1868), 17n, 217; for a contemporary description of the plan, see Reed, Washington, to Pickering, January 20, 1812, Pickering Papers. For roll call analysis of House "war measures" during the spring of 1812, see Reginald Horsman, "Who Were the War Hawks?", *Indiana Magazine of History*, 60 (1964), 121-136, and Hatzenbuehler, "Party Unity and the Decision for War," *WMQ*, 29 (July 1972), 367-390.

45. EQ, *Quincy*, 240. That Quincy was not alone in this view that Madison had no desire for war, see Leverett Saltonstall Jr., Salem, to Leverett Saltonstall, January 10, 1812, Saltonstall Papers. See also James A. Bayard, Washington, to William H. Wells, January 12, 1812, in "Papers of James A. Bayard," *Annual Report of the American Historical Association for 1913* (2 vols., Washington, 1915), II, 188.

46. JQ, "Speech in Relation to Maritime Protection, January 25, 1812," in JQ, *Speeches*, 291-328; Abijah Bigelow, Washington, to his wife, January 25, 1812, AAS *Procs.*, 40 (October 1930), 327; JA, Quincy, to JQ, February 21, 1812, in EQ, *Quincy*, 248; *New York Spectator*, January 28, 1812; EQ, *Quincy*, 240; *AC*, 12th, 1st, 1115, 1127: February 28 and March 2, 1812.

47. Foster, Washington, to Lord Wellesley, January 16, 1812, memorandum no. 3, FO 5/84, British Public Records Office, London. Professor Morison earlier arrived at the same conclusion that Quincy was the Federalist Foster was citing in his memoranda to London; see his *DAB* article on JQ.

48. Foster, Washington, to Wellesley, December 11 and 18, 1811, nos. 30, 31, in Précis Book of Foster Correspondence, Special Collections, NYPL.

49. AAS *Procs.*, n.s. 33 (April 1923), 377: January 20, 1812; Samuel Eliot Morison, "The Henry-Crillon Affair of 1812," MHS *Procs.*, 69 (1947-1950), 207-231.

50. *AC*, 12th, 1st, 1162-1184: March 9, 1812; JQ, Washington, to Otis, March 19, 1812, Otis Papers; Perkins, *Prologue to War*, 364.

51. JQ, Washington, to his wife, March 22, 1812, in EQ, *Quincy*, 253.

52. *AC*, 12th, 1st, 1606: April 3, 1812; JQ, Washington, to Wolcott, April 12, 1812, Wolcott Papers; E. S. M. Quincy, Braintree, to JQ, April 10, 1812, in E. S. M. Quincy, *Memoir*, 153.

53. Taggart, Washington, to Pickering, April 3, 1812, Pickering Papers.

54. Eliza Quincy, Boston, to Winthrop, June 30, 1879, Winthrop Papers; *AC*, 12th, 2nd, 167-173, 540-573, 659-677.

55. Quotation from Adams, *Randolph*, 306.

Notes to Chapter 5: Between Jobs

1. Eliza Quincy, "Journal," November 28, 1814, Quincy Family Papers.

2. *Public Documents of the Legislature of Massachusetts Containing the Speech of His Excellency Governor Strong* ... (Boston, 1813), copy in Massachusetts Archives, State House, Boston; [JQ], *The New States, or a Comparison*

of the Wealth, Strength and Population of the Northern and Southern States (Boston, 1813), 36; JQ, Boston, to Pickering, June 28, 1813, Pickering Papers; *Columbian Centinel,* June 16, 19, and 26, 1813. See also Morison, *Dissent,* 3-31.

3. EQ, *Quincy,* 324; H. Adams, *History of the United States,* VII, 64-66; Otis, Washington, to Phillips, February 3, 1818, Otis Papers. The resolution was expunged from the Senate Journal in 1824.

4. William A. Robinson, "Washington Benevolent Society in New England," MHS *Procs.,* 49 (1916), 274-286; Fischer, *American Conservatism,* 110-128; Minutes of the Proceedings of the Washington Benevolent Society of Massachusetts (1812-1824), MS., MHS.

5. *New England Palladium,* April 29 and May 3, 1814; Minutes of the Benevolent Society, 55.

6. EQ, *Quincy,* 346-347; Eliza Quincy, "Journal," September 28, 1814, Quincy Family Papers. See also James B. Gardner, "New England Guards," Bostonian Society *Publications,* 4 (1907), 9-53; Walter Kendall Watkins, "The Defense of Boston in the War of 1812," *ibid.,* 2 (1899), 35-74.

7. Morison, *Otis,* II, 68; JQ, *Oration Delivered before the Washington Benevolent Society of Massachusetts, April 30, 1813* (Boston, 1813), 18; *Independent Chronicle,* January 31, 1814; JA, Quincy, to Jefferson, June 28, 1812, in Cappon, *Adams-Jefferson Letters,* II, 311; JQA, St. Petersburg, to Abigail Adams, October 25, 1813, in Ford, *Writings of JQA,* IV, 528-530; William Bentley, *Diary* (4 vols., Salem, Essex Institute, 1905-1914), IV, 104.

8. Morison, *Otis,* II, 66-67; Morison, *Dissent,* 26-27. See also John Lowell, Boston, to Otis, February 25 and 26, 1823, Otis Papers.

9. Randolph, Richmond, to JQ, March 22, 1814, Randolph Papers; East, "Economic Development," *NEQ,* 10 (September 1937), 430-446; Warren, *Jacobin and Junto,* 255.

10. East, "Economic Development," 440-446.

11. JQ, *Oration before the Washington Benevolent Society,* 29; Caroline Ware, *Early New England Cotton Manufacture* (Boston, Houghton Mifflin, 1931), 60-66; Carl Seaburg and Stanley Paterson, *Merchant Prince of Boston: Colonel T. H. Perkins, 1764-1854* (Cambridge, Mass., Harvard University Press, 1971), 245-246; Morison, *Otis,* II, 66-67.

12. Carey, *Olive Branch,* 77, 78, 365.

13. EQ, *Quincy,* 255, 301. See, for comparative purposes, the organizing sentiments expressed in Glyndon Van Deusen, "Some Aspects of Whig Thought and Theory in the Jacksonian Period," *AHR,* 63 (January 1958), 305-322; Lynn L. Marshall, "The Strange Stillbirth of the Whig Party," *ibid.,* 72 (January 1967), 452.

14. JQ, "Travel Journal (1801)," in MHS *Procs.,* 2nd ser., 4 (May 1888), 124; ———, *The Rich Men of Massachusetts* (Boston, 1852), 55-56.

15. Randolph, Roanoke, to JQ, July 1, 1814, Randolph Papers. For Quincy's doubts about unrestricted immigration, see JQ, Boston, to Wolcott, March 11, 1821, Wolcott Papers.

16. Morison, *Otis,* II, 125-139; Banner, *To the Hartford Convention,* 350; EQ, *Quincy,* 357-358.

17. Eliza Quincy, "Journal," February 13 and 22, 1815, Quincy Family Papers; E. S. M. Quincy, *Memoir,* 181-182; *Columbian Centinel,* February 22, 1815.

18. Minutes of the Benevolent Society, 67, 74.

19. EQ, *Quincy*, 261.

20. Morison, *Otis*, I, 286-320, II, 139; Fischer, *American Conservatism*, 273; *Columbian Centinel*, April 8, 1813; Gore, Waltham, to King, October 5, 1812, in King, *Rufus King*, V, 282.

21. [JQ], *Address to the Independent Electors of Massachusetts, February 27, 1815* (Boston, 1815), 5. On Federalist politicians' accommodations in Massachusetts, see Shaw Livermore Jr., *The Twilight of Federalism: The Disintegration of the Federalist Party, 1815-1830* (Princeton, Princeton University Press, 1962), 49-86, and Morison, *Otis*, II, 200-206.

22. Journal of the Massachusetts Senate, June 15, 1816, MS., Massachusetts Archives, State House, Boston; Edward Stanwood, "Separation of Maine from Massachusetts," MHS *Procs.*, 31 (June 1907), 125-164; JQ, "Diary" (1818-1827), 152: September 28, 1825, JQ Papers, MHS; EQ, *Quincy*, 373-375.

23. Quincy quoted in Walker, "Quincy," MHS *Procs.*, 9 (1866-1867), 106-107n; William Tudor, Boston, to King, February 12, 1820, King, *Rufus King*, VI, 273.

24. To gauge the change, compare Richard Beale Davis, "The Early American Lawyer and the Profession of Letters," *Huntington Library Quarterly*, 12 (February 1949), 191-205, and Clement Hugh Mill, "Memoir of Rufus Choate," MHS *Procs.*, 2nd ser., 11 (1896-1897), 124-155.

25. For Quincy's involvement in the management of the Middlesex Canal, see "Report to the Board of Directors, April, 1817," Middlesex Canal Corporation Papers, Kress Room, Baker Library, Harvard Business School.

26. J. P. Mayer, ed., *Journey to America* (New Haven, Yale University Press, 1962), 202-203; Goodman, "Ethics and Enterprise," *American Quarterly*, 18 (Fall 1966), 438; J. C. Ropes, "Memoir of the Hon. John Chipman Gray LL.D.," MHS *Procs.*, 2nd ser., 4 (1887-1888), 22-37; James C. Merrill, "Memoir of James Bowdoin," MHS *Colls.*, 9 (1846), 224-225.

27. Mayer, *Journey to America*, 203; John Lothrop Motley, Vienna, August 7, 1864, to EQ, in EQ, *Quincy*, 548; JQ, "Massachusetts Institutions," *North American Review*, 2 (March 1816), 309-319; Charles Knowles Bolton, "Memoir of Francis Calley Gray," MHS *Procs.*, 47 (1914), 529-534.

28. JQ, "Agriculture," *North American Review*, 8 (December 1818), 138; JQ, Boston, to Pickering, June 20, 1811, and Pickering, Wenham, to JQ, December 15, 1819, Pickering Papers; *The Centennial Year (1792-1892) of the Massachusetts Society for Promoting Agriculture* (Salem, 1892), 37.

29. Ferris Greenslet, *The Lowells and Their Seven Worlds* (Boston, Houghton Mifflin, 1946), 134; JQ, *Essay on the Soiling of Cattle* (Boston, 1859); JQ, "On the Field Culture of Vegetables," "On the Culture of Potatoes," *Massachusetts Agricultural Repository and Journal*, 4 (1817), 211-217, and 5 (1819), 64. See also Percy W. Bidwell, "The Agricultural Revolution in New England, 1800-1860," *AHR*, 26 (July 1921), 683-702.

30. JQ, "Agriculture," 137; JQ, "Review of *A Statistical View of the Commerce of the United States*, by Timothy Pitkin," *North American Review*, 3 (September 1816), 345-354; JQ, Boston, to Cummington Society of Husbandmen and Manufacturers, June 6, 1824, Bryant Family Papers, Special Collections, NYPL. See also Jane Maloney Johnson, "Through Change and Storm: A Study of Federalist-Unitarian Thought, 1800-1860," 153-167, unpub. diss., Radcliffe College, 1958, HUA.

31. JQ, *An Address Delivered before the Massachusetts Agricultural Society*

at the Brighton Cattle Show, October 12, 1819 (Boston, 1819), 2-3, 15; Randolph, Roanoke, to JQ, July 1, 1814, Randolph Papers.

32. JQ, *Brighton Address*, 1; Eliza Quincy, "Journal," interlineations in the January 1820 entries, especially 162, Quincy Family Papers. These were made by her in the late 1870's.

33. *Ibid.*, 175.

34. E. S. M. Quincy, *Memoir*, 188.

35. JQ, Boston, to Harmanus Bleecker, August 2, 1820, in H. L. P. Rice, *Harmanus Bleecker—An Albany Dutchman* (Albany, privately printed, 1924), 45-46; JQ, Quincy, to Samuel Cabot, July 14, 1819, Cabot Family Papers; [JQ], "Annual Report" (January 1820), MS., Athenaeum Letters, II, 4, Boston Athenaeum.

36. Eliza Quincy, "Journal," 175: October 2, 1820, Quincy Family Papers; JQ, "Diary" (1818-1827), May 31, 1819, JQ Papers, MHS.

37. *Columbian Centinel*, March 29, 1820; EQ, *Quincy*, 375; *Boston Town Records, 1814-1822* (RCCB *Rpts.*, 37), 5, 28, 56, 71, 97, 115.

38. Eliza Quincy, "Journal," 164-165: January 1820, Quincy Family Papers; [Boston] *Daily Advertiser*, April 18 and May 16, 1820; *Columbian Centinel*, April 11 and May 13, 1820; *Boston Town Records, 1814-1822*, 141.

39. Eliza Quincy, "Journal," 165: January, 1820, Quincy Family Papers.

40. JQ, *Brighton Address*, 11; JQ, Boston, to Cummington Society, June 6, 1824, Bryant Family Papers, Special Collections, NYPL.

41. Eliza Quincy, "Journal," 195-196: January 22, 1821, Quincy Family Papers.

42. *Resolves of the General Court of the Commonwealth of Massachusetts* (Boston, 1820), 221-232. For evidence of Quincy's earlier concern with such problems, see his *Address to the Trustees of the Massachusetts General Hospital to the Public* (Boston, 1814).

43. JQ, *Municipal History*, 35.

44. Samuel Eliot Morison, "History of the Constitution of Massachusetts," *A Manual for the Constitutional Convention* (Boston, State of Massachusetts, 1917), 28-38; *Columbian Centinel*, June 17, October 11 and 18, 1820; *Boston Town Records, 1814-1822*, 157-181.

45. Chilton Williamson, *American Suffrage: From Property to Democracy, 1760-1860* (Princeton, Princeton University Press, 1960), 190-194; Morison, *Otis*, II, 235; *Journal of Debates and Proceedings in the Convention of Delegates Chosen to Revise the Constitution of Massachusetts, November 15, 1820-January 9, 1821* (Boston, 1853), 40, 42.

46. *Ibid.*, 123.

47. JQ, *Address Delivered at the Fifth Anniversary of the Massachusetts Peace Society, December 25, 1820* (Cambridge, 1821); Eliza Quincy, "Journal," 192: January, 1821, Quincy Family Papers; *Columbian Centinel*, December 27, 1820; JQ, Boston, to Wolcott, March 11, 1821, Wolcott Papers.

48. *Columbian Centinel*, January 13, 1821; Eliza Quincy, "Journal," 195-196: January 10 and 22, 1821, Quincy Family Papers.

49. JQ, *Report of General Court Committee on Pauper Laws* . . . (Boston, 1821), 3-5. On the general question, see Robert W. Kelso, *The History of Public Poor Relief in Massachusetts, 1620-1920* (Boston, Houghton Mifflin, 1922).

50. JQ, *Municipal History*, 35-39; JQ, *Remarks on Some of the Provisions of the Laws of Massachusetts, Affecting Poverty, Vice and Crime* (Cambridge,

1822); JQ, "Report on House of Industry," October 22, 1821, *Boston Town Records, 1814-1822*, 241-250. For Quincy's place in the history of institutionalization of "deviant" and dependent members of the community, see David J. Rothman, *The Discovery of the Asylum* (Boston, Little, Brown, 1971), 31, 157-169.

51. *Independent Chronicle*, June 2, 1821; Oscar Handlin and Mary F. Handlin, *Commonwealth; A Study of the Role of Government in the American Economy: Massachusetts, 1774-1861* (New York, New York University Press, 1947), 173-194; *Columbian Centinel*, January 14, March 6 and 13, 1822.

52. Sullivan, Boston, to Otis, January 13, 1822, Otis Papers.

53. Otis, Washington, to Sullivan, January 19, 1822, Otis Papers.

Notes to Chapter 6: Back to Work

1. JQ, Boston, to Bleecker, May 6, 1823, in Rice, *Bleecker*, 46-47.

2. JQ, *Municipal History*, 1-19; "Protests against the Incorporation of Boston, 1714," Colonial Society of Massachusetts *Publications*, 10 (1904-1906), 345-356; Timothy Dwight, *Travels in New England and New York* [1821], ed. Barbara Miller Solomon (4 vols., Cambridge, Mass., Harvard University Press, 1969), I, 362-363.

3. Darrett Rutman, *Winthrop's Boston: Portrait of a Puritan Town* (Chapel Hill, University of North Carolina Press, 1965), 64-66; Arthur W. Brayley, *A Complete History of the Boston Fire Department* (Boston, 1889), 18; Kelso, *Poor Relief*, 115-116; John B. Blake, *Public Health in the Town of Boston, 1630-1822* (Cambridge, Mass., Harvard University Press, 1959), 167.

4. John Fairfield Sly, *Town Government in Massachusetts* (Cambridge, Mass., Harvard University Press, 1930), 112; JQ, *Municipal History*, 18; James A. Henretta, "Economic Development and Social Structure in Colonial Boston," *WMQ*, 22 (January 1965), 75-92; Allan Kulikoff, "The Progress of Inequality in Revolutionary Boston," *ibid.*, 28 (July 1971), 375-412; Kirker and Kirker, *Bulfinch's Boston*, 76-100; Blake, *Public Health*, 235; Robert Dahl, *Who Governs? Democracy and Power in an American City* (New Haven, Yale University Press, 1961), 17.

5. Walter Muir Whitehill, *Boston: A Topographical History* (Cambridge, Mass., Harvard University Press, 1968), 37-38, 47-48, 73-74; Oscar Handlin, *Boston's Immigrants: A Study in Acculturation*, 2nd ed. (Cambridge, Mass., Harvard University Press, 1959), 25-53.

6. Firey, *Land Use*, 43-45. For a discussion of the distribution of wealth in Boston of the 1820's, see Edward Pessen, "The Egalitarian Myth and American Social Reality: Wealth, Mobility, and Equality in the 'Era of the Common Man,' " *AHR*, 76 (1971), 111-112.

7. Whitehill, *Boston*, 94.

8. *Columbian Centinel*, November 10, 1821; [Samuel Alonzo Knapp], *Extract from the Journal of Travels in North America by Ali Bey* (Boston, 1818), 40-41; JQ, *Municipal History*, 29.

9. Otis, Washington, to Sullivan, January 19, 1822, Otis Papers.

10. Kirker and Kirker, *Bulfinch's Boston*, 268-270.

11. Blake, *Public Health*, 229-242; *Columbian Centinel*, December 12, 1821.

12. *Journal of Debates, 1820-1821*, 615; *Boston Town Records, 1814-1822* (RCCB *Rpts.*, 37), 254-255.

13. *Columbian Centinel*, January 9, 1822; JQ, *Municipal History*, 31-33.

14. Sullivan, Boston, to Otis, January 6, 1822, and Perkins, Boston, to Otis, April 5, 1822, Otis Papers.

15. Morison, *Otis*, II, 207-218, 234-237.

16. Otis, Washington, to Sullivan, January 19, 1822, Otis Papers.

17. Otis to Sullivan, January 8, 1822, *ibid.*

18. Edward L. Ballantyne, "The Incorporation of Boston, 1784-1822," 32, unpub. honors thesis, Harvard College, 1955, HUA; *Independent Chronicle*, March 2, 1822.

19. *Ibid.*, March 22, 1822. On Middling Interest, see *An Exposition of the Principles and Views of the Middling Interest in the City of Boston* (Boston, 1822); *Defense of the Exposition of the Middling Interest* (Boston, 1822); Morison, *Harrison Gray Otis*, 436; *Daily Advertiser*, March 5, 6, and 30, 1822; Emerson, Boston, to John Boynton Hill, March 11, 1822, in Ralph L. Rusk, ed., *Letters of Ralph Waldo Emerson* (6 vols., New York, Columbia University Press, 1934), I, 110-112; *Boston Patriot*, March 9, 1822.

20. *Independent Chronicle*, February 16 and March 2, 1822; Otis, Washington, to Sullivan, March 21, 1822, Otis Papers; *Boston Town Records, 1814-1822*, 264.

21. [Boston] *New England Galaxy*, March 29, 1822.

22. EQ, *Quincy*, 393; Sullivan, Boston, to Otis, January 13, 1822, Otis Papers.

23. Eliza Quincy, Quincy, to Winthrop, October 29, 1879, Winthrop Papers.

24. EQ, *Quincy*, 393; Eliza Quincy to Winthrop, October 29, 1879, Winthrop Papers.

25. Sullivan, Boston, to Otis, January 13, 1822, Otis Papers. Edmund Quincy's rendering of this episode, to borrow Morison's polite phrasing, is "misleading" and stresses his father's ingenuousness rather than his ingenuity. See Morison, *Otis*, II, 239n.

26. *New England Galaxy*, March 29, 1822.

27. Webster, Boston, to Story, April 5, 1822, in *Writings and Speeches of Daniel Webster* (18 vols., Boston, Little, Brown, 1903), XVI, 68; *Columbian Centinel*, April 10, 1822.

28. Webster to Story, April 6, 1822, Story Papers. See also Leverett Saltonstall, Salem, to James C. Merrill, April 9, 1822, Saltonstall Papers.

29. Perkins to Otis, April 5, 1822, Otis Papers; *Columbian Centinel*, April 8, 1822.

30. JQ, Boston, to James Lloyd, April 9, 1822, JQ Papers, Houghton Library; *Columbian Centinel*, April 10, 1822; Eliza Quincy, Quincy, to Winthrop, October 29, 1879, Winthrop Papers.

31. *Independent Chronicle*, April 10, 1822; *Columbian Centinel*, April 19, 1822; *Selectmen's Minutes, 1818-1822* (RCCB *Rpts.*, 39), 251; JQ, *Municipal History*, 42-57, 373-374.

32. John Lowell, Boston, to Otis, February 25 and 26, 1823, Otis Papers; *Columbian Centinel*, April 12 and 16, 1823.

33. Eliza Quincy, Quincy, to Winthrop, October 29, 1879, Winthrop Papers; RCB, I, 175-176.

34. JQ, *Municipal History*, 375, 42-57; Blake, *Public Health*, 235; RCB, I, 29: May 24, 1822.

35. JQ, *Municipal History*, 375-376.

36. RCB, I, 189: May 5, 1823; Blake, *Public Health*, 237; *Columbian Centinel*, December 12, 1821; JQ, *Municipal History*, 65.

37. *Columbian Centinel*, March 1 and 5, 1823; JQ, *Municipal History*, 378, 381; RCB, I, 228-229: May 29, 1823.

38. Blake, *Public Health*, 229.

39. JQ, *Municipal History*, 385; Roger Lane, *Policing the City: Boston, 1822-1885* (Cambridge, Mass., Harvard University Press, 1967), 16-17; *Columbian Centinel*, April 16, 1823, and June 2, 1824.

40. JQ, *Municipal History*, 382; Otis, "Report to the Common Council," January 4, 1830, *ibid.*, 304; Blake, *Public Health*, 212-213; RCB, I, 311-338: August 4, 1823; JQ, "Address on Taking Final Leave of the Office of Mayor, January 3, 1829," JQ, *Municipal History*, 266. The relative good health of Boston is also attested in Charles E. Rosenberg, *The Cholera Years* (Chicago, University of Chicago Press, 1962), 37.

41. Brayley, *Boston Fire Department*, 18, 80, 125; JQ, *Municipal History*, 28, 44, 60.

42. Brayley, *Boston Fire Department*, 140; JQ, *Municipal History*, 153-154.

43. Brayley, *Boston Fire Department*, 142; RCB, I, 452, 493-499: November 23, 1823; JQ, Boston, to Melville, November 16, 1823, and Melville, Boston, to JQ, November 17, 1823, Rare Book Room, BPL; JQ, *Municipal History*, 155-195.

44. Brayley, *Boston Fire Department*, 148-149; JQ, *Municipal History*, 160; *Daily Advertiser*, April 9 and 11, 1825.

45. *Boston Patriot*, July 7, 1825; *Daily Advertiser*, July 2 and 7, 1825; *Columbian Centinel*, July 7, 1825; Brayley, *Boston Fire Department*, 154-157.

46. *Ibid.*, 155.

47. JQ, *Municipal History*, 263-265, 191; Edward H. Savage, *Police Records and Recollections; or, Boston by Daylight and Gaslight for Two Hundred and Forty Years* (Boston, 1873), 65: March 3, 1826; *Boston News-Letter and City Record*, April 8, 1826.

48. JQ, *Municipal History*, 378; RCB: Common Council, I, 413, II, 388; "City Administration," *Boston Patriot*, December 8, 1828.

49. Kirker and Kirker, *Bulfinch's Boston*, 195-196; *Selectmen's Records, 1818-1822* (RCCB *Rpts.*, 39), 218; JQ, *Municipal History*, 11, 13, 74-75.

50. RCB, I, 299-310, 524-527, 528: July 31 and December 8, 1823; JQ, *Municipal History*, 74-81. The most complete history of the Quincy Market is to be found in Elizabeth R. Amadon *et al.*, *The Faneuil Hall Markets: An Historical Study* (Boston, Boston Redevelopment Authority, 1968).

51. RCB, II, 21-23: January 12, 1824; *Independent Chronicle*, December 9, 1823; *Boston Patriot*, January 13 and 16, 1824; *Columbian Centinel*, January 17, 1824.

52. JQ, *Municipal History*, 256, 289-293, 415; RCB, II, 267-268: July 15, 1824; Nathan Matthews Jr., *The City Government of Boston* (Boston, 1895), 244-245; *Boston News-Letter and City Record*, April 8, 1826.

Notes to Chapter 7: Quincy's Boston

1. JQ, "Diary" (1818-1827), 171: February 4, 1827, JQ Papers, MHS; Savage, *Police Records*, 62: May 3, 1823; *Columbian Centinel*, December 12, 1828; Josiah Quincy Jr., *Figures of the Past*, 86-93; RCB, II, 330-331: August 24, 1824; Shattuck, Boston, to his son George, August 24, 1825, Shattuck Papers, MHS.

2. Shattuck to his son, August 24, 1825, *ibid.*; Lane, *Policing the City*, 14-25.

3. On Quincy's later and more somber thoughts about urban life, see his *Considerations on Annexation*, 6-9.

4. JQ, *Remarks Affecting Poverty*, 3, 21. For corroboration of this analysis of the "conservative" character of urban reform in the 1820's, see M. J. Heale, "The New York Society for the Prevention of Pauperism, 1817-1823," NYHS *Quarterly*, 55 (April 1971), 153-176; Rothman, *Discovery of the Asylum*, 195.

5. *Boston Town Records, 1814-1822* (RCCB, *Rpts.*, 37), 267-272; RCB, I, 7-9, 30-31, 79-86, 103-114.

6. *Ibid.*, I, 138-143: January 13, 1823; JQ, *Report on Pauper Laws*, 5; JQ, *Municipal History*, 34-39, 48-54.

7. RCB, I, 296-297: July 28, 1823; II, 436-443, 465-486; JQ, *Report of the Committee of the City Council on the Relations of the Overseers of the Poor* (Boston, 1824), copy in Massachusetts State Library; JQ, *Municipal History*, 88-96.

8. *Ibid.*, 142-145.

9. RCB, III, 124-126: April 25, 1825; JQ, *Municipal History*, 91-96, 271.

10. JQ, *Remarks Affecting Poverty*, 2; JQ, *Municipal History*, 380.

11. William Jenks, "Report on Prostitution in the Town of Boston," *Fourth Annual Report of the Boston Society for the Moral and Religious Instruction of the Poor* (Boston, 1821); copies of later reports in Jenks Papers. See also J. Leslie Dunstan, *A Light to the City: 150 Years of the City Missionary Society of Boston* (Boston, Beacon Press, 1966), 26-43, and Lane, *Policing the City*, 47.

12. *Selectmen's Minutes, 1818-1822* (RCCB *Rpts.*, 39), 45; Savage, *Police Records*, 63: June 19, 1823.

13. JQ, *Municipal History*, 380; RCB, I, 207-216: May 15, 1823; Lane, *Policing the City*, 23-24.

14. Jenks, "Eleventh Annual Report of City Missionary Society," 14, MS., Jenks Papers; Lane, *Policing the City*, 20.

15. JQ, *Remarks Affecting Poverty*, 19; Savage, *Police Records*, 65: February 6, 1826; JQ, Boston, to Griscom, December 2, 1825, Griscom Papers; JQ, *Municipal History*, 53, 106, 256, 269.

16. Nathan Dane, Boston, to JQ, May 6, 1822, Autograph Letter Book No. 3, Quincy Family Papers; RCB, I, 347-363: August 14, 1823; JQ, *Remarks Affecting Poverty*, 21. For contrast with later reformers, see Stanley Elkins, *Slavery: A Problem in American Institutional and Intellectual Life* (Chicago, University of Chicago Press, 1959), 140-206; John L. Thomas, "Romantic Reform in America, 1815-1865," *American Quarterly*, 17 (Winter 1965), 656-681.

17. *Independent Chronicle*, December 9, 1826; JQ, *Municipal History*,

391-395; RCB, II, 187: May 29, 1824; *Boston News-Letter and City Record*, October 28, 1826.

18. JQ, *Municipal History*, 383, 392-396.

19. *Ibid.*, 398-406.

20. Charles K. Dillaway, "Education, Past and Present," in Winsor, *Memorial History*, IV, 235-278; [Henry Oliver], *Report on Public Schools, May, 1826* (Boston, 1826); "Girls in the Public Schools of Boston," *Barnard's Journal of Education*, 13 (1863), 243-266.

21. JQ, *Municipal History*, 377; RCB, I, 103-114, 456-458: October 21, 1822, and November 1, 1823.

22. Dillaway, "Education," 246; Joseph M. Wightman, *Annals of the Boston Primary School Committee* (Boston, 1860), 14-35; Merle Curti, *The Social Ideas of American Educators* (New York, Scribner's, 1935), 41-49, 101-168; JQ, *Municipal History*, 271; SCR, 258: June 28, 1825.

23. *Ibid.*, 158-159: May 10 and June 22, 1825.

24. RCB, II, 258-259, 280-281: June 28 and August 22, 1825; JQ, Boston, to Griscom, February 27, 1828, Griscom Papers. For Quincy's views on the monitorial system, see Stanley K. Schutz, *The Culture Factory: Boston Public Schools, 1789-1860* (New York, Oxford University Press, 1973), 265-268.

25. Bailey, Boston, to School Committee, December 5, 1825, SCR; Minutes of School Committee, October 26, 1825, and February 28, 1826, SCR; [E. Bailey], *An Account of the High School for Girls* (Boston, 1826), 15-16.

26. [John Pierpont], "Report of the Sub-committee on High School for Girls," August 26, 1826, SCR; Minutes of School Committee, 195: August 26, 1826, SCR.

27. SCR, 199: October 3, 1826.

28. Questionnaire and responses from fourteen headmasters in SCR: November 17, 1826.

29. The failure to implement monitorial instruction was generally attributed to opposition to the method on the part of Boston teachers. See JQ, Boston, to Griscom, March 11, 1828, Griscom Papers; John Lowell Jr., Boston, to JQ, April 1, 1828, SCR.

30. Response of Abraham Andrews, Bowdoin School, October 21, 1826, SCR. See similar remarks of Elisha Webb, Sears C. Walker, Eliot School, SCR: October 23, 1826.

31. [Oliver], *Report on Public Schools*, 15-16.

32. JQ, "Report of the Subcommittee on the High School for Girls," SCR: November 17, 1826. *The Boston Patriot*, December 19, 1827, later called Quincy's use of the questionnaires "insidious."

33. Bailey, Boston, to JQ, November 17, 1826, SCR.

34. RCB, II, 381: October 30, 1826; Barney Smith, "Petition regarding the Establishment of a High School for the Education of the Children of the Coloured Citizens," January 12, 1827; David Francis, "Memorial for French, Spanish and German Instruction in Boston Public Schools," February 22, 1827; James Savage, "Report," May 8, 1827, MSS., SCR.

35. JQ, *Municipal History*, 406-407, 409. Quincy's reasons for opposing the girls' high school are more forthrightly presented in his "Address on Taking Final Leave of the Office of Mayor, January 3, 1829," JQ, *Municipal History*, 269-270.

36. Minutes of meetings, January 10, February 12 and 21, 1828, and

[Thomas Welsh], "Committee Report on the Expediency and Practicality of a High School for Girls," June 22, 1825, SCR.

37. Eliza Quincy, Quincy, to Winthrop, October 29, 1879, Winthrop Papers.

38. JQ, *Municipal History*, 58, 121, 167, 197, 210, 228; RCB, III, 398: December 12, 1825; IV, 431: December 12, 1826; V, 180: December 11, 1827. The most complete listing of election returns is in C. W. Ernst's collection of Mayors' Addresses—City of Boston, 1822-1855, I, inside cover, BPL.

39. *Boston Patriot*, December 8, 1828; JQ, *Municipal History*, 304; JQ, Boston, to John Pray, March 1, 1826, Miscellaneous Manuscripts, Rare Book Room, BPL.

40. *Boston Patriot*, December 6, 11, 19, 27, 1827, and January 12, 1828; *Columbian Centinel*, April 12, 1828.

41. James Savage, "Report," March 7, 1827, SCR; Ebenezer Bailey, *Review of the Mayor's Report on the Subject of Schools so Far as It Relates to the High School for Girls* (Boston, 1828), 6-11.

42. *Ibid.*, 5. On Jacksonian exertions in Boston in 1827-1828, see Arthur B. Darling, *Political Changes in Massachusetts, 1824-1848* (New Haven, Yale University Press, 1925), 67-73.

43. *Columbian Centinel*, December 6 and 10, 1828; *Boston Patriot*, December 8, 1828.

44. *Look to your Interest!*, Broadside Collection, Rare Book Room, BPL.

45. *Independent Chronicle*, December 8, 1828; *Boston Patriot*, December 8, 1828; RCB, IV, 371: December 9, 1828.

46. *Columbian Centinel*, December 12, 1828; *Daily Advertiser*, December 13, 1828; Charles Francis Adams, *Diary*, vols. I and II, ed. Aida DiPace Donald and David Donald (Cambridge, Mass., Harvard University Press, 1964), II, 321; Shattuck, Boston, to his son George, December 14, 1828, Shattuck Papers.

47. *Worse and Worse!!*, Broadside Collection, Rare Book Room, BPL; *Columbian Centinel*, December 17, 1828; RCB, III, 380: December 16, 1828; JQ, *Municipal History*, 257-258.

48. James M. Hubbard, "Boston's Last Town Meetings and First City Election," *Bostonian Society Publications*, 6 (1910), 99; James M. Bugbee, "Boston Under the Mayors, 1822-1880," in Winsor, *Memorial History*, IV, 217-292.

49. Roland N. Stromberg, "Boston in the 1820's and 1830's," *History Today*, 11 (September 1961), 591-598; Handlin, *Boston's Immigrants*, 18; JQ, *Municipal History*, 261. For a contemporary evaluation of Boston, see *The Journals of Bronson Alcott*, ed. Odell Shepard (Boston, Little, Brown, 1938), 15.

50. JQA, Washington, to JQ, January 15, 1829; Pickering, Salem, to JQ, January 7, 1829; Webster, Washington, to JQ, January 15, 1829, all in Autograph Letter Book No. 3, Quincy Family Papers; Mellen Chamberlain, *Josiah Quincy: The Great Mayor* (Boston, 1889); Barbara M. Solomon, *Ancestors and Immigrants* (Cambridge, Mass., Harvard University Press, 1956), 84-85.

Notes to Chapter 8: The Making of a Schoolmaster

1. JQ, Cambridge, to Sir Thomas C. Banks, November 10, 1829, JQ Papers, Houghton Library.

2. Both Professor Morison (*Three Centuries*, 195-221) and Josiah Quincy (*Harvard*, II, 344-353) understate the difficulties at Harvard in the 1820's. Morison's earlier "The Great Rebellion in Harvard College and the Resignation of President Kirkland" (Colonial Society of Massachusetts *Publications*, 27 (1928), 54-112) is more revealing. The two best sources for the period are Quincy's 41-page memorandum on the "general state of Harvard University antecedent to . . . June 1829," in his "Memorandum Book" (1825-1847), written after he published his *History*, and Nathaniel Bowditch's "College History," written in 1828 and apparently used to force the retirement of College Treasurer Davis and to hasten the departure of Kirkland. Both manuscripts are in the Harvard University Archives.

3. John Thornton Kirkland, "Literary Institutions—University," *North American Review*, 7 (1818), 270-278. The article was actually written by Edward Everett, thereby keeping intact Kirkland's record of writing nothing while at Harvard. See David B. Tyack, *George Ticknor and the Boston Brahmins* (Cambridge, Mass., Harvard University Press, 1967), 86.

4. *Ibid.*, 43-83; Paul Revere Frothingham, *Edward Everett: Orator and Statesman* (Boston, Houghton Mifflin, 1925), 33-60; Mark A. DeWolfe Howe, *The Life and Letters of George Bancroft* (2 vols., New York, Scribner's, 1908), I, 31-154; [Joseph Green Cogswell], "On the Means of Education, and the State of Learning, in the United States of America," *Blackwood's Edinburgh Magazine*, 4 (February 1819), 550. See also Orie Long, *Literary Pioneers: Early American Explorers of European Culture* (Cambridge, Mass., Harvard University Press, 1935); Cynthia Stokes Brown, "The American Discovery of the German University: Four Students at Göttingen, 1815-1822," unpub. diss., Johns Hopkins University, 1964.

5. JQ, *Harvard*, II, 112-114, 293, 307; Morison, *Three Centuries*, 212-213; Thomas Metcalf, ed., *The General Laws of Massachusetts* (Boston, 1823), 251-252, 312-313, 347, 358.

6. JQ, *Harvard*, II, 312-333; Goodman, "Ethics and Enterprise," *American Quarterly*, 18 (Fall 1966), 437-452; George Ticknor, *Remarks on Changes Lately Proposed or Adopted, in Harvard University* (Boston, 1825), 3.

7. "Charts on Harvard Admissions" (1725-1859), comparisons with Yale and Princeton, and the percentage of students admitted from outside New England have been compiled by Clifford K. Shipton and are in the Harvard University Archives.

8. Morison, *Three Centuries*, 195-196; John Pierce, "Memoir of John Thornton Kirkland," MHS *Procs.*, 2nd ser., 9 (1894), 143-157; Ralph Waldo Emerson, Concord, to William Emerson, April 3, 1828, in Rusk, *Letters of Emerson*, I, 230.

9. Morison, *Three Centuries*, 190, 195; Eliza Quincy, Quincy, to Winthrop, July 7, 1879, Winthrop Papers.

10. Bowditch, "College History," 6-8, 116, HUA.

11. Morison, "The Great Rebellion," 58; Pierce, "Kirkland," 144-157, 151. For a sullen undergraduate's view of Kirkland as "an intolerable bore," see CFA, *Diary*, I, 375.

12. [Cogswell], "On the Means of Education," 549; Morison, "The Great Rebellion," 93-94; Ticknor, *Remarks on Changes*, 9-10.

13. ————, *The Rebelliad, or Terrible Transactions at the Seat of the Muses [1818]*, (Boston, 1842); CFA, *Diary*, I, 184-186; Josiah Quincy Jr.,

Figures of the Past, 16-43; "Frederick West Holland Diary, 1827-1828," *Harvard Alumni Bulletin*, 30 (September-October 1927), 7-11, 35-39; George Paul Schmidt, *The Liberal Arts College: A Chapter in American Cultural History* (New Brunswick, Rutgers University Press, 1957), 93.

14. Francis Wayland, *Thoughts on the Present Collegiate System in the United States* (Boston, 1842); Frederick Rudolph, *The American College and University* (New York, Knopf, 1962), 201-240; [Cogswell], "On the Means of Education," 549; Ticknor, Boston, to William Prescott, July 31, 1821, Ticknor Papers. See also Oscar Handlin and Mary F. Handlin, *The American College and American Culture* (Berkeley, University of California Press, 1970), 19-42.

15. Pierce, "Kirkland," MHS *Procs.*, 2nd ser., 9 (1894), 150-156; Andrew P. Peabody, *Harvard Reminiscences* (Boston, 1888), 9-17.

16. Randolph, Richmond, to JQ, December 11, 1813, Randolph Papers; Jedidiah Morse, *An Appeal to the Public on the Controversy respecting the Revolution in Harvard College* (Charleston, 1814); N. A. Haven, Portsmouth, N. H., to Ticknor, September 15, 1821, Ticknor Papers; *Columbian Centinel*, September 1 and 22, November 10, December 5, 1821.

17. Mary Orne Pickering, *Life of John Pickering* (Boston, 1887), 230-231; Thomas Tracy, "Commonplace Book," MS., July 7, 1815, HUA.

18. Russel B. Nye, *George Bancroft: Brahmin Rebel* (New York, Knopf, 1944), 64-66; Faculty Recs., X, 26: April 23, 1823; Cogswell, Cambridge, to Kirkland, October 21, 1822, Coll. Papers, X, 40; Everett, Cambridge, to Story, April 13, 1821, in Frothingham, *Everett*, 71; Howe, *Bancroft*, I, 163.

19. Sidney Willard, "State of Learning in the United States," *North American Review*, 10 (1819), 240-269; Willard, *Memories*, I, 326; Jeannette R. Graustein, *Thomas Nuttall, Naturalist* (Cambridge, Mass., Harvard University Press, 1967), 207; Cornelius C. Felton, ed., *A Memorial of the Rev. John Snelling Popkin, D.D.* (Cambridge, 1852); James Freeman Clarke, *Autobiography*, ed. Edward Everett Hale (Boston, 1891), 36-37.

20. On Ticknor's marginal place in Cambridge, see JQ, Cambridge, to Gallatin, November 29, 1830, Gallatin Papers.

21. Tyack, *Ticknor*, 117.

22. Ticknor, *Remarks on Changes*, 10, 43-45. See also letter signed "G." to the *Daily Advertiser*, August 7, 1821, praising West Point; a clipping of it is in the Ticknor Papers.

23. Ticknor to Prescott, July 31, 1821, Ticknor Papers. These recommendations, only slightly modified, are repeated in his *Remarks on Changes* and "Comments on the President's Report," April 11, 1827, Corp. Papers.

24. Morison, "The Great Rebellion," 54-112; JQA, Washington, to Kirkland, May 19, 1823, Corp. Papers, X, 58.

25. Harvard Corporation Representation to the General Court, February 9, 1824, copied into the Corp. Minutes, VI, 120-125; Quincy, *Harvard*, II, 357-359; Andrews Norton, Cambridge, to Channing, September 10, 1824, Ticknor Papers.

26. Shipton charts, HUA; Ticknor, *Remarks on Changes*, 8; John Thornton Kirkland, *The Annual Report of the President of Harvard University for the Academical Year 1825-26* (Cambridge, 1827), 38-45; Ticknor, "Remarks on the President's Report," Ticknor Papers.

27. Edward Everett et al., "Memorial of the Resident Instructors," May 31, 1824, Overseers Recs., VII (1825), 102-162; *Report of Overseers to the Memorial of the Resident Instructors, January 6, 1825* (Boston, 1825); [John

Lowell], *Remarks on the Memorial of the Officers of Harvard College* (Boston, 1824); [John Lowell], *Further Remarks on the Memorial* . . . (Boston, 1825). For a defense of the instructors' position, see Andrews Norton, *In Behalf of the Resident Instructors* (Boston, 1825); for the Corporation's position, see JQ, *Harvard*, II, 338-353.

28. Tyack, *Ticknor*, 115; Ticknor, Boston, to John Lowell, November 6, 1822, Ticknor Papers; Ticknor, *Remarks on Changes*, 27; John Snelling Popkin, Cambridge, to John Pickering, October 17, 1825, in Pickering, *Life of Pickering*, 306; Bowditch, "College History," 13, 70-71, HUA.

29. *Ibid.*, 10-23, 36-37; Kirkland, Cambridge, to Pickering, June 13, 1826, Corp. Papers; JQ, On the state of Harvard University, "Memorandum Book," JQ Papers, HUA; Eliza Quincy, Quincy, to Winthrop, July 7, 1879, Winthrop Papers; Charles Saunders, Cambridge, to Ebenezer Francis, June 25, 1828, Coll. Papers, III, 44.

30. Gerald T. Dunne, *Justice Joseph Story and the Rise of the Supreme Court* (New York, Simon and Schuster, 1970), 248-251; JQ, *Harvard*, II, 362-368; JQ, On the state of the University, "Memorandum Book," JQ Papers, HUA; Bowditch, "College History," 20, HUA; microfilm of Davis' reconstructed Treasurer's books, Corp. Papers; Overseers Recs., VII, 320: January 18, 1827; Corp. Minutes, VII, 66-67: March 27, 1828.

31. Everett, Washington, to Isaac Parker, January 22, 1829, Everett Papers; R. W. Emerson, Concord, to William Emerson, April 3, 1828, in Rusk, *Letters of Emerson*, I, 230; Overseers Recs., VII, 405-417: January 17, 1828; Coll. Papers, II, 68-69: August 31, 1827.

32. Eliza Quincy, Quincy, to Winthrop, July 7, 1879, Winthrop Papers; Bowditch, "College History," 37, HUA.

33. Morison, "The Great Rebellion," 110; Overseers Recs., VII, 419: May 8, 1828; [Boston] *Evening Gazette*, April 5, 1828; [Boston] *Evening Bulletin*, April 9, 1828; *Columbian Centinel*, June 7, 1828.

34. Tyack, *Ticknor*, 122; Ann Gilman Storrow, Boston, to Jared Sparks, January 23, 1829, in Frances Bradshaw Blanshard, ed., "Letters of Ann Gilman Storrow to Jared Sparks," *Smith College Studies in History*, 6 (1921), 236; Story, Washington, to Webster, April 13, 1828, Story Papers; Story, Boston, to Bowditch, January 1, 1829, Coll. Papers, III, 188; Peter Chardon Brooks, Medford, to Everett, April 14, 1828, Everett Papers; John Lowell, Roxbury, to Ticknor, October 9, 1825, Ticknor Papers.

35. Emerson to John Haskins Ladd, April 18, 1828, in Rusk, *Letters of Emerson*, I, 232; Brooks, Medford, to Everett, April 14, 1828, Everett Papers.

36. Everett, Washington, to Brooks, May 9, 1828, and Everett, Charlestown, to Alexander Hill Everett, September 15, 1828, *ibid.*

37. Ticknor, Boston, to Nicholas Biddle, July 9, 1828, Ticknor Papers; *Columbian Centinel*, October 8, 11, 15, 18, 1828; Charles Saunders, Cambridge, to Francis, July 16, 1828, Coll. Papers, III, 77.

38. Story to Webster, April 13, 1828, Story Papers.

39. "Journal of Eliza Susan Quincy," excerpts in Cambridge Historical Society *Publications*, 4 (October 1909), 90; Robert Elton Berry, *Yankee Stargazer: The Life of Nathaniel Bowditch* (New York, McGraw-Hill, 1941), 203-210.

40. "Journal of Eliza Quincy," 91; Brooks, Medford, to Everett, January 8, 1829, Everett Papers; JQ, Cambridge, to Sir Thomas C. Banks, November 10, 1829, JQ Papers, Houghton Library; Corp. Minutes, VII, 105: January 15, 1829.

41. Everett, Washington, to A. H. Everett, January 18, 1829, and to Isaac Parker, January 22, 1829, Everett Papers; R. W. Emerson, Cambridge, to William Emerson, February 2, 1829, in Rusk, *Letters of Emerson*, I, 262; Ann Gilman Storrow to Sparks, January 23, 1829, "Letters of Ann Storrow," 236.

42. *Boston Recorder*, January 17 and 29, 1829; *Boston Statesman*, January 23 and 26, 1829; Shattuck, Boston, to R. Shurtleff, June 3, 1829, Shattuck Papers, MHS. The Overseers confirmed Quincy's election by a vote of 40 to 26 (Overseers Recs., VII, 459: January 29, 1829).

43. "Journal of Eliza Quincy," 90; Overseers Recs., VII, 479: June 4, 1829.

44. JQ, "Diary of a Journey" (February 3-March 6, 1829), JQ Papers, MHS; "Original Papers in Relation to a Course of Liberal Education [The Yale Report]," *American Journal of Science*, 15 (1829), 297-345. See also George Paul Schmidt, "Intellectual Crosscurrents in American Colleges, 1825-1855," *AHR*, 42 (1936), 46-53.

45. "Yale Report," 305, 308, 312, 317.

46. JQ, "Diary of a Journey," 2-16, 17-23, JQ Papers, MHS: JQ, Boston, to EQ, January 1, 1823, EQ Papers.

47. JQ, "Inaugural Address," June 2, 1829, JQ Papers, HUA; *Boston Courier*, June 5, 1829; Pierce, "Memoir," 5 (June 2, 1829), Pierce Papers. Because Nathaniel Bowditch took exception to Quincy's generous remarks about Kirkland, the Inaugural Address was not published. See Eliza Quincy's margin note on manuscript copy in HUA.

48. JQA, "Diary," September 10, 1829, reel no. 39, Adams Papers; JQ, "Memorandum on Aggregate of the Weight of Scale . . . ," Corp. Papers (folder for 1829, 1830); Peabody, *Reminiscences*, 30-31; R. H. Dana, Newport, to R. H. Dana Jr., October 24, 1831, Dana Papers.

49. Benjamin Peirce, Cambridge, to JQ, May 13, 1833, JQ Papers, HUA; Faculty Recs., XI, 50: October 3, 1836; Morison, *Three Centuries*, 260.

50. JQ, "Abstract of Petitions against Rank," Coll. Papers, VI (1834), 109-110. Opposition to instilling "a spirit of emulation" in the students was also found in the faculty; see "Rough Minutes of Remarks of Faculty on Rank-Emulation," March 31, 1834, JQ Papers, HUA.

51. "Yale Report," 303; Robert F. Lucid, ed., *The Journal of Richard Henry Dana Jr.* (3 vols., Cambridge, Mass., Harvard University Press, 1968), I, 22-24; George E. Channing, Cambridge, to Dana, June 2, 1832, and Dana, Cambridge, to Channing, March 21, 1832, Dana Papers.

52. JQ, "Diary of a Journey" (1829), 22-23, JQ Papers, MHS; "Yale Report," 303; Corp. Minutes, VI, 303: July 20, 1826; Faculty Recs., X, 124: June 12, 1826.

53. JQ, "Address Delivered to the Students," October 1829, outline in JQ Papers, HUA.

54. Corp. Minutes, September 29, 1829; JQ, "Address," October 1829, JQ Papers, HUA.

55. George Moore, "Diary" (1828-1836), March 17, 1831, HUA.

56. *Ibid.*, March 18, 1831.

57. Lucid, *Journal of Dana*, I, 20-22.

58. *Ibid.*, 22; Moore, "Diary," March 3, 5, 10, 1832; JQ, "Account of the Disturbances in Harvard College, March, 1832," and "Argument before the Overseers on the Necessity of Making the Undergraduates of a College Amenable to the Laws of the State," JQ Papers (1832), HUA.

59. Moore, "Diary," March 8, 1834.

60. *Ibid.*, May 23, 1834; Faculty Recs., II, 138-139: May 21 and 26, 1834; JQ, "Communication to Parents and Guardians regarding a Series of Trespasses . . . ," June 4, 1834, copy in Massachusetts State Library, Boston.

61. Moore, "Diary," May 27, 1834.

62. "Sophomore Memorial to Faculty," March, 1834, Coll. Papers, VI, 115-117; Faculty Recs., XI, 140: May 26, 1834.

63. JQ, "Statement to Overseers," July 31, 1834, Overseers Recs., VIII, 170-175.

64. Moore, "Diary," May 27, 1834.

65. *Ibid.*, May 29, 1834; Faculty Recs., XI, 140-141: May 30, 1834.

66. Moore, "Diary," May 29, 1834.

67. *Ibid.*, May 30, 1834.

68. Faculty Recs., XI, 146: May 31, 1834; Moore, "Diary," May 31, 1834.

69. Faculty Recs., XI, 146: June 2, 1834; Moore, "Diary," May 31, 1834.

70. *Ibid.*, June 2, 1834. On June 6, 1834, Massachusetts Attorney General James Trecothick Austin offered the college the use of "public officers to preserve and vindicate the public peace." See Coll. Papers, VI, 180, and JQ, Cambridge, to Austin, June 6, 1834, Norcross Collection.

71. ———, *A Circular of the Senior Class of Harvard College on the Recent Disturbances* (Boston, 1834), 8.

72. [Boston] *Evening Transcript*, June 16, 1834; *Boston [Daily] Advocate*, June 18, 1834; *Mercantile Journal*, June 18, 1834; *Boston Courier*, June 19, 1834; *Columbian Centinel*, June 16, 1834.

73. JQ, Cambridge, to Charles Upham, June 21, 1834, JQ Papers, HUA.

74. Faculty Recs., XX, 143-164: May 30-July 7, 1834. Characteristically, Quincy insisted on keeping the minutes of all faculty meetings and recording the divisions on all matters brought to a vote.

75. George W. Spindler, *Life of Charles Follen: A Study in German-American Cultural Relations* (Chicago, University of Chicago Press, 1917), 10-93; Peabody, *Reminiscences*, 122; Lewis Feuer, *The Conflict of Generations* (New York, Basic Books, 1969), 59-66. See also Elizabeth Bancroft Schlesinger, "Two Early Harvard Wives: Eliza Farrar and Eliza Follen," *NEQ*, 18 (June 1965), 147-167.

76. Eliza Quincy, "Journal," interlineations made in 1870's on November 28, 1814 entry, Quincy Family Papers; Sibley, "Journal," 791: May 28, 1868, Sibley Papers; Eliza Cabot Follen, *Life of Charles Follen* (Boston, 1844), 228; Samuel Cabot, Brookline, to JQ, May 21, 1834, Coll. Papers, VI (1833-1835), 172; Corp. Minutes, VII, 361: June 19, 1834. It was Ticknor who brought Follen to Harvard as an instructor, assuring Kirkland that he had been expelled from Germany "for political causes entirely." See Ticknor to Kirkland, September 26, 1825, Ticknor Papers.

77. Andrew McFarland Davis, "Jackson's LL.D.—A Tempest in a Teapot," MHS *Procs.*, 2nd ser., 20 (December 1906), 490-512; Josiah Quincy Jr., *Figures of the Past*, 303-304; Overseers Recs., VII, 130: June 22, 1833; JQA, "Diary," June 17, 1833, reel no. 42, Adams Papers.

78. Pierce, "Memoir," 6 (1833-1836), 31-32, Pierce Papers. For national reaction to the event, see Ward, *Andrew Jackson*, 83-86.

79. Simon Greenleaf, Cambridge, to Story, January 23, 1834, Story Papers; Overseers Recs., VIII, 154-164: February 6 and 13, 1834; *Boston [Daily] Advocate*, January 11, 1834; "Commencement Journal of the Rev. Dr. John

Pierce," MHS *Procs.*, 2nd ser., 5 (January 1890), 213; Leverett Saltonstall, Salem, to Story, September 24, 1835, Saltonstall Papers; JQ, Cambridge, to Austin, February 8, 1834, G. L. Paine Papers, MHS.

80. Overseers Recs., VIII, 167-176: July 17 and 31, 1834; JQA, "Diary," August 8, 19, 21, 1834, reel no. 42, Adams Papers.

81. Overseers Recs., VIII, 178-195: August 25, 1834. Two anonymous pamphlets published during the summer of 1834, both taking exception to John Quincy Adams' Report, further suggest that Everett was waiting in the wings: *Remarks on a Pamphlet entitled Proceedings of the Overseers of Harvard University* (Boston, 1834), and *Remarks Occasioned by the Publication of a Pamphlet Entitled Proceedings of the Overseers of Harvard University* (Boston, 1834). The copies of the pamphlets in the Adams Papers were brought to my attention by Mr. Marc Friedlander, the Associate Editor of the Adams Papers.

82. JQA, "Report to the Overseers," August 25, 1834, Overseers Recs., VIII, 178-196.

83. JQA, "Diary," July 26, 1834, reel no. 42, Adams Papers; Moore, "Diary," July 15 and 19, August 11, 1834. See also CFA, "Diary," August 23, 1834, reel no. 62, Adams Papers.

84. Moore, "Diary," August 20 and 23, 1834.

85. *Ibid.*, August 27, 1834; JQA, "Diary," August 27, 1834, reel no. 42, and CFA, "Diary," August 27, 1834, reel no. 62, Adams Papers.

86. Faculty Recs., XI, 140, 200: September 4 and October 6, 1834.

87. JQA, "Diary," October 15, 1834, reel no. 42, Adams Papers.

Notes to Chapter 9: Toward a University

1. Palfrey, Boston, to JQ, September 12, 1845, Palfrey Papers.

2. "Yale Report," 229. "Nursery of orthodoxy" is used pejoratively by E. S. Gannett in his "Harvard College—Sectarianism," *Christian Examiner*, 39 (September 1845), 269. On the general dissatisfaction with American colleges, see Richard J. Storr, *The Beginnings of Graduate Education in America* (Chicago, University of Chicago Press, 1953), 29-45; Rudolph, *The American College*, 201-220.

3. JQ, *Harvard*, II, 284-285; Morison, *Three Centuries*, 187-191.

4. John Brazer, *Discourse Delivered before the Society for the Promotion of Christian Education in Harvard University, August 28, 1825* (Boston, 1825), 18, 20; Increase N. Tarbox, ed., *Diary of Thomas Robbins, D.D.* (2 vols., Boston, 1886-1887), I, 974; [Boston] *New England Puritan*, February 28, 1845.

5. *Boston Statesman*, January 26, 1829; James D. Knowles, *An Address Delivered before . . . the Newton Theological Institution, November 14, 1832* (Boston, 1832). Estimates on the number of Harvard graduates entering the ministry are derived from *Triennial Catalogue of Harvard University, 1854-1863* (Cambridge, 1864), which still listed clerical alumni in italics. For additional evidence of the declining role of the clergy, from someone who bemoaned the fact, see Pierce's "Commencement Journal," MHS *Procs.*, 2nd ser., 5 (January 1890), 167-263.

6. Francis Calley Gray, *Letter Written to Governor Levi Lincoln in Relation to Harvard University* (Boston, 1831), 49.

7. JQ, "Argument against passing act of March 28, 1834—making Christians

of all denominations eligible to the clerical part of the Board of Overseers," February 2, 1843, JQ Papers, HUA; JQ, Cambridge, to Palfrey, October 25, 1845, Palfrey Papers; JQ, Cambridge, to Corporation, March 19, 1845, Corp. Minutes, VIII, 257.

8. "Yale Report," 350; Storr, *Graduate Education*, 5-6.

9. For Bigelow, see *DAB*, II, 257-258; Bigelow, "Inaugural Address," *North American Review*, 4 (1816), 271-275.

10. Bigelow, Boston, to JQ, February 5, 1830, Coll. Papers, V, 53-54.

11. George Ticknor shared Bigelow's views, as he showed earlier in his *Remarks on Changes*, and may properly be thought a utilitarian. See his letter to JQ, April 20, 1834, JQ Papers, HUA.

12. Channing, Boston, to JQ, February 14, 1834, *ibid*. These views were not newly acquired by Channing; see his "Thoughts on the Proper Methods of Instruction at the University, May, 1825," *ibid*. (1811-1828 folder).

13. JQ, Cambridge, to Channing, February 14, 1834, JQ Papers, HUA. For the same views, see also JQ, Cambridge, to Beck, November 16, 1835, Coll. Papers, VII, 203.

14. JQ, "Address upon Inauguration as President," June 2, 1829, MS., 17, JQ Papers, HUA.

15. Tyack, *Ticknor*, 126; JQ, *Report of the President . . . [on] a General Plan of Studies, Conformably to a Vote of the Board of Overseers . . . February 4, 1830* (Cambridge, 1830), 3 *et passim*; JQ, Cambridge, to Gallatin, November 29, 1830, Gallatin Papers.

16. Story, Washington, to JQ, January 25, 1830, JQ Papers, HUA; James A. Hillhouse, *Dramas, Discourses, and Other Pieces* (Boston, 1839), 129. See also Story, Washington, to John Lowell, October 10, 1834, Corp. Papers, and Dunne, *Joseph Story*, 235-237, 280-281.

17. JQ, *Report on a Plan of Studies*; JQ, *Fifth Annual Report of the President of Harvard University, 1829-1830* (Cambridge, 1831), 5; JQ, Cambridge, to Palfrey, April 11, 1835, Palfrey Papers. Enrollment figures compiled from *Annual Reports* (1829-1835); Morison, *Three Centuries*, 253.

18. JQ, Draft of statement to Corporation on "special students," May 15, 1834, Corp. Papers, V; Faculty Report on Probationary Admissions, Coll. Papers, VII: May 2, 1836; F. C. Gray, Boston, to JQ, May 14, 1833, JQ Papers, HUA.

19. JQ, Cambridge, to James Marsh, May 18, 1833, *ibid*.

20. R. W. Emerson, Cambridge, to William Emerson, February 2, 1829, Rusk, *Letters of Emerson*, I, 262; Peabody, *Reminiscences*, 70-73; Carl L. Johnson, *Professor Longfellow at Harvard* (Eugene, University of Oregon Press, 1944), 8-15; Beck, Cambridge, to JQ, June 16, 1838, Coll. Papers, VIII.

21. Benjamin Peirce, "The Arrangement of Mathematical Studies," 1832, Coll. Papers, V, 57; *DAB*: "Benjamin Peirce"; Sven R. Petersen, "Benjamin Peirce: Mathematician and Philosopher," *Journal of the History of Ideas*, 16 (January 1955), 89-112; Moses King, ed., *Benjamin Peirce: A Memorial Collection* (Cambridge, 1891).

22. Peirce, Cambridge, to JQ, May 13, 1833, JQ Papers, HUA; Peirce, Cambridge, to JQ, October 14, 1835, Corp. Papers, V; Peirce to JQ, August 1839, Coll. Papers, IX, 294.

23. Peabody, *Reminiscences*, 182-183; George F. Hoar, *Autobiography of*

Seventy Years (2 vols., New York, Scribner's, 1903), I, 99-100; Petersen, "Peirce," 93.

24. JQ, *Report on a Plan of Studies*, 6.

25. Peirce to JQ, October 14 and 21, 1835, Corp. Papers; "Yale Report," 300.

26. JQ, Cambridge, to Walker, November 21, 1835, Corp. Papers.

27. CFA, "Diary," August 5, 1837, reel no. 63, Adams Papers.

28. *DAB*: "Charles Beck"; Peabody, *Reminiscences*, 124-126; William Newell, *The Christian Citizen: A Discourse Occasioned by the Death of Charles Beck* (Cambridge, 1866).

29. Beck, Cambridge, to JQ, July 16, 1831, JQ Papers, HUA. For a discussion of Beck's seminary, see Storr, *Graduate Education*, 25-28.

30. Storr, *Graduate Education*, 26; Pierce, *Sumner*, I, 199,245. For Quincy's defensiveness about Harvard's "predilection for foreigners" on the faculty, see JQ, Cambridge, to Charles W. Upham, June 21, 1834, JQ Papers, HUA.

31. Beck, Cambridge, to Corporation, Summer, 1832, Coll. Papers; Storr, *Graduate Education*, 28.

32. Beck to JQ, October 17, 1835, Coll. Papers.

33. Beck to JQ, March 14, 1835, JQ Papers, HUA; Corporation Committee Report on Limiting Study of Classics to First Two Years, May 18, 1835, Coll. Papers, VII, 87-89.

34. Peirce to JQ, January 21, 1838, Coll. Papers.

35. Peirce to JQ, March 15, 1835, JQ Papers, HUA.

36. Beck to JQ, June 16, 1838, Coll. Papers; Corp. Minutes, May 20 and June 2, 1838.

37. JQ to Beck, June 16, 1838, Coll. Papers.

38. Beck to JQ, June 16, 1838, *ibid*.

39. *Ibid*.

40. Peabody, *Reminiscences*, 171; G. S. Hillard, "Memoir of Cornelius Conway Felton," MHS *Procs*., 10 (1868), 352-368; Morison, *Three Centuries*, 263; Felton to JQ, June 30, 1838, Coll. Papers.

41. Corp. Minutes, August 19, 1838; Felton to JQ, August 16, 1839, JQ Papers, HUA.

42. Theophilus Parsons, *Report of the Corporation Committee . . . respecting the Introduction of the Voluntary System in the Studies of Mathematics, Latin, and Greek* (Cambridge, 1841), 2.

43. John Pickering, *Report of the Overseers Committee respecting the Introduction of the Voluntary System* (Cambridge, 1841); JQ, *Remarks on the Nature and Probable Effects of Introducing the Voluntary System . . .* (Cambridge, 1841).

44. JQ, *Harvard University—Notice to Parents and Guardians in Relation to Elective Studies* (Cambridge, 1843), copy in JQ Papers, HUA. See also Benjamin A. Gould to Peirce, 1843, Peirce Papers. For Everett's opposition to the elective system, see Everett to Charles W. Upham, May 11, 1846, Edward Everett Papers, I (1846-1848), HUA, and his inquiries on the subject among the faculty, Coll. Papers, 1846-1847. See also Preston C. Combs, "Harvard College, 1846-1869: An Age of Transition," unpub. honors thesis, Harvard College, 1950, HUA. Both Morison and Combs, in my judgment, understate the significance and the success of Quincy's efforts to modernize the curriculum.

45. Walker, "Quincy," MHS *Procs.*, 9 (1866-1867), 134. The best survey of the development of the elective system at Harvard is contained in Charles William Eliot, *Annual Report of the President of Harvard College*, [1883-1884] (Cambridge, 1885), 16-18. See also C. W. Eliot, "Remarks," MHS *Procs.*, 57 (1923-1924), 6.

46. JQ, *Remarks on the Voluntary System*, 7; Peirce, Cambridge, to JQ, February 14, 1845, JQ Papers, HUA; Petersen, "Peirce," 94.

47. Gray, *Letter to Lincoln*, 9-16; JQ, *Considerations Relative to the Library of Harvard University Respectfully Submitted to the Legislature of Massachusetts* (Cambridge, 1833); JQ, *Harvard*, II, 599-601; Henry Ware, Cambridge, to JQ, June 6, 1832, and Corporation to Ware, July 17, 1832, Coll. Papers, V, 129-130 and 165-169.

48. ———, *A Brief View of the American Education Society with an Appeal to the Christian Public* (Andover, 1826); "Beneficiaries for 1836-1837," *American Quarterly Register*, 10 (August 1837), 95-97. See also JQ, Cambridge, to Samuel A. Eliot, August 30, 1838, JQ Papers, HUA.

49. Margery Somers Foster, *"Out of Smalle Beginnings... " An Economic History of Harvard College in the Puritan Period* (Cambridge, Mass., Harvard University Press, 1962), 106-128; JQ, *Harvard*, I, 40, II, 555; Ticknor, Boston, to JQ, April 20, 1834, Ticknor Papers; JQ, On the state of the university prior to June 1829, "Memorandum book," JQ Papers, HUA.

50. JQ, *Harvard*, II, 594-595; JQ, *President's Annual Report, 1835-1836*, 2.

51. JQA, "Diary," September 13, 1834, reel no. 42, Adams Papers.

52. Eliza Quincy, Cambridge, to Sir Thomas C. Banks, January 7, 1837, JQ Papers, Houghton Library; Harvard Alumni Association Materials (folder no. 1), HUA; JQ, *Harvard*, II, 639; CFA, "Diary," September 8, 1836, reel no. 63, Adams Papers.

53. JQ, Proposal for disbursing beneficiary fund, undated, Coll. Papers, VI (1833-1835), 147-148; JQ, Cambridge, to F. C. Gray, April 22, 1834, *ibid.*, 145-146; JQ, Cambridge, to Samuel A. Eliot, August 30, 1838, JQ Papers, HUA.

54. JQ, Cambridge, to W. E. Channing, February 14, 1834, *ibid.*; JQ, Memorandum to Corporation, April 16, 1834, Coll. Papers, VI, 132-135.

55. JQ to Eliot, August 30, 1838, JQ Papers, HUA.

56. Edward Wigglesworth, "First Report of the Trustees of the Fund for Assisting Students at Harvard College," December 30, 1840, Coll. Papers, X, 173-174; Shipton Charts on admissions, HUA.

57. JQ, Cambridge, to Lemuel Shaw, November 2, December 3 and 20, 1841, Lemuel Shaw Papers, MHS; Solon I. Bailey, *The History and Work of the Harvard Observatory* (New York, McGraw-Hill, 1931), 2-10; Hindle, *Pursuit of Science*, 99-100.

58. Bailey, *Harvard Observatory*, 10-14; *DAB*: "William Cranch Bond."

59. JQ, *Memoir of the Life of John Quincy Adams* (Boston, 1858), 287-293. See also Richard H. Shryock, "American Indifference to Basic Science during the Nineteenth Century," *Archives Internationales d' Histoire des Sciences*, 28 (October 1948), 50-65; Donald Fleming, "American Science and the World Scientific Community," *Journal of World History*, 8 (1965), 669.

60. William Cranch Bond, "History and Description of the Astronomical Observatory of Harvard College," *Annals of the Astronomical Observatory*, 1 (1856), lxxii-lxxxviii; JQ, *Harvard*, II, 392, 637; Bessie Z. Jones, *Lighthouse of the Skies* (Washington, Smithsonian Institution, 1965), 13-16. See also Bessie Z.

Jones and Lyle Gifford Boyd, *The Harvard College Observatory: The First Four Directorships, 1839-1919* (Cambridge, Mass., Harvard University Press, 1971), 36-57.

61. Bond, "Astronomical Observatory," vi-xiv; Bailey, *Harvard Observatory*, 16.

62. *Ibid.*, 17-22.

63. Thomas T. Bouvé, "Historical Sketch of the Boston Society of Natural History," *Anniversary Memoir of the Boston Society of Natural History* (Boston, 1880), 12; JQ, Boston, to Winthrop, February 27, 1855, Papers Relating to the Observatory, JQ Papers, HUA. See Edward Weeks, *The Lowells and Their Institute* (Boston, Little, Brown, 1966), 3-54; Howard S. Miller, *Dollars for Research: Science and Its Patrons in Nineteenth-Century America* (Seattle, University of Washington Press, 1970), 36-37.

64. Bailey, *Harvard Observatory*, 50-67; E. Richardson, n.pl., to JQ, October 25, 1849, Papers Relating to the Observatory, JQ Papers, HUA.

65. Bessie Z. Jones, ed., "Diary of the Two Bonds, 1846-1849," *Harvard Library Bulletin*, 15 (October 1967), 368-386; 16 (1968), 49-71, 178-207; Bailey, *Harvard Observatory*, 30, 31; JQ, Boston, to Sparks, November 5, 1849, Papers Relating to the Observatory, JQ Papers, HUA.

66. John Gorham Palfrey, "Review of Josiah Quincy's *History of Harvard University*," *North American Review*, 12 (April 1841), 339; Francis Parkman, "Review of *History of Harvard University*," *Christian Examiner*, 30 (March 1841), 56-57.

67. JQ, *Harvard*, I, 1-2; Eliza Quincy, to Samuel A. Drake, September 22, 1873, Quincy Family Papers; JQA, "Diary," September 9, 1836, reel no. 43, Adams Papers; Parkman, "Review," 57. Quincy was assisted in his labors by his daughter and his wife, both of whom wielded the blue pencil to good effect when he "got hung up on the Mathers." See Eliza Quincy, Quincy, to Winthrop, September 12, 1877, Winthrop Papers.

68. JQ, *Harvard*, I, 226-227, 324, II, 4, 182-197; JQ, Cambridge, to Daniel A. White, June 30, 1841, JQ Papers (folder on *Harvard*), HUA.

69. JQ, *Harvard*, I, 3-5, 20.

70. *Ibid.*, 44-230, 226-227.

71. *Ibid.*, II, 39-71, 52.

72. *Ibid.*, 284-287, 358-359; I, 5.

73. *Ibid.*, II, 461-708; JQ, Cambridge, to Corporation, December 26, 1840, JQ Papers, HUA.

74. Parkman, "Review," 56-62; Palfrey, "Review," 338-384; Enoch Pond, "Review of *History of Harvard University*," *American Biblical Repository*, 3 (July 1841), 178-196, and 4 (October 1841), 109-140; Rogers' comment reprinted in *Christian Register*, March 31, 1849. For Quincy's rejoinder, see JQ to Rogers, March 23, 1849, JQ Papers, HUA.

75. JQ, Cambridge, to Palfrey, May 25, 1838, *ibid.*; JQ, Boston, to Palfrey, October 25, 1845, Palfrey Papers. On Quincy's religious moderation, see Walker, "Quincy," MHS *Procs.*, 9 (1866-1867), 155. Quincy's religious latitudinarianism did not extend, however, to the point that he looked with favor upon all sects sharing equally in Harvard's management. See his "Speech to the Overseers," February 16, 1843, Overseers Recs., VIII.

76. Eliza Quincy, Quincy, to Winthrop, September 12, 1877, Winthrop Papers; JQ, Cambridge, to White, June 30, 1841, JQ Papers, HUA.

77. Eliza Quincy, Boston, to S. A. Drake, December 22, 1873, Quincy Family Papers; CFA, "Diary," April 27, 1841, reel no. 64, Adams Papers.

78. Darling, *Political Change*, 289-291; Saltonstall, Boston, to JQ, February 12, 1845, JQ Papers, HUA.

79. Overseers Recs., VIII, 388: February 2, 1843; undated clipping on "old tory Harvard," contrasting it with Brown, in Palfrey Papers. See also Nye, *Bancroft*, 129.

80. Overseers Recs., VIII, 407-411: February 8, 1844.

81. *Ibid.*, 415: February 22, 1844; CFA, "Diary," February 8, 1844, reel no. 67, Adams Papers.

82. Darling, *Political Change*, 318-319; George Morley, "Visiting Committee Report," Overseers Recs., VIII, 422-425, 427: January 16, 1845.

83. George Bancroft, *Report on Diminishing the Cost of Instruction in Harvard College* (Boston, 1845), 10; *Boston Courier*, February 7, 1845; Overseers Recs., VIII, 435: February 7, 1845. See Bancroft's quite different sentiments prior to his identification with Jackson, in "The Harvard Library," *North American Review*, 33 (1831), 216-226.

84. Loring, Boston, to JQ, March, 1845, JQ Papers, HUA; Leverett Saltonstall, *Report of a Committee of Overseers concerning the Requirements for Admission* (Salem, 1845); James Savage, *Report of a Committee of Overseers on Impact of Voluntary System upon the Health of the Undergraduates* (Boston, 1845).

85. JQ, *Speech . . . before the Board of Overseers . . . February 25, 1845, on the Minority Report of the Committee of Visitation, Presented . . . by George Bancroft, Esq., . . .* (Boston, 1845), 7, 19-26; Papers relating to the Investigation of Student Expenses, JQ Papers (1844-1845 folder), HUA; John Pierce, "Memoir" (1803-1848), III, 78, Pierce Papers.

86. JQ, *On the Minority Report*, vi-vii; Morison, *Three Centuries*, 289.

87. JQ, Cambridge, to Corporation, March 19, 1845, and JQ, Cambridge, to John Chipman Gray, February 18, 1845, JQ Papers, HUA. Undergraduate reminiscence included in undated newspaper review among "Reviews of *Life of Josiah Quincy*," EQ Papers.

88. Ralph Waldo Emerson, *Journals*, ed. Edward Waldo Emerson and Waldo Emerson Forbes (10 vols., Boston, Houghton Mifflin, 1909-1914), VII, 168: May 1, 1846; Morison, *Three Centuries*, 275.

Notes to Chapter 10: A Final Eminence

1. JQ, Cambridge, to Longfellow, June 21, 1845, in Johnson, *Longfellow*, 54.

2. EQ, *Quincy*, 486; Henry Adams, *The Education of Henry Adams* (Boston, Houghton Mifflin, 1918), 15.

3. Jones, "Diary of the Two Bonds," *Harvard Library Bulletin*, 15 (October 1967), 372, 375; 16 (April 1968), 179. JQ's diary, which ran to three octavo volumes, is presumed to have been destroyed by President James Walker after he had used it for his *Memoir* of Quincy. See Sibley, "Journal," II, 791: May 28, 1868, Sibley Papers.

4. JQ, "Memoir of James Grahame, LL.D.," MHS *Colls.*, 2nd ser., 9 (1895), 2-41; JQ, *Memoir of John Bromfield* (Cambridge, 1850); JQ, *The History of the*

Boston Athenaeum, with Biographical Notices of its Deceased Founders (Cambridge, 1851); JQ, *Municipal History*; JQ, *Memoir of JQA*; JQ, *On the Soiling of Cattle*; JQ, Quincy, to Mrs. Robert C. Waterston, August 3, 1856, Quincy Family Papers; Lucid, *Journal of Dana*, I, 386.

5. Sibley, "Journal," I, 116, 118-119: April 1 and 10, 1847, Sibley Papers; Everett, Cambridge, to Webster, July 6, 1846, and to White, April 24, 1847, Everett Papers; [JQ], *A Plea for Harvard: showing that the name "The University at Cambridge" was not that established for this seminary . . .* (Boston, 1849); JQ, Quincy, to Sparks, June 7, 1849, JQ Papers, HUA.

6. [JQ], *Remarks on "An Act to Establish the Superior Court of the City of Boston," Passed by the General Court of Massachusetts* (Boston, 1849); JQ, *Remarks on the Act in Relation to the Organization and Powers of the City Council of the City of Boston* (Cambridge, 1851); James M. Bugbee, "Boston under the Mayors," in Winsor, *Memorial History*, III, 260.

7. JQ, Boston, to Seaver, September 10, 1852, Miscellaneous Manuscripts, Rare Book Room, BPL; *Boston Evening Transcript*, June 11, 1873; Will of Josiah Quincy (1864), Probate No. 45572, Suffolk County Probate Court, Boston.

8. [JQ], *Considerations on Annexation*, 2, 6-7.

9. W. W. Wheildon, *A Brief Review of 'Considerations on the Proposed Annexation . . . '* (Boston, 1854), 3, 11; Winsor, *Memorial History*, III, 570.

10. JQ, *Athenaeum*; "An Old Proprietor," *Daily Advertiser*, March 14, 1853; JQ, *An Appeal in Behalf of the Boston Athenaeum, Addressed to the Proprietors* (Boston, 1853). See also Tyack, *Ticknor*, 210.

11. JQ, "Speech . . . February, 1858, before . . . the Massachusetts Legislature . . . [on] the Petition of the New England Historic-Genealogical Society for a Change of Their Corporate Name, and the Remonstrance of the Massachusetts Historical Society," MHS *Procs.*, 3 (1855-1858), 344-351; George D. Wolkins, "The Prince Society," *ibid.*, 66 (1936-1941), 223-254; Samuel G. Drake, *Narrative Remarks, Expository Notes, and Historical Criticisms on the New England Historical and Genealogical Society and Incidentally on the Massachusetts Historical Society* (Albany, 1874), 38, 47.

12. Sibley, "Journal," I, 421-422: August 10, 1857, Sibley Papers.

13. E. S. M. Quincy, *Memoir*, 248-249; "Tribute to the Memory of Mrs. Quincy," *Christian Examiner*, 14 (November 1850), 251; CFA, "Diary," September 3, 1850, reel no. 72, Adams Papers; EQ, *Quincy*, 499-500.

14. Mark A. DeWolfe Howe, ed., *The Articulate Sisters* (Cambridge, Mass., Harvard University Press, 1946); J. P. Quincy, "Memoir of Robert C. Waterston," MHS *Procs.*, 2nd ser., 8 (1892-1894), 292-302.

15. James Cameron, *The Public Service of Josiah Quincy Jr. (1802-1882)* (Quincy, privately printed, 1964), 3-4; Josiah Quincy Jr., *Figures of the Past*, 16-50; Robert W. Tolf, "Edmund Quincy: Aristocrat Abolitionist," 14-40, unpub. diss., University of Rochester, 1957.

16. Cameron, *Quincy*, 5-10; Tolf, "Edmund Quincy," 81.

17. Loring, *Boston Orators*, 495-499; Stephen Salsbury, *The State, the Investor, and the Railroad: The Boston and Albany 1825-1867* (Cambridge, Mass., Harvard University Press, 1967), 148-154.

18. Bugbee, "Boston under Mayors," in Winsor, *Memorial History*, III, 251-254; Lane, *Policing the City*, 62-64; Solomon, *Ancestors and Immigrants*, 5; Handlin, *Boston's Immigrants*, 120.

19. Cameron, *Quincy*, 15-17; Josiah Quincy Jr., *Letter to the Shareholders of the Vermont Central Railroad* (Boston, 1852); CFA, "Diary," January 19 and February 12, 1852, reel no. 72, Adams Papers; Josiah Quincy Jr., Boston, to John Jay, January 28, 1859, Miscellaneous Manuscripts, Columbiana Room, Columbia University.

20. Kinley J. Brauer, *Cotton versus Conscience: Massachusetts Whig Politics and Southwestern Expansion, 1843-1848* (Lexington, University of Kentucky Press, 1967), 87; Josiah Quincy Jr., *Eulogy on the Life and Character of the Late Zachary Taylor* (Boston, 1850); CFA, "Diary," July 14, 1856, reel no. 74, Adams Papers; D. Weston, Boston, to A. W. Weston, April 7, 1851, Anti-Slavery Weston Papers, Rare Book Room, BPL.

21. EQ, Dedham, to Richard D. Webb, May 27, 1869, EQ Papers.

22. J. P. Quincy, "Memoir of Edmund Quincy," MHS *Procs.*, 2nd ser., 18 (1903-1904), 409; Lowell, "A Great Public Character," *Atlantic Monthly*, 20 (November 1867), 625.

23. Tolf, "Edmund Quincy," chapter 10; Emerson, "Chardon Street Convention," in Ralph Waldo Emerson, *Complete Works* (14 vols., Boston, 1883-1893), X, 351-354.

24. Tolf, "Edmund Quincy," 334; and see *ibid.*, 216, for p. 17 of [EQ], *Annual Report of the Massachusetts Anti-Slavery Society* (Boston, 1843).

25. JQ, *The Duty of Conservative Whigs in the Present Crisis: A Letter to the Honorable Rufus Choate by a Conservative Whig* (Boston, 1856), 1-2; Pierce, "Commencement Journal," MHS *Procs.*, 2nd ser., 5 (January 1890), 247; JQ, Boston, to Sumner, November 21, 1845, Sumner Papers.

26. CFA, "Diary," July 14, 1856, reel no. 74, Adams Papers; Nathaniel Southgate Shaler, *Autobiography* (Boston, Houghton Mifflin, 1909), 112, 198-199; Mason Wade, ed., *The Journals of Francis Parkman* (2 vols., New York, Harper, 1947), I, 292; Van Deusen, "Whig Thought," *AHR*, 63 (January 1958), 305-322; Lane, *Policing the City*, 62-64; Tolf, "Edmund Quincy," 371-372; JQ, *JQA*, 233.

27. Adams, *Education of Henry Adams*, 29. On Whig accommodationist bent, see Lynn Marshall, "The Strange Stillbirth of the Whig Party," *AHR*, 72 (January 1967), 445-468.

28. [EQ], "War with England," *National Anti-Slavery Standard*, October 25, 1849, quoted by Tolf, "Edmund Quincy," 215. That Quincy Sr. and Edmund remained on good terms throughout this period is suggested by JQ, Cambridge, to EQ, April 24, 1843, JQ Papers, Houghton Library.

29. Sibley, "Journal," 335-336: April 13, 1854, Sibley Papers; JQ, *JQA*, 40-41; EQ, *Quincy*, 505.

30. JQ, *JQA*, 343-348.

31. *Ibid.*, 95-119, 106.

32. *Ibid.*, 104.

33. *Ibid.*, 395; *AC*, 9th, 2nd, 183-184: December 18, 1806; JQ, *The New States, or a Comparison of the Wealth, Strength and Population of the Northern and Southern States* (Boston, 1813). On the nature of the Federalists' anti-slavery beliefs generally, see Kerber, *Federalists in Dissent*, 23-66.

34. JQ, *JQA*, 94-95; EQ, *Quincy*, 65-66; JQ, *Address on the Slave Power*, 31; J. T. Bixby, "Review of *Life of Josiah Quincy*," *Christian Examiner*, 83 (1967), 369.

35. JQ, *Memoir*, 56-112. For restored version, see JQ Jr., "Southern

Journal," MHS *Procs.*, 49 (1916), 433-470. For Quincy's explanation, see *Daily Advertiser*, July 18, 1863.

36. JQ, Cambridge, to JQA, July 13, 1836, in MHS *Procs.*, 2nd ser., 15 (1901), 459-460. For Adams' sentiments supporting the abolitionist views of EQ, see JQA, Quincy, to EQ, July 28, 1838, Nicholas Brown Scrapbook, Brown University Library.

37. Bemis, *Adams*, 524-546; JQ, Boston, to James M. Broome, March 27, 1848, in EQ, *Quincy*, 496-497.

38. CFA, "Diary," October 14, 1850, reel no. 72, Adams Papers; D. Weston, Boston, to Carol Weston, October 21, 1850, Anti-Slavery Weston Papers, Rare Book Room, BPL.

39. David D. Van Tassell, "Gentlemen of Property and Standing: Compromise Sentiment in Boston in 1850," *NEQ*, 23 (1950), 319; Lucid, *Journal of Dana*, II, 428.

40. *Ibid.*, 438; CFA, "Diary," April 27, 1852, reel no. 72, Adams Papers; EQ, *Quincy*, 502.

41. Lucid, *Journal of Dana*, II, 618-619; CFA, "Diary," February 23, 1854, reel no. 73, Adams Papers; Pierce, *Sumner*, III, 365.

42. [Charles Gordon Greene], *The Identity of the Hartford Convention Federalists with the Modern Whig, Harrison Party* (Boston, 1840), failed to make a case for Quincy as a Whig. On Quincy's relations with Webster, see Eliza Quincy, "Journal," January 1820, interlineations, Quincy Family Papers.

43. Pierce, *Sumner*, II, 262, 365; David Donald, *Charles Sumner and the Coming of the Civil War* (New York, Knopf, 1960), 172; Eliza Quincy, Boston, to Louisa Loring, November 20, 1864, Ellis Gray Loring Papers, Schlesinger Library, Radcliffe College.

44. CFA, London, to EQ, October 18, 1867, EQ Papers; Lucid, *Journal of Dana*, II, 671-672. For a discussion of the bifurcation of the Boston Whig community, see Brauer, *Cotton versus Conscience*, 159-180.

45. Lucid, *Journal of Dana*, II, 438; JQ, Quincy, to Samuel H. Walley, May 24, 1854, Washburn Autograph Collection.

46. CFA, "Diary," August 16, 1854, reel no. 73, Adams Papers; Lucid, *Journal of Dana*, II, 258; JQ, *Speech Delivered before the Whig State Convention . . . August 16, 1854* (Boston, 1854), 5, 7.

47. Duberman, *CFA*, 198; Lucid, *Journal of Dana*, II, 671-672. On Massachusetts Know-Nothingism, see William Gleason Bean, "Party Transformation in Massachusetts with Special Reference to the Antecedents of Republicanism, 1848-1860," 344-350, unpub. diss., Harvard University, 1922, HUA; the author of *Francis William Bird* (privately printed, Boston, 1897) describes Quincy as the gubernatorial candidate on "The Honest Man's Ticket," an anti-Know-Nothing group (47-48).

48. EQ, *Quincy*, 511-512.

49. CFA, "Diary," June 5, 1856, reel no. 74, Adams Papers; Richard Webb, Dublin, to "my dear Friend," September 27, 1856, Anti-Slavery Weston Papers, Rare Book Room, BPL; JQ, *Address on the Slave Power*, 30, 32.

50. *Ibid.*, 2; [JQ], *Duty of Conservative Whigs*, 17; JQ, *Remarks on the Letter of the Hon. Rufus Choate to the Whig State Committee of Maine* (Boston, 1856), 7.

51. JQ, Quincy, to White, August 14, 1856, JQ Papers, HUA. On the conservative element brought into the Republican party, see Eric Foner, *Free*

Soil, Free Labor, Free Men: The Ideology of the Republican Party before the Civil War (New York, Oxford University Press, 1970), 186-225.

52. JQ, *Whig Policy Analyzed and Illustrated* (Boston, 1856), 13; JQ, Boston, to Sumner, August 22, 1856, Sumner Papers; Donald, *Sumner*, 319.

53. EQ, *Quincy*, 515; JQ, Boston, to H. C. Cary, September 21, 1856, Miscellaneous Manuscripts, Special Collections, NYPL; JQ, Quincy, to Benjamin Silliman, August 9, 1856, Washburn Autograph Collection; Nicholas B. Wainwright, ed., *A Philadelphia Perspective: The Diary of Sidney George Fisher Covering the Years 1834-1871* (Philadelphia, Historical Society of Pennsylvania, 1967), 260: September 8, 1856; *The Republican Scrapbook* (Boston, 1856), 45-51; *Democratic Handbook* (n.pl., 1856), 15-17. For Quincy's impact, see also Peterson, *The Jefferson Image*, 201.

54. Donald, *Sumner*, 322; Duberman, *CFA*, 209; JQ, Boston, to A. P. Peabody, November 17, 1856, JQ Papers, HUA.

55. Edward Dicey, "Review of Life of Josiah Quincy," *Spectator*, 41 (April 25, 1868), 500; MHS *Procs.*, 9 (1866-1867), 155.

56. *Daily Advertiser*, July 17, 1862; JQ, Boston, to Samuel H. Walley, February 10, 1863, Washburn Autograph Collection. See also Edmund's obituary in New York *Daily Tribune*, July 4, 1864.

57. Eliza Quincy, Quincy, to Sumner, May 15, 1864, Sumner Papers; *Daily Advertiser*, July 17, 1862; Tolf, "Edmund Quincy," 314.

58. Samuel Arthur Bent, "Eulogy on Samuel Miller Quincy, May 24, 1887," Bostonian Society *Procs.*, 1 (1887), 7-27; J. P. Quincy, Boston, to Samuel Miller Quincy, July 2, 1864, Quincy Family Papers.

59. *Daily Advertiser*, July 17, 1862; JQ, *Address to the Members of the Union League of Boston*, February 27, 1863, copy in Sumner Papers. Quincy's growing concern with the humanitarian aspects of the struggle fits with the attitudes described by George Fredrickson (*The Inner Civil War: Northern Intellectuals and the Crisis of the Union* (New York, Harper and Row, 1968), 79-97).

60. JQ, Quincy, to President Abraham Lincoln, September 7, 1863, in EQ, *Quincy*, 538-539.

61. Sibley, "Journal," 666: November 12, 1863, Sibley Papers; Walker, "Quincy," MHS *Procs.*, 9 (1866-1867), 154; Eliza Quincy, Quincy, to Sumner, July 2, 1864, Sumner Papers; EQ, *Quincy*, 541.

62. New York *Daily Tribune*, July 4, 1864, 1, 2; *Boston Journal*, July 4, 1864; *Daily Advertiser*, July 20, 1864; Ezra Stiles Gannett, *A Discourse Occasioned by the Death of the Hon. Josiah Quincy, July 10, 1864* (Boston, 1864), 6; Richard Henry Dana, "Memorial Services for Josiah Quincy, July, 1864," MHS *Procs.*, 7 (1863-1864), 398; *Proceedings of the Government of Harvard University on the Death of the Hon. Josiah Quincy* (Cambridge, 1864); *Proceedings of the City of Boston on the Death of the Hon. Josiah Quincy* (Boston, 1864).

Index

Harvard Historical Studies

84. *Marvin Arthur Breslow.* A Mirror of England: English Puritan Views of Foreign Nations, 1618–1640. 1970.
85. *Patrice L.-R. Higonnet.* Pont-de-Montvert: Social Structure and Politics in a French Village, 1700–1914. 1971.
86. *Paul G. Halpern.* The Mediterranean Naval Situation, 1908–1914. 1971.
87. *Robert E. Ruigh.* The Parliament of 1624: Politics and Foreign Policy. 1971.
88. *Angeliki E. Laiou.* Constantinople and the Latins: The Foreign Policy of Andronicus, 1282–1328. 1972.
89. *Donald Nugent.* Ecumenism in the Age of Reformation: The Colloquy of Poissy. 1974.
90. *Robert A. McCaughey.* Josiah Quincy, 1772–1864: The Last Federalist. 1974.